LITERATURE

and the IRRATIONAL

A Study in Anthropological Backgrounds

WAYNE SHUMAKER

Department of English
University of California at Berkeley

Englewood Cliffs, N.J.

PRENTICE-HALL, INC.

1960

Printed in the United States of America

5 3 7 5 4 – C

ROBERTO

filio dilectissimo
qui juvenis primaevus
patris cognitionibus de rebus primaevis
inconscius contribuit
necnon tum cum ille scribendi labore vexatus
iracundiae dominationem animi dederat
nugis levibus serenitatem domi restituebat
hunc librum gravem
do et dedico

Primarily language does not express thoughts or ideas, but feelings and affections.

—ERNST CASSIRER, *An Essay on Man*

What is the meaning of a "scientific fact"? Obviously no such fact is given in any haphazard observation or in a mere accumulation of sense data. The facts of science always imply a theoretical, which means a symbolic, element. Many, if not most of those scientific facts which have changed the whole course of the history of science have been hypothetical facts before they became observable facts.

—CASSIRER, *An Essay on Man*

Unconscious mental processes, Freud found, are of fundamental significance and frequency in human behavior. . . . Every behavior pattern of man has a cause, and it is most likely that the cause will be unconscious.

—ROBERT A. HARPER, *Psychoanalysis and Psychotherapy: 36 Systems*

Preface

The essay that follows has resulted from a study of books
and articles which as recently as ten years ago I should
not have expected to find relevant to the understanding
of literature, and it proposes conclusions which at that
time I might have found disconcerting.

So far as I can remember, the initial impulse to the
reading came not from a critical treatise but from a novel,
Raoul Faure's *The Spear in the Sand*. The slow decline
into savagery, described in that work, of an isolated and
finally marooned man did curious things to my mind. Although exclusion from civilization necessarily entailed the
loss of many precious human values, I wrote down a
query, which is still among my notes: "Can an entire
philosophy of literary form be based on the assumption
that man yearns unknowingly for the unitary consciousness of the brute state?" I thought of the obvious reluctance of children to think with the cortex only, of T. S.
Eliot's phrase about the dissociation of sensibilities, of
the Christian myth of a prelapsarian state in which the
mind and body were at one, and of much else which
tended to suggest an affirmative answer. While the notion
was still in my mind, I came upon Ernst Cassirer's *Language and Myth,* which analyzes savage perception in
terms remarkably applicable to aesthetic contemplation.
The still-untranslated second volume, *Das Mythische
Denken,* of the same author's *Philosophie der Symbol-*

ischen Formen drew my attention next; and from that I worked gradually into the rich body of anthropological, psychological, and aesthetic writings reflected in the following pages.

To my astonishment, I found that for many years the thought of scholars in several intellectual disciplines had been converging upon a view of literature which as yet has had comparatively little effect upon critical attitudes. I trust that my readers will not decide immediately that the view is prejudicial to literature. On the contrary, it leads not only to a more lively appreciation of creative works but also to the delineation of an area in which literary art has a secure and permanent autonomy. It is true that the pool into which several distinct streams of scholarship have emptied looks black, deep, and perhaps, at first sight, rather foul; but the search for an understanding of human experience cannot afford to follow only comfortable trails. In the end, one turns back to trimmed grass and the clear sky with a relief not untinged with nostalgia.

It is only fair to add that in spite of the heavy reliance placed upon anthropological data in the central and longest portion of the study, I lay no claim to special competence in any other kind of anthropology than the very curious kind presented here. I should acknowledge also that my knowledge of Greek is very slight; for that reason the section on Greek tragedy has received the criticism of Professor Joseph Fontenrose, and the section on Greek epic that of Professor Elroy L. Bundy. The chapters on the language of literature were read by still another colleague, Professor David W. Reed, whose careful and sympathetic appraisal has also been helpful—particularly his assurance that my discussion lies mostly outside the area of general linguistics and hence can be said, at worst, not to have to do with language at all. Under such a criticism I can breathe, since I am not particular about the rubric under which the data are collected. To these scholars, and to Professor Josephine Miles, who read the whole manuscript with understanding and made useful suggestions, I am grateful. I am grateful also to the University of California for research grants which permitted me to have the manuscript typed and to receive help in filing an unwieldy collection of note cards, and, not least, for the opportunity to work under conditions and in an atmosphere conducive to study.

WAYNE SHUMAKER
Berkeley, July 14, 1959

vi

THANKS ARE DUE TO THE FOLLOWING PUBLISHING HOUSES
AND PERSONS FOR PERMISSION TO CITE EXCERPTS FROM
THE WORKS NOTED:

Abelard-Schuman, Ltd. (New York, *Thespis: Ritual, Myth and Drama
in the Ancient Near East*, by Theodor H. Gaster. Appleton-Century-Crofts,
Inc. (New York), *The Beginnings of Art*, by Ernest Grosse. Edward Arnold
& Co. (London), *The Origin of Attic Comedy*, by Francis MacDonald Cornford. Mme L. Autran, *Homère et les origines sacerdotales de lèpopée
grecque*, by Charles Autran. Beacon Press (Boston), *Fiction and the Un-
conscious*, by Simon O. Lesser. Bollingen Foundation, Inc. (New York),
The Hero with a Thousand Faces, by Joseph Campbell, and *The Myth of
the Eternal Return*, by Mircea Éliade. Cambridge University Press, Amer-
ican Branch (New York), *The Heroic Age*, by H. M. Chadwick, and *From
Ritual to Romance*, by Jessie L. Weston. Bruno Cassirer Publishers, Ltd.
(Oxford), *Philosophie der Symbolischen Formen, Zweiter Teil, Das
Mythische Denken*, by Ernst Cassirer. City Light Books (San Francisco),
"Transcription of Organ Music," from *Howl and Other Poems*, by Allen
Ginsberg. Columbia University Press (New York), *The Individual and His
Society*, by Abraham Kardiner and Ralph Linton. Cornell University Press
(Ithaca, N. Y.), *The New Science of Giambattista Vico*, translated by
Thomas Goddard Bergin and Max Harold Fisch. J. M. Dent & Sons, Ltd.
(London), *Heart of Darkness*, by Joseph Conrad. *The Encyclopaedia Britan-
nica*, Inc. (Chicago), article on "Homer," by Gilbert Murray. Grandt and
Grandt, Inc. (New York), Agent for the Estate of Maxwell Anderson, "The
Essence of Tragedy," by Maxwell Anderson. Harcourt, Brace & Company,
Inc. (New York), *Poets at Work*, by Rudolf Arnheim, W. H. Auden, Karl
Shapiro, and Donald A. Stauffer; also *Theory of Literature*, by René Wellek
and Austin Warren. Harper & Brothers (New York), *Language and Myth*,
by Ernst Cassirer, translated by Susanne K. Langer, and *The Horse's Mouth*,
by Joyce Cary. D. C. Heath and Company (Boston), *General Anthropol-
ogy*, by Franz Boas. Dr. W. Hoffer, President, British Psycho-Analytical
Society, and Freud Copyright Ltd. (London), "Der tragische Held und der
Verbrecher," by Leo Kaplan. Houghton Mifflin Company (Boston), *Pat-
terns of Culture*, by Ruth Benedict, and "The End of the World," from
Streets in the Moon, by Archibald MacLeish. B. W. Huebsch (New York),
Dreams, by Henri Bergson, translated by Edwin E. Slosson. Humanities
Press Inc. (New York), *Language and Thought of the Child*, by Jean Piaget,
translated by Marjorie Gabain. Indiana University Press (Bloomington,
Ind.), "The Structural Study of Myth," by Claude Lévi-Strauss, from *Myth:
A Symposium*, edited by Thomas A. Sebeok. *The Journal of Aesthetics and
Art Criticism* (Cleveland, Ohio), "The Essence and Origin of Tragedy,"
by Helen Adolf. Alfred Kröner Verlag (Stuttgart), *Elemente der Völkerpsy-
chologie*, by Wilhelm Wundt. John Lane, The Bodley Head Ltd. (London),
"Notes on Sculpture," by Henry Moore, from *The Painter's Object*, by
Myfanwy Evans. Lawrence & Wishart, Ltd. (London), *Aeschylus and
Athens: A Study in the Social Origins of Drama*, by George Thomson.

Louise Lewisohn, *A Modern Book of Criticism*, by Ludwik Lewisohn. Longmans, Green & Co., Ltd. (London), *Myth, Ritual and Religion*, by Andrew Lang. The Macmillan Company (New York), *The Golden Bough: A Study in Magic and Religion*, by Sir James George Frazer, and *The Cutting of an Agate*, by William Butler Yeats. J. C. B. Mohr (Paul Siebeck), Tübingen, "Kunst and Gefühl," by Otto Baensch. John Murray (London), *Origins of Sacrifice*, by E. O. James. Martinus Nijhoff (The Hague), *Art and Analysis: An Essay toward a Theory in Aesthetics*, by Edward G. Ballard, Oxford University Press (London), *Ancient Art and Ritual*, by Jane Ellen Harrison (published as part of the Home University Library); *The Homeric Odyssey*, by Denys Page; and *La Mentalité primitive: The Herbert Spencer Lecture Delivered at Oxford 29 May, 1931*, by Lucien Lévy-Bruhl. R. Piper & Co. Verlag (Munich), *Vom Wesen der Kunst*, by Konrad Fiedler. Princeton University Press (Princeton, N. J.), "The Composer and His Message," by Roger Sessions, from *The Intent of the Critic*, edited by Augusto Centano. Lord Raglan, his own work, *The Hero*. Dietrich Reimer (Andrews & Steiner), Berlin, *Unter den Naturvölkern Zentral-Brasiliens*, by Karl von den Steinen. Ernst Reinhardt Verlag (Munich), *Die Upsprünge der Lyrik*, by Heinz Werner. Rinehart & Company, Inc. (New York), *The Forgotten Language*, by Erich Fromm. Routledge & Kegan Paul Ltd. (London), *The Primitive Mind and Modern Civilization*, by Charles Roberts Aldrich, and *Language and Thought of the Child*, by Jean Piaget, translated by Marjorie Gabain. Charles Scribner's Sons (New York), *The Wings of the Dove*, by Henry James, and *The Story of a Novel*, by Thomas Wolfe. The Technology Press (Cambridge, Mass.), Benjamin Lee Whorf, "Languages and Logic," now available in *Language, Thought, and Reality*, copyright by The Massachusetts Institute of Technology and published jointly by the Technology Press of The Massachusetts Institute of Technology and John Wiley and Sons, Inc. (New York). University of California Press (Berkeley, Cal.), *Folk Tale, Fiction and Saga in the Homeric Epics*, by Rhys Carpenter; *Hupa Texts*, by Earle Pliny Goddard; "Comedy and Laughter," by Benjamin Harrison Lehman, from *Five Gayley Lectures, 1947-1954;* and *Selected Writings of Edward Sapir*, edited by David G. Mandelbaum. The University of Chicago Press (Chicago, Ill.), An *Appraisal of Anthropology Today*, edited by Sol Tax, Loren C. Eiseley, Irving Rouse, and Carl F. Voegelin. The Viking Press, Inc. (New York), "All Day I Hear," from *Collected Poems* by James Joyce; also *Letters to an Artist: From Vincent van Gogh to Anton Ridder van Rappard*, translated by Rela van Messel. A. P. Watt & Son, literary agents for Mrs. W. B. Yeats, "A Prayer for Old Age," from *A Full Moon in August*, by William Butler Yeats. Heinz Werner (Clark University, Worcester, Mass.), his own *Comparative Psychology of Mental Development*, now published by International Universities Press (New York), and *Die Ursprünge der Lyrik*, originally published by Ernst Reinhardt Verlag (Munich). Yale University Press (New Haven, Conn.), *An Essay on Man*, by Ernst Cassirer, and *The Philosophy of Symbolic Forms*, Vol. I, language, by Ernst Cassirer, translated by Ralph Manheim.

Contents

8. CONCLUSION: LITERATURE AND FEELING 240

1

The Cognitive Value of Literature

Everyone who is deeply interested in literature must remember times when his absorption in a book was virtually complete and everything but the literary work itself slipped to the extreme verge of consciousness. At such a moment, the walls of the room fade or recede, the chair in which the reader is sitting has little tactile substance, and the printed pages of the book itself exist as objects only to the extent that they offer obstacles to the smooth continuity of the experience—as, for instance, when an important word is illegible or by accident two leaves are flipped over together. The foreground of consciousness, in which the literary imagination is active, is brilliantly lighted, the background of practical reality so dim that it hardly has psychological reality. In a sense, the reader's world is radically foreshortened, since the immediate experience has only as much history as is implicit in the literary universe. Yet the total feeling is one of fullness, of extraordinary vitality, of psychic richness and depth. The "unitary consciousness" lamented by recent critics as no longer attainable has been achieved, and will continue until broken by an intrusion from the background, the perception of destructive flaws in the foreground, or fatigue.

How frequently such absorption occurs in a relatively intense form can only be guessed. Some readers are perhaps not capable of it. Others will remember knowing it as children but will pride themselves on having acquired enough maturity to hold art off at a cool distance. Aestheticians, while acknowledging that virtually complete absorption is possible, may deplore it as critically improper. If children were questioned, some would no doubt be incredulous that books could ever be so interesting, whereas others, perhaps more intelligent and certainly more imaginative, would at once exclaim, "Oh, yes!" To everyone, however, except the few lumpish people too phlegmatic ever to become vitally alive, psychic absorption of some kind will be credible, if only because of memories preserved across an expanse of dully sensed years. A boy may have known absorption while staring down, in fascinated horror, at the gently rippling water of a swimming pool from a twenty-foot diving platform. A lover may have known it during courtship, a fisherman while playing a steelhead, a politician while maneuvering frantically against odds at a convention. Whatever the external circumstances, however, the psychic mark of the experience is a rapt focusing of attention on something outside the self. In so far as conscious selfhood continues, it is as process rather than state. The boundaries between personality and the situation melt away, and whatever in the background has no relevance to the absorbing object ceases to exist for consciousness.

FEELING TONES.   The fact that literature is capable of producing such states is critically significant and must be reckoned with in an adequate aesthetic—and this regardless of whether the most intense degrees of absorption are ultimately to be approved or discouraged. What especially deserves notice is the play, in the aroused state, not only of ideas but also of feelings. The evoked perceptions have affective valences, as it were, and tend to become structured in terms of feeling relationships. Clearly, what happens unmistakably in aroused contemplation happens to some extent in all aesthetic transactions and is responsible for one of their distinguishing qualities. Just as the fisherman, in playing his steelhead, makes physical adjustments which are not preceded or accompanied by trains of discursive thought, so the perceptive reader of a book can follow the development of a literary situation without rationalizing all the formal and material tensions. That literary experience is suffused with feeling tones is, in fact, a commonplace of discussion; and that the tones modify both perceptions and rational processes can be taken for granted.

THE COGNITIVE ELEMENT. All this would hardly be worth saying had there not, for several decades, been a tendency in aesthetic theory—induced, perhaps, by a wish to vindicate art in a social order which finds unrivaled usefulness in science—to play down the affective element in aesthetic experience in favor of a cognitive element. That the cognitive element is also present can be granted happily. As Kant recognized, the mind is active in its contacts with the external world and does not register passively the impulses that impinge on the nerve endings. Instead, it transforms the impulses into impressions, which enter into combinations as *Gestalten* and are registered finally as knowledge, the total process, apparently, having a good deal of similarity to aesthetic creation generally and even more similarity to the verbal and imaginal creation which produces literature. Ernst Cassirer made much of the basic Kantian insight in *Philosophie der Symbolischen Formen,* which has already had a considerable impact on aesthetics; and other men as well, philosophers, linguists, and critics, have contributed to a recognition that all thought, no matter how strictly "scientific," on an ultimate level is mythical. In so far as we succeed in making a cosmos of the sensory impressions that reach us, we do so very much as a poet creates a poem,[1] by fitting together sensory images and the counters provided us by a symbolic language in such a way as to make a whole. Neither is there much doubt that philosophers and scientists, as well as poets, often feel connections before rationalizing them. Without subscribing to a now thoroughly outdated view that the poet, or any artist, tries merely to give ornamented expression to a notion or feeling which has pre-existed the compositional process and survives it unchanged, it is impossible to deny that art, and a fortiori the art whose medium is words, has cognitive value.

At the same time, it is very far from established that poetry, or any other art, is significant wholly or even chiefly as cognition. The efforts of literary critics to demonstrate that in the future we must look to poetry as a substitute for religion, or philosophy, or ethics, or science have won few converts. Attempts to show that specific works contain many superimposed layers of meaning have been more successful; but the technique lends itself easily to parody, as in the writings of William Empson, and often results in a dissipation of exactly the sense of effective wholeness which tends to permeate absorbed reading—that wholeness which led John Dewey, himself a distinguished proponent of aesthetic cognition, to find the most fundamental characteristic of aesthetic experience in its "consummatory" quality. At any rate, literature is not *merely* cognitive; and, if it is not, an adequate aesthetic must take account of whatever else enters into the total process.

"Virtual" autonomy of the art work

An indication that aesthetic meanings have a very limited and special cognitive significance can be found, indeed, in another principle which is very popular just now and has often been inconsistently associated with an emphasis on aesthetic cognition. Again and again, in recent years, it has been insisted that literary works have autonomy, are *selbständig,* admit no responsibility to the extra-

---

[1] An early recognition of the similarity between aesthetic and non-aesthetic thought appears in S. T. Coleridge's famous comment on the primary and secondary imaginations in *Biographia Literaria,* chap. xiii.

aesthetic universe. Virginia Woolf, in a well-known essay, objected to the novels of H. G. Wells, John Galsworthy, and Arnold Bennett because "they leave one with so strange a feeling of incompleteness and dissatisfaction" and make one feel that it is necessary to "do something—to join a society, or more desperately, to write a cheque." It is different, she believes, with such a novel as *Tristram Shandy* or *Pride and Prejudice,* which is "self-contained" and "leaves one with no desire to do anything, except indeed to read the book again, and to understand it better." [2] The point of view is familiar, and is given weight by the empirical fact that, immediately after one has emerged from what Susanne Langer calls the "virtual" world of a good piece of art, the only appropriate comment seems, for a few charmed moments, to be "Well!" Whatever its other values, aesthetic cognition has little importance as practical wisdom. The closed-off world of aesthetic contemplation is often so discontinuous with the everyday world that a passage from one to the other requires basic readjustments. The "truth-to" theories of art no longer have eloquent advocates, at least in their simpler formulations. If a convincing argument is to be made for the utility of aesthetic cognition, it cannot rest on the assumption that what is true in and for a specific art work is also true outside it.

Aesthetic distance

A related concept which also seems important to contemporary aestheticians is that of aesthetic distance. The emphasis here is on the awareness, throughout a "proper" aesthetic transaction, that the art work is "there" and the percipient "here"; on the necessity that a play be sensed as "staged," a picture as "framed," a novel as "fictive," all art works as "art" and not "reality." Paradoxically, such awareness is by no means incompatible with aesthetic absorption even in its most intense degrees. Writers have more than once shown in creative works a realization that the aesthetic illusion must never become delusion. The classic development of this theme

---

2 Virginia Woolf, "Mr. Bennett and Mrs. Brown," in Mark Schorer, Josephine Miles, and Gordon McKenzie (eds.), *Criticism: The Foundations of Modern Literary Judgment* (rev. ed.; New York: Harcourt, Brace and Company, Inc., 1958), p. 70.

is in *Don Quixote;* but there are many other treatments. In *Huckleberry Finn,* Tom Sawyer is shown to be emotionally absorbed in playing robber without in the least wishing actually to decapitate, burn, and scatter in pieces any member of the band who betrays its secrets. When the threat of betrayal becomes practical, the malcontent is pacified with a nickel. It is Huck, the unimaginative realist, who is constitutionally unable to distinguish between fact and fancy, Huck who is disappointed when a band of Spaniards, together with two hundred elephants and six hundred camels, turns out to be nothing but small girls on a Sunday School picnic. Tom, who invented the fiction and played it out to the end, was never for a moment deceived. Readers who co-operate emotionally with art may, indeed, be enabled to do so precisely by their confident hold on actuality. At any rate, there is little danger, for nonpathological readers, in aiming at affective participation. To cold intelligence, the laws which hold the fictive universe together must remain obscure in the exact proportion in which they are laws not of the reason but of feelings. If participation required the destruction of aesthetic distance, a serious problem would arise. Fortunately it does not. One can feel sensitively at a distance, exactly as one can perceive and think at a distance. The principle of aesthetic distance must be invoked when literature is confused with life, not when readers are moved by their contacts with books.

The role of affections in creation

That good reading demands intellectual co-operation will be granted readily by contemporary critics; that it demands emotional participation will, I fear, be resisted in certain quarters. T. S. Eliot, in a passage which seems often to have been read inaccurately, insisted that poetry is an escape from emotion; and the interest of aestheticians in cognition offers another barrier. Yet there is widespread realization that, as Samuel Alexander urged,[3] aesthetic appreciation is identical in kind with aesthetic creation. If creation can be shown to be flooded with affective tonality, a disposition

---

[3] Samuel Alexander, *Beauty and Other Forms of Value* (London: Macmillan & Co., Ltd., 1933), p. 30.

may be created to admit that in aesthetic contemplation the feelings as well as the intellect must be active.

In such a collection of statements about the psychic experiences of artists as is to be found in Brewster Ghiselin's *The Creative Process,* the emphasis on feelings is surprisingly strong. It is true that there is emphasis also on the necessity of much puttying up after the creative idea has "come to" the artist; but the seizure of the artist by his subject provides a motif which runs through most of the descriptions, and the seizure appears regularly to be accompanied by excitement. If the subject is cognized, it is also felt; so strongly felt, indeed, that the more purely cognitive struggles which follow upon the original seizure, and which may extend over a period of months or years, often have a compulsive character.

The case is very clear for the art with which we are here especially concerned, literature. "All good poetry," said Wordsworth, "is the spontaneous overflow of powerful feelings." In different words, the basic significance of this statement, *that poetry has much to do with the feelings,* is supported by nearly everything that has been written about poetic creation. According to A. E. Housman, poetry is "more physical than intellectual." [4] In the opinion of Amy Lowell, a poet may be defined as "a man of an extraordinarily sensitive and active subconscious personality, fed by, and feeding, a non-resistant consciousness." Sometimes there is no conscious awareness of the initial impulse to composition, or the impulse may have been forgotten; "but whatever it is, emotion, apprehended or hidden, is a part of it, for only emotion can rouse the subconscious into action." [5] W. B. Yeats puts an emphasis on sensation, which in context we may understand to mean excited perception:

> Art bids us touch and taste and hear and see the world, and shrinks from what Blake calls mathematic form, from every abstract thing, from all that is of the brain only, from all that is not a fountain jetting from the entire hopes, memories, and sensations of the body. . . .

---

[4] Brewster Ghiselin, *The Creative Process: A Symposium* (Berkeley, Calif.: University of California Press, 1954), p. 90.
[5] *Ibid.,* p. 111.

> God guard me from those thoughts men think
> In the mind alone;
> He that sings a lasting song
> Thinks in a marrow-bone.[6]

Ghiselin himself, while working on "Bath of Aphrodite," at one point went over the fragments he had already written, "partly in expectation of revising them, but mostly in order to rouse *the images that made me feel my life*." [7] And these statements suggest not only the compositional process as it appears to individual poets, but also the impact on the reader's consciousness of whole segments of world poetry. Arabic poetry "dealt with the feelings spinning around an event or fact," [8] Japanese and Chinese poetry are recognized to be instinct with feeling.

Much the same thing is true of prose. On his fifth trip to Europe, Thomas Wolfe felt more desperately homesick than ever before; and (he writes), "I really believe that *from this emotion, this constant and almost intolerable effort of memory and desire,* the material and the structure of the books I now began to write were derived." While he was writing in New York, at times in despair, he nevertheless lived with extraordinary fullness. "My powers of *feeling and reflection*—even the sense of hearing, and above all, my powers of memory, had reached the greatest degree of sharpness that they had ever known." [9] His whole psyche was aroused, not his intellect alone. "One thing," remarks Gertrude Stein, "which I have tried to tell Americans is that there can be no truly great creation without passion"; and again, in replying to the question, "What has passion got to do with choosing an art form?" she said "Everything. There is nothing else that determines form." [10] Dorothy Canfield testifies that, "broadly viewed," her stories "all have exactly the same genesis," and she confesses that she "cannot conceive of any creative fiction written from any other beginning . . . that of a generally intensified emotional sensibility." When—for ex-

---

6 *Ibid.,* pp. 107 and 108.
7 *Ibid.,* p. 130 (my italics).
8 A. L. Kroeber, *Configurations of Culture Growth* (Berkeley, Calif.: University of California Press, 1944), p. 518.
9 Ghiselin, *Creative Process,* pp. 192 and 200 (my italics).
10 *Ibid.,* pp. 168 and 170.

ample—after much preliminary thought, she began to write "Flint and Fire," she found, after four hours that had seemed to her only a half hour, that "my cheeks were flaming, my feet were cold, my lips parched." [11] According to Katherine Anne Porter, the creative question is "how to convey a sense of whatever is *there*, as feeling, within you, to the reader." [12] Of drama, John Galsworthy writes that it is "that imaginative expression of human energy, which, through technical concretion of feeling and perception, tends to reconcile the individual with the universal, by exciting in him impersonal emotion"; and, he adds, "the greatest art is that which excites the greatest impersonal emotion in an hypothecated perfect human being." [13] Nietzsche describes vividly the state of heightened emotionality in which he wrote *Zarathustra:* "There is an ecstasy whose terrific tension is sometimes released by a flood of tears." [14]

The citations could be multiplied endlessly. Anyone who has read widely about literary inspiration will recognize these quotations as typical—not, indeed, typical of all that is said about the birth of a poem, play, or novel, but typical of one part or aspect of nearly all such descriptions.

Practitioners of the other arts have described their creative experiences in very similar terms. Julian Levi sees in his own painting a union of thought and emotion:

> I am seeking an integration between what I feel and what I have learned by objective criteria . . . above all I hope to resolve the polarity which exists between an essentially emotional view of nature and a classical, austere sense of design.[15]

Picasso's painting seems to the painter himself to be passionate: "I order things in accordance with my passions. . . . What I want is that my picture should evoke nothing but emotion." When he walks in a forest he contracts "an indigestion of greenness" and "must empty this sensation into a picture." [16] The perception be-

---

[11] *Ibid.,* pp. 174 and 178.
[12] *Ibid.,* p. 206.
[13] Quoted in Ludwig Lewisohn (ed.), *A Modern Book of Criticism* (New York: Boni and Liveright, 1919), p. 118.
[14] Ghiselin, *Creative Process,* p. 210.
[15] *Ibid.,* p. 56.
[16] *Ibid.,* pp. 49–51.

comes painfully *full*. Van Gogh recognized his successful drawings by sensing feelings in them:

> When I have a model who is quiet and steady and with whom I am acquainted, then I draw repeatedly till there is one drawing that is different from the rest, which does not look like an ordinary study, but more typical and with more feeling. All the same it was made under circumstances similar to those of the others, yet the latter are just studies with less feeling and life in them. . . . As to *The Little Winter Gardens,* you said yourself they had so much feeling; all right, but that was not accidental—I drew them several times and there was no feeling in them. Then afterwards— after I had done the ones that were so stiff—came the others.[17]

A sculptor whose work is at the opposite extreme from romantic denies that form is an end in itself: "I am very much aware that associational, psychological factors play a large part in sculpture." For example,

> rounded forms convey an idea of fruitfulness, maturity, probably because the earth, women's breasts, and most fruits are rounded. . . . My sculpture is becoming less representational, less an outward visual copy, and so what some people would call more abstract; but only because I believe that in this way I can present the human psychological content of my work with the greatest directness and intensity.[18]

A dancer gives her testimony:

> My purpose is not to "interpret" the emotions. . . . My dances flow rather from certain states of being, different stages of vitality which release in me a varying play of the emotions, and in themselves dictate the distinguishing atmospheres of the dances.

When working with a group, her purpose is "to seek out a common feeling." [19] An "intellectual" composer of music adds his voice:

> These bars from the Prelude to Tristan do not express for us love or frustration or even longing: but they reproduce for us, both

---

17 *Ibid.*, pp. 46–47.
18 Henry Moore, quoted *ibid.*, pp. 72–73.
19 Mary Wigman, quoted *ibid.*, pp. 74–76.

qualitatively and dynamically, certain gestures of the spirit which are to be sure less specifically definable than any of these emotions, but which energize them and make them vital to us.

So it seems to me that this is the essence of musical expression. "Emotion" is specific, individual and conscious; music goes deeper than this, to the energies which animate our psychic life, and out of these creates a pattern which has an existence, laws, and human significance of its own.[20]

Everywhere in the literature which describes aesthetic creation, reports include some such statement as those which have been quoted; and the impression is borne out by the observed conduct of artists. That art also includes a cognitive element, and that this too is important, has already been granted. But that aesthetic cognition grows out of, or at intense moments is accompanied by, feelings is quite as significant for the aesthetic theorist. The editor of the collection of reports from which many of the foregoing quotations have been taken sums up his findings by saying flatly, "Production by a process of purely conscious calculation seems never to occur." [21] Connections can be *felt* as well as thought; and, though the ultimate art work has cognitive value, it is also an embodiment of feelings.

Critical recognition of feeling in art

The foregoing quotations have intentionally been drawn, for the most part, from the published writings or conversations of recent artists, since the importance of the emotional element in aesthetic experience has been brought into question only recently. The emphasis of classical, neoclassical, and romantic criticism on feelings is too well known to require documentation. In our own century, too, while influential aestheticians have been urging the importance of aesthetic cognition, other theorists have continued to stress the role of feeling. A few of these must be named, for I am anxious to avoid giving the impression that the approach taken in the present book is either wholly new or, even in the immediate climate of opinion, eccentric.

---

20 Roger Sessions, quoted *ibid.*, p. 36.
21 *Ibid.*, p. 5.

We may begin with philosophical aestheticians, of whom there is space to mention only a few. Samuel Alexander, a critical realist, in *Beauty and Other Forms of Value,* asserted that "the impulse to creation is based upon the material passions provoked by the subjects, but is distinguishable from them and is formal." The creative process itself, however, "arises from the excitement caused by the subject matter." [22] These statements are significant because Alexander believes art to be cognitive and throughout his discussion shows an especially lively interest in aesthetic form, going so far, at one point, as to recommend that in the reading of poetry no effort be made to throw feeling into the words, lest "the undisturbed appreciation of beauty" be obscured by "over-excitement of the material passions." [23] But if the creative process is accompanied by excitement, and if, as he himself has urged, there is "no difference in kind between aesthetic appreciation and aesthetic creation," there must be some feeling in appreciation also. We can understand his emphasis on a certain coolness in aesthetic contemplation to be motivated by a desire to keep the feelings evoked by an art object in the aesthetic universe instead of allowing them to spill over into the world of practical activity. The example is instructive. In all probability, most, if not all, of the contemporary de-emphasis of emotion in art springs from similar motives, and the very men who have done most to discourage empathetic sensitivity to the affective curves of literary works would admit, if pressed, that of course there is feeling in literature.

Another exponent of aesthetic cognition, John Dewey, speaks frequently about feelings in *Art as Experience*: as, for example, in pointing out that "when excitement about subject matter goes deep, it stirs up a store of attitudes and meanings derived from prior experience." [24] Here again a desire to resist the popular misconception that art has to do *merely* with the emotions has led an influential aesthetician to adopt modes of expression which allow a misreading of his total theory. One other example taken from

---

22 Alexander, *Beauty and Other Forms of Value,* p. 72.
23 *Ibid.,* p. 131.
24 John Dewey, *Art as Experience* (New York: Minton, Balch & Co., 1934), p. 65.

philosophic aesthetics will perhaps serve for all. Wilhelm Worringer's *Abstraktion und Einfühlung,* which stresses the effort in much art to render objects in their "restricted material individuality" by such means as approximation to "crystalline" form,[25] might easily be misread as an argument for purely intellectual appreciation of art. In fact, however, Worringer is much interested in the psychological needs served by art, calls for a "history of world-feeling," and wishes to analyze not the technical abilities of artists but their aesthetic drives (*Kunstwollen*).[26] Probably no aesthetician of importance has really thought that the aesthetic transaction was or should be completely devoid of feeling. A stressing of the desirability that in aesthetic contemplation a certain composure be maintained is susceptible, however, of misunderstanding.

More directly influential in literary circles have been the ideas of literary theorists—men who sometimes (though by no means always) have some acquaintance with philosophical aesthetics but adapt the principles for a specific use. For example, Louis Cazamian, the French critic and literary historian, would make criticism turn on the *idées génératrices* of literary works, which are "almost always an emotion of some kind."[27] Paul Goodman, in a recent volume called *The Structure of Literature,* thinks that in art "there is less anxiety and withdrawal" than in real life, so that "the meaning of the emotion can flower. . . . Works of plastic and musical art are pure language of the emotions."[28] Richard Moritz Meyer emphasizes excitement in the creative process:

> If we compare but for a moment the birth of a poem among such primitive men as can still be observed with the birth of one within the zones of our civilization, we shall find that there remain but two things common to the two processes, two inevitable circumstances: the element of subjective excitement; the object that induces the excitement.[29]

---

25 Wilhelm Worringer, *Abstraktion und Einfühlung: Ein Beitrag zur Stilpsychologie* (3d ed.; Munich: R. Piper & Co. Verlag, 1911), p. 41.

26 See *ibid.,* esp. pp. 9 and 14.

27 Louis Cazamian, *Criticism in the Making* (New York: The Macmillan Company, 1929), p. 31.

28 Paul Goodman, *The Structure of Literature* (Chicago: The University of Chicago Press, 1954), p. 5.

29 Quoted in Lewisohn (ed.), *Modern Book of Criticism,* p. 60.

Another German, Richard Mueller-Freienfels, finds that "in most literature the true significance lies in the images, feelings, passions, volitional stimuli which are merely communicated by" language.[30] Sir Herbert Read, creative artist as well as sensitive critic, once wrote sweepingly: "To render emotion exactly—there is no need to insist on that phrase as the definition of all art whatsoever that is worthy of the name." [31] Rémy de Gourmont, who has had considerable influence among the New Critics of England and America, distinguishes two kinds of style, one visual and one emotional.

> If a writer possesses the emotional in addition to the visual memory, if, while evoking a material spectacle he has also the power of replacing himself into the precise emotional state which the spectacle produced in him, he is master of the whole art of writing.[32]

A recent critic of the psychological novel, Leon Edel, believes that "the critical reader who intellectually apprehends a book but has achieved no particular feeling in the process usually has only a ledger-book concept of the work." [33] He suggests that the stimulus to the technical inventiveness of such a novelist as Dorothy Richardson (and perhaps also James Joyce, Marcel Proust, William Faulkner, and Virginia Woolf) was the failure of traditional fictive techniques to render feelings adequately.[34] Without forgetting the part of the aesthetic transaction which has tended to slip from incautious formulations, Jane E. Harrison, after examining the primitive roots of art, expressed what has probably been in the minds of most persons who have objected to an overemphasis on affections: Let the artist

> feel strongly, and see raptly—that is, in complete detachment. Let him cast this, his rapt vision and his intense emotion, into outside

---

30 Quoted in Lewisohn, *ibid.,* pp. 76–77.

31 Sir Herbert Read, *Phases of English Poetry* (London: Hogarth Press, Ltd., 1928), p. 121.

32 Quoted in Lewisohn (ed.), *Modern Book of Criticism,* pp. 31–32.

33 Leon Edel, *The Psychological Novel, 1900–1950* (Philadelphia: J. B. Lippincott Company, 1955), p. 101.

34 *Ibid.,* p. 111.

form, a statue or a painting; that form will have about it a nameless thing, an unearthly aroma, which we call beauty.[35]

With this quotation the series may be brought to an end. Here are to be found all the elements that have been brought centrally into the present discussion: the absorption experienced in a "good" or "proper" aesthetic transaction; the maintenance at the same time of aesthetic distance—a realization that the art work exists in a universe different from that of everyday experience; and the "vision," or cognitive insight, which has played so important a role in critical theory of the last few decades. For once, all the elements have been brought into combination (together with the concept of beauty, about which nothing has been said). We must leave the matter here, for our purpose is not to review aesthetic speculation in detail but only to say what is necessary to relate the present work to others which have affected the reflective atmosphere in which it will be encountered.

It remains, before proceeding with the task which will occupy us in following chapters, to observe that more than one aesthetician has gone far toward basing a theory of art fundamentally on the recognition of affective patterns. Thus Susanne Langer, in *Feeling and Form*, begins from the premise that art works are symbols of human feelings. Even a simple decorative frieze is structurally similar to an affective pattern. The book has been favorably received: in the *Kenyon Review*, which is edited by one of the staunchest defenders of the art-equals-cognition view, it was reviewed under the heading, "This May Be the Book." Rudolph Arnheim, a psychologist, has not only written brilliantly about art works as isomorphs of feelings but has challenged the naïve realism of Ruskin's nineteenth-century strictures about the pathetic fallacy. The phrase "pathetic fallacy," he has urged,

> implies a painful misunderstanding based on a conception of the world which stresses material differences and neglects structural analogies. When Torquato Tasso relates the wailing of the wind and the dewdrops shed by the stars to the departure of his love

---

[35] Jane E. Harrison, *Ancient Art and Ritual* (New York: Henry Holt and Company, Inc., 1913), pp. 212–13.

he is not pretending to believe in a fallacious animism, which endows nature with sympathetic feeling, but is using genuine structural similarities of the perceivable behavior of wind and water on the one hand and the experience and expression of grief on the other.[36]

Baensch on the cognition of feelings

I wish to dwell especially, however, on a remarkable article on "Kunst und Gefühl" to which attention has been called by Mrs. Langer, for in this the contrary emphases on cognition and feeling are reconciled through the perception that aesthetic constructs offer the best possible opportunities precisely for the cognizing of feelings.

The author, Otto Baensch, begins by announcing his object.

It will be shown that art, like philosophy, is a spiritual activity through which we raise the world-substance to communal consciousness, and that, moreover, it is the special task of art to accomplish this work for the affective content of the world. According to this view the function of art is not to gratify the percipient in any way—not even the loftiest way—but to make known to him something of which he is ignorant.[37]

Art is thus cognitive, but what it cognizes is feelings. For example, when we say that a landscape has a "mood," we think our real meaning to be that the contemplation of the landscape arouses in us a feeling which we can then read back into it.

This, however, is theory. The immediate, empirical datum suggests to us, at first, nothing of such an objectifying process. What in theory appears to be the result of an objectifying process enters the consciousness as a fact which is simply there, without manifesting itself as something created by us. . . . The landscape does not express a mood, it has the mood; the mood surrounds it, fills it, and pervades it like the light with which it shines, the odor which streams from it; the mood belongs with the total impres-

---

[36] Rudolf Arnheim, W. H. Auden, Karl Shapiro, and Donald A. Stauffer, *Poets at Work* (New York: Harcourt, Brace and Company, Inc., 1948), p. 151.
[37] Otto Baensch, "Kunst und Gefühl," *Logos,* XII (1923), 1.

sion and can be separated from it as a part of the whole only by abstraction.[38]

All this does not, of course, mean that the mood would exist in the landscape if no observer were present. Rather, the landscape objectifies a feeling in such a way that it can produce the feeling in spectators who do not come to it with the feeling already prepared. The world as it impinges on human consciousness has affective tones which rather impress themselves on the human psyche than emanate into it from the psyche.[39] Such feelings are the special province of art, which by nonrational processes (at least in part) allows them to be contemplated and hence, in a fashion, *known*.

Baensch's development of this thesis is worked out largely in terms of music and need not be recapitulated in detail; but we may follow briefly his generalization of the aesthetic process. How is it possible, he inquires, to give unity to the qualitatively rich, but formless, impressions received from experience?

> The answer is that we can do this by creating objects in which we embody the feelings to be isolated as objective feelings, so that the embodied feelings must come to the consciousness of every empathetic observer of the objects in the mode of affective intuitions.

Such objects are art objects, and the activity which brings them into being is artistry.

> The feelings, both subjective and objective, come to the artist's consciousness, as to every man's, in the forward and backward fluctuations already described between the self and the non-self. . . . It is incumbent upon the artist, however, to give them form (*Gestalt*). . . . Out of the fullness of his experience he must extract and give relief to complexes which he feels as internally cohering structures. At the same time, out of the endless internal multiplicity of the structures so extracted and given relief, he must undertake a process of abstraction and condensation and set up internal limits, must divide the structures into cohering groups and sub-groups. Because

---

[38] *Ibid.*, p. 2.
[39] E.g., we are sometimes offended by the sight of a cheerful landscape when our spirits are depressed; we may say of a picture, "Life isn't that bitter"; etc.

of the peculiar nature and mode of consciousness of the feelings, however, this task cannot be given over wholly and directly to the feelings themselves. The division and the selective condensation, together with the inner framework of the feeling complexes to be structured, can be handled only in such a way that the object in which the feeling complex wins objective status is created and formed at the same moment. In practice the structuring of the feeling and that of the object in which the feeling is to be embodied falls together into a single activity.[40]

Thus the art object and the feeling to be embodied in it gain clarity simultaneously, and artistry at once defines the feeling for the artist's consciousness and makes it accessible to the consciousness of others.

The insight expressed in this analysis is important for aesthetics. If it is perhaps not the whole truth about art (what truth is the whole truth?), it is at least a truth which very much needs emphasizing at present. Indeed, the dignifying and exalting of art that seems to be intended by the exponents of aesthetic cognition can very likely be served best by an aesthetic theory which assigns to art an area of conscious activity that is peculiar to it rather than an area which is shared by such other branches of rational inquiry as philosophy and science. The discipline which most nearly intrudes upon that of philosophical aesthetics as here defined is psychology; but psychology aims at causal explanation, whereas art aims at the contemplation of the thing-in-itself, at the communication and comprehension not so much of its mode of becoming as of its mode of being. If the realm of art is primarily that of the feelings, or of consciousness in which feelings play an active and formative role, that realm is securely and permanently its own.

---

[40] Baensch, *op. cit.*, pp. 14–15.

2

Literature and the Unified Sensibility

At the beginning of the previous chapter it was observed that in absorbed reading the mind tends to submit itself to the laws of an aesthetic universe as completely as the universe itself permits, so that relationships can be appreciated which at cooler moments, when logical thought processes are dominant, would seem puzzling or inexplicable. But how can the irrational processes which are active in excited reading be submitted to rational analysis? Literary theory is a branch of aesthetics, which in turn is a branch of philosophy; and philosophy, as contrasted with art or mysticism, is persistently, even doggedly, logical.

The approach through psychology

One kind of entry into the nonrational consciousness can be made through psychology. Since psychology has recently interested many writers and some critics, the possibility of using it is attractive. Unfortunately, there are reasons why as yet psychology is inadequate, by itself, for the task to be undertaken. In general, most really successful psychological analyses of literature have had a narrow scope, and they tend to concentrate on writers concerning whom a good deal of biographical information is accessible—that is to say, on writers of the comparatively recent past. If what is in view is rather an inclusive theory of literature than a series of case histories, the effort to work into the problem through psychology would appear to be unpromising. Even if the difficulties were surmounted, there is a strong possibility that literature, and indeed all art, would appear from this point of view to be little more than wish fulfillment. That conclusion, however, is ruled out by the apparently valid discovery that art has cognitive significance. Many insights obtained from psychology will undoubtedly be incorporated in a complete description of what goes on in states of aesthetic absorption; but at the moment it seems that a description based entirely, or mostly, on data obtained from psychology would be unsatisfactory.

The approach through anthropology

A better course will be to see what can be learned through anthropology. On the hypothesis that a desire to construe the universe of human experience in purely rational terms is a comparatively late evolutionary development, nonrational psychic activities are residual from, or continuous with, psychic patterns common at an earlier stage of development and therefore can be studied most conveniently in primitive minds. This is not to say, of course, that savages do not think or that even the most "advanced" member of our own society is a purely rational creature; but if Homo sapiens as we know him developed gradually from something rather like one of the lower anthropoids, his psychic habits were less rational at an earlier stage of development than now. An earlier stage of development could be observed not long ago, and in many parts of the world can be observed still, in societies that we call "primitive" or "savage"; and anthropologists have studied many such societies carefully. The relevant literature is in fact enormous. By observing the human psyche as it exists, or existed recently, in savages, we can arrive at conclusions about the irrational tendencies in the modern consciousness. The method is that of all genetic studies, and as such requires no detailed justification. At the same time, it is economical to study a phenomenon at the point of greatest density, where it is least complicated by modifying factors. I propose, therefore, to see whether something can be learned about psychic activities in states of literary absorption by comparing the irrational elements in literary experience with the irrational elements in primitive thought.

Reductionism and holism

At this point, what will appear to some readers to be a serious difficulty must be met honestly. At present, many anthropologists are strongly disinclined to generalize about the savage mind or savage behavior. The causes of their reluctance are chiefly two. First, although much evidence is at hand, much more remains to be gathered; and what has already been investigated might often be studied afresh, from a new point of view or by more responsible methods. Secondly, since primitive societies are disappearing rapidly, it is felt that they must be studied at all costs while they still exist, the enormous and complicated task of putting together the total bodies of evidence not being given a high priority in the meantime. Everyone will agree that the considerations are weighty. Moreover, when generalization has been attempted, it has often proved to be untrustworthy. Yet, potentially, generalization is, of course, possible unless the class concept "primitives" has no objective content; and postponement of synthesis in almost any area of knowledge can always be urged on the ground that findings are incomplete. The real issue here is not between possibility and impossibility but between two scientific methods, one favored, generally, by American and British anthropologists, the other by Continental scholars; and it bears not only on anthropology but also on psychology, which, although subsidiary in the present study, is also of importance to it.

The nature of the issue can be indicated by a comment of Gordon W. Allport in the Foreword to an English version of a German psychological work which will be much quoted in following pages. There are, says Allport, broadly speaking, "two contrasting approaches to the subject matter of psychological science," of which one may be called mechanistic and the other organic. If there are important differences of outlook within the two schools, the divergence between them is much greater: one is "bent on the discovery of elementary detail, the other on the discovery of significant complex structures in mental life." Of the two approaches, the more familiar to American students is the mechanistic.

> The reasons need not concern us here; suffice it to say that they are bound up with the pragmatic emphasis upon habits and capacities so characteristic of the American ethos. . . . Around the central concept of *Struktur* there had grown up in Germany in the first quarter of the present century the movements known as *Gestalt* psychology, the psychology of the *Komplex-qualität*, the *Geisteswissenschaften*, and *Personalistik*. Although there were differences to mark these schools, all of them agreed on the basic tenet that the study of mental *patterns* should take precedence over the study of mental *elements*. The introduction of this general point of view into American psychology has been taking place gradually during the past two decades.[1]

Americans must, I think, recognize what Allport calls their "cultural predilection for the reductionistic and mechanistic approach"[2]—a preference which may go so far as to stigmatize as "unscientific" any research that follows a basically different method and proceeds toward a different goal. As a people, we tend to feel at home with figures and apparatus and to accept readily discoveries made with their assistance. The methods of Sigmund Freud and Carl Jung,

---

[1] For the excerpt, see Heinz Werner, *Comparative Psychology of Mental Development* (rev. ed.; Chicago: Follett Publishing Co., 1948), ix.
[2] *Ibid.*

although known to the educated public, appear to receive remarkably little attention in university courses in psychology.[3] In no other country or time, probably, has there been so positivistic an intellectual temper. Its result has been substantial achievements which no one would wish to discredit. Yet it is patent that truths are accessible by methods other than reductionism, and no irreparable harm will be done the American public if it is now and then exposed to reflections based on scientific disciplines not predominantly sanctioned by its institutions.

Much the same comment can be made about anthropology, which in both Germany and France has long been investigated by holistic methods not often used in America. Emile Durkheim and Lucien Lévy-Bruhl in France, Ernst Cassirer, Heinz Werner (who was Austrian by birth), and others in Germany have studied patterns rather than elements, with consequences of the first importance for certain areas of learning.[4] Undoubtedly, some of the conclusions have been dubious, and none of the men just mentioned was a field worker. In compensation, their philosophical sophistication has tended to outrun that of their American and British colleagues; so that, if something is lost in one direction, something is gained in another. The Continental scholars are not unintelligent and not lacking in industry; on the contrary, their knowledge is often astonishing in range, in detail, and in profundity. Moreover—and for the present study, at least, the consideration is crucial—their findings are *usable* in a way that those of American anthropologists are not. No immediately recognizable significance for literary studies attaches to most of the data gathered by American anthropologists. This fact is not discreditable to the anthropologists, for they do not work with the needs of literary scholars in mind. When, however, the literary theorist finds in the writings of Continental scholars well-documented assertions about primitives which bear obviously and directly on his own interests,

---

[3] E.g., at my own university, the names of Sigmund Freud, Carl Jung, Alfred Adler, and other Continental depth psychologists do not (1958–59) appear in eight pages of course titles and descriptions. Yet the Department of Psychology is a distinguished one.

[4] The American "configurational" anthropologists differ in tending to study one culture at a time or else in emphasizing contrasts rather than similarities.

he can hardly be blamed for wanting to appropriate them. He will check the assertions in whatever ways he can and in the process will find some to be evidently unsound and others to be supported by anthropological writings oriented differently. He need not, however, determine finally to credit only the methods and findings of his countrymen. He will console himself also by the reflection that in scholarship, as in clothing, much depends on fashion. As a distinguished American psychologist has said, the noting of likenesses is not popular today "because of a fashion of thought according to which it is more scientific to talk about differences than about similarities." [5] But likeness is as real and important an element in the world and in human experience as difference, and a desire to study it is not really naïve.

Resemblance between literary absorption and primitive psychic habits

The first task is to establish that literary absorption does in fact have points of resemblance to the psychic states of primitive men. For the moment we must be satisfied to describe absorption as characterized by a kind of total awareness in which the senses and feelings, as well as the discursive reason, are active—a state, that is, of "unitary" consciousness, in which there is no room in the awakened parts of the psyche for anything but what is engrossing attention. The transition from a rational grasp of the object to an affective or merely sensory grasp of it, and back again, can be made smoothly when required because what controls the situation is not a sophisticated desire to cognize in any particular way but a felt need, generated by a compulsive interest, to maintain contact by any possible means. Is it true that primitive men are susceptible to this state? They do not, of course, sit in armchairs and read books; but if in the course of other activities they achieve an absorption which seems to resemble that of aesthetic seizure, we may proceed to look for similarities between their mental processes and those of absorbed readers.

---

[5] Rudolf Arnheim, *Art and Visual Perception* (Berkeley, Calif.: University of California Press, 1954), p. 134.

That savages are often absorbed is beyond question. To be sure, the moments of absorption tend to alternate with moments of lethargy, so that to white observers members of primitive races often appear to be either indolent or frantic, either fully committed to an activity or not committed to it at all. A. B. Ellis, writing of the Ewe-speaking tribes of the African Slave Coast, notes:

> They are usually deficient in energy. . . . Many of these moral deficiencies may be attributed to the relaxing influences of a hot climate, which besides being primarily inimical to physical and mental energy, causes on the other hand a greater amount of intensity whenever the state of indolence is overcome, to which the savage outbursts of passion and the frantic excesses of the Negro in moments of excitement are due.[6]

The Ewe tend, that is, to be bored whenever they are not absorbed. R. R. Marett generalizes the comment: "Certain it is that the observers of rude races incline to put down most of them as apathetic, when not tuned up to concert-pitch by a dance or other social event."[7] Bronislaw Malinowski comments on the intensity with which the savage throws himself into the performance of certain magical practices. A very widespread act of magic consists of pointing, or throwing, or thrusting some pointed object toward an enemy; but "the emotional setting, the gestures and expressions of the sorcerer during the performance, have been but seldom described. Yet these are of the greatest importance." The magician acts angry, he operates with "an intense expression of fury and hatred." Similarly, in love magic the performance "reproduces the behavior of a heart-sick lover," in war magic there is a show of combative passion, in exorcisms there is an atmosphere of terror.[8] Nothing is held back; all the resources of consciousness are brought to bear on the matter in hand. The readiness of primitive minds to be *invaded* by objects of special interest, to become *enthralled*

---

6 A. B. Ellis, *The Ewe-Speaking Peoples of the Slave Coast of West Africa* (London: Chapman & Hall, Ltd., 1890), p. 10.

7 R. R. Marett, *Anthropology* (New York: Henry Holt and Co., ?1912), pp. 91–92.

8 Bronislaw Malinowski, *Magic, Science and Religion and Other Essays,* selected by Robert Redfield (Boston: The Beacon Press, 1948), pp. 52–53.

in such communal activities as dancing and religious ceremonies, and, even in such a pursuit as solitary hunting, to *rivet* their attention on something external to the self (as a cat is oblivious of human observers while stalking a mouse), is in fact written so large in anthropological literature that self-consciousness has often been asserted to exist only in advanced cultures. In less highly developed communities, interest tends either to be very strong or hardly to exist at all.

That this is so can be suggested to persons who have done little reading in anthropology by an appeal to direct observation. For example, the Indian dances which can still be watched in the western half of the United States are performed with a seriousness that is almost comic. "Don't they know how silly they look?" a spectator may wonder, glancing sideways at his neighbor to see whether his own impulse to laugh is shared. The dancers' feet shuffle monotonously in simple patterns, the gourds and tambourines are shaken steadily, the feathers and other properties are moved into grotesque positions, yet the whole consciousness of the performers is plainly engrossed in the ceremony—and this after many of the Indians have gone to public schools administered by white men and are sometimes (one suspects) more at home in English than in the language they are chanting. One is reminded of the absorption shown by children in play that seems incomprehensible or trivial to adults.

The impression is deepened by the moving pictures of primitive peoples now sometimes exhibited publicly. Whenever the event being filmed is ceremonial, or even merely social, the faces caught by the camera are likely to wear rapt expressions, and the bodily postures to reveal intense concentration. Javanese farmers invoking good harvests, Calypso singers and dancers, an island people praying for the safe return of fishermen, a blood-drinking tribe of Central Africa celebrating a communal festival, a Dayak in the interior of Borneo demonstrating by a dance performed in his bride's village the martial prowess that makes him a fit husband— in fact, any person or group in a society which has not developed a sophisticated awareness that personality can be asserted by maintaining a psychic distance between the actor and the activity

—is likely to show outwardly, when doing something important, the inner rapture which accompanies a wholehearted commitment of the self to a compelling interest.

Even in the "civilized" white communities of the United States, absorption is not infrequently attained. It can be observed at a teen-age dance, at a revival meeting, at sports events, at a political convention, or whenever groups of people share an interest which is deepened by social communion. In general, the susceptibility to rapture increases toward the lower, or more "primitive," end of the social and educational scale. A Negro jazz band performing in a night club is less self-consciously separate from the music it is producing than a symphony orchestra performing in a concert hall. Among actual savages there appears to be little rational self-criticism in the course of any deeply interesting activity. The feelings are so strongly aroused that resistance to them is hardly evoked at all by a desire to let conduct be monitored steadily by the reason.

That the primitive consciousness tends, when interested, to become enthralled by the object of attention has often been remarked. Thus Cassirer, in contrasting the mythical thought of primitives with the empirico-theoretical reflections of Western sophisticates, finds an essential difference to be the dominance of the immediate present in the former.

In this mode, thought does not dispose freely over the data of intuition, in order to relate and compare them to each other, but is captivated and enthralled by the intuition which suddenly confronts it. It comes to rest in the immediate experience; the sensible present is so great that everything else dwindles before it. For a person whose apprehension is under the spell of this mythico-religious attitude, it is as though the whole world were simply annihilated; the immediate content, whatever it be, that commands his religious interest so completely fills his consciousness that nothing else can exist beside and apart from it. The ego is spending all its energy on this single object, lives in it, loses itself in it. Instead of a widening of intuitive experience, we find here its extreme limitation; instead of expansion that would lead through greater and greater spheres of being, we have here an impulse toward concentration; instead of extensive distribution, intensive compression.

This focusing of all forces on a single point is the prerequisite for all mythical thinking and mythical formulation.[9]

Discursive thought proceeds mainly outward from specific objects or ideas: the individual is subsumed under a species, from which, however, it remains distinct. "Every concept has a certain 'area' that belongs to it and whereby it is distinguished from other conceptual spheres." Accordingly, the intellectual process expands over a widening sphere of perception and contemplation. In the nondiscursive reflection of savages—as in aesthetic cognition—"the mental view is not widened, but compressed; it is, so to speak, distilled into a single point." [10] What brings it to a point is rapture. Attention is so engrossed that there is no leisure for comparison, for classification, for the analytic isolation of strands.

A compatible conclusion has been arrived at by Heinz Werner, who, because he brought to his anthropological investigations the special competencies of a trained and brilliant psychologist, is an especially authoritative guide here. The earliest psychic experience is an emotionally toned motor reaction.[11] In adult primitives, affections are more intimately related to physical movements than in modern sophisticates; [12] so that—for example—in primitive laments sorrow is bound up with bodily activity.[13] The tendency of external stimuli to mingle with, and become indistinguishable from, the motor reactions they induce is accompanied by a merging of perceptions and ideas.[14] The mind-body tends thus to be less readily divisible than among educated Westerners, the basis of unity being a feeling which bridges the dichotomies of the mental and the physical, the stimulus and the response.

In brief, primitive thinking is not only concrete but affective as well. The structure of primitive thought is concretely determined

---

[9] Ernst Cassirer, *Language and Myth,* trans. Susanne K. Langer (New York: Harper & Brothers Publishers, 1946), pp. 32–33.

[10] *Ibid.,* p. 90.

[11] Heinz Werner, *Die Ursprünge der Metapher* (Leipzig: Wilhelm Englemann, 1919), p. 36.

[12] Cf. Werner, *Comparative Psychology,* p. 83.

[13] See the remarks about the expression of sorrow by the Ceylonese Veddas, *ibid.*

[14] Cf. Werner, *Comparative Psychology,* p. 148.

in so far as it has a tendency to configurate pictorially, and it is emotionally determined in so far as it unites that which is affectively related.[15]

Interest compels a *total* activation of the psyche (not to mention the body, which in aesthetic contemplation can make only small muscular adjustments). As in aesthetic absorption, the transition from a rational grasp of the object to a merely sensory grasp of it, if necessary at all (the seizure at given moments being less than total), occasions no difficulty because interest is accompanied by an affection which permeates the whole transaction and gives it a felt unity.

The singleness even of complex situations as they are experienced by primitives is suggested by a further observation of Werner's. The narration of a series of incidents by savages is so disturbed by an interruption that the story cannot be picked up where it was broken off but must be started again at the beginning.[16] No analytic rearrangement of parts is attempted, for the entire sequence is sensed as organically single; the parts are inseparable from the whole.[17] A similar observation is made by Franz Boas:

> A Pueblo [Indian] will say, "You cannot say, 'he entered the house,' for he must first climb up the ladder, then down into the house. He must greet those present properly and receive the proper courteous reply." None of these steps may be omitted. . . . The Kwakiutl cannot say, "Then he spoke," but they would say "Then he arose, spoke and said." They do not allow a person to arrive at a place without first letting him start and travel. An epic diffusiveness, an insistence on details is characteristic of most free primitive narrative.[18]

The coherence of details in complexes is too powerful to be disrupted. Experiences are gulped down whole, not laid apart into elements, of which some may be excised as nonessential. The

---

[15] *Ibid.*, p. 302.

[16] Cf. *ibid.*, pp. 159–60.

[17] "Diffuse imagery has a global character which colors each individual part, a pervasive quality in which all the constituent parts are embedded."—*Ibid.*, p. 160.

[18] Franz Boas, *Primitive Art* (New York: Dover Publications, 1955), pp. 308–309.

psyche is so completely caught up into the immediate present that it is incapable, while the spell lasts, of keeping a part of itself cognitively distant. It exists *in* the situation, not outside it in some deliberately chosen vantage point of consciousness.

Synesthesia as regressive

From these considerations it appears probable that the highly differentiated sensorium of adult Westerners has developed out of something simpler.[19] Synesthesia is a case in point: it appears to have been more common formerly than now and is still commoner in children than in adults. The basis of association in synesthesia appears to be not so much the triggering of one actual sense response by another qualitatively different one as the similar expressive value of the two for a feeling. Thus a man who associates a certain tone with a certain color will often say that the color "is not really optically present but is somehow *felt*." [20] Feeling is primary and basic, differentiated cognitive activity, later and derived. In aesthetic absorption, there is partial regression to earlier psychic patterns. For the deeply involved reader of a poem or novel, as for the primitive engaged in religious ceremonial or warfare, the partitions between psychic compartments tend to melt away, and the experience to fuse into singleness.

Recapitulation of primitive psychic states by children

Additional support is given to the foregoing analysis by the apparent tendency of young children to recapitulate primitive stages of consciousness. Ludwig von Holzschuher remarks on this fact in *Praktische Psychologie*.

If we consider the *ontogeny of a man of our race,* we recognize in the early stages of his development certain parallels with primi-

---

[19] Cf. Werner, *Comparative Psychology,* pp. 86–103.

[20] Heinz Werner, *Einführung in die Entwicklungspsychologie* (3d ed.; Munich: Johann Ambrosius Barth, 1953), p. 66. This passage in the later German edition does not appear in the English translation, called *Comparative Psychology,* etc., which has been quoted elsewhere for the reader's convenience.

tives. . . . The child is similarly characterized by a high degree of impulsiveness and lack of governance, by absorption in the immediate present and inconsistency, and also, of course, by incompetence in logical and critical thought. Feelings and wish-images flow, in the child, without sharp boundaries into sensations and perceptions of reality. The child lives in his own magical world and dreams, as it were, with open eyes; he remains still predominantly in the "primitive consciousness," into which the adult only occasionally relapses. . . . This developmental process leads to the conclusion that in *the small child the primitive person rules exclusively.*[21]

So undifferentiated, in fact, are the psychic states of a very young child that, as Werner remarks, "it is difficult to say, for instance, whether a very young baby is frightened, angry, or pleasantly excited." [22] At first there is only excitement—or passivity; and from the affectively toned excitement distinguishable feelings develop only gradually.[23] Savages, who are "apathetic when not tuned up to concert-pitch," develop less far from the aboriginal pair of psychic states than civilized Westerners; and, to the degree that they remain psychically infantile, their consciousness is less differentiated.

Another similarity between primitives and Western children appears in the fondness of both for invariable routines and repetitive experiences. Every parent knows the tendency of small children to insist that habitual actions be performed in a single way; and the inability or reluctance of savages to modify routines and the design of cult objects is notorious. The unanalyzed total experience would be destroyed by the change of a detail.

There is an inner relation between the global manner in which the child experiences objective situations, and his well-known conservatism. . . . A global interpretation of a situation implies that the situation is the result of numerous unanalyzed elements. . . . Such a "whole-structure" tends to a rigid traditionalism, since any

---

21 Ludwig von Holzschuher, *Praktische Psychologie: Die Primitivperson im Menschen* (2d ed.; Seebruck am Chiemsee: Im Heering-Verlag, 1955), p. 106.
22 Werner, *Comparative Psychology*, p. 86.
23 Cf. *ibid.*: "Emotions develop out of a general, undifferentiated affect which [Katherine Bridges] calls 'excitement.' "

element that is changed or left out may completely transform the total situation to which the child is adjusted.[24]

And again, for the savage:

For the primitive man a trivial variation in the appearance of some object of daily use or of cult significance in his house or in his local world is interpreted not as a mere transposition or transformation of an unessential detail, but as a revision of the whole, a revolutionary change in the impression of the totality.[25]

As a child cannot sleep if a customary blanket is in the wash, so the primitive is deeply disturbed by an alteration in his environment. Thus

immediate significance and object constitute a homogeneous complex of such a kind that it would never be possible for the primitive to resolve the homogeneity into a duality consisting of the meaning of the process itself and the meaning of what the process presents objectively.[26]

In exactly the same way literary meanings tend, in absorbed reading, to appear inseparable from processes and incidents. Only when the spell has been deliberately or accidentally disrupted or is incomplete can the document be critically analyzed.

Simultaneity of datum and meaning

The simultaneity for the primitive mind, as for the sensitive Western mind during aesthetic absorption, of datum and meaning is very likely responsible for the well-documented dislike of savages for rigidly logical thought patterns—a dislike illustrated, for example, by the preference of many African Negroes for the English system of weights and measures over the metric system.[27] The metric system keeps the mind on the plane of abstraction, whereas the unequal leaps between pence, shillings, and pounds, or between inches, feet, and yards, is more congenially arbitrary. Sensory

---

[24] *Ibid.*, pp. 130–31.
[25] *Ibid.*, p. 141.
[26] Werner, *Ursprünge der Metapher*, p. 69.
[27] Cf. L[ucien] Lévy-Bruhl, *La Mentalité primitive* (Paris: Librairie Félix Alcan, 1922), p. 7.

impressions sink into the primitive consciousness tinged, or satu-rated, with an affective tonality which seems more important than relationships deducible from a purely cortical understanding of such concepts as value or space.

All this suggests that in primitive societies, as in literature, there is less tendency to abstraction than in empirico-theoretical reflec-tion, a stronger impulse to react in terms of sensory clusters which are to some extent isolated, because of the intense interest they generate, from experiences which to the scientific intelligence would appear to be continuous with them. Rudolf Arnheim con-trasts the sensory emptiness of sophisticated concepts with the specificity of primitive languages. Concepts, he says, are useful for human communication because their emptiness

> permits statements that imply no other characteristics than the few on which the speaker and the listener are agreed. To be able to tell of "a man who showed me to the station" without having to com-municate the details of his appearance is helpful in keeping the information to its essentials. . . .
>
> Different needs and interests lead to linguistic differentiation in varying areas. The Eskimos have different words for "snow on the ground," "falling snow," "drifting snow," "a snowdrift" (Franz Boas). . . . Again, a primitive language may possess a score of particular words indicating different varieties of gait. . . . Western man does not possess the corresponding specific terms or when he does he uses them rarely because, under the influence of modern natural science, the "physiognomic" qualities of shape, movement, etc., have lost their vital importance for effective deal-ing with the problems of daily life.[28]

It is notorious, however—a point of which more will be made in a later chapter—that in creative literature, as in primitive lan-guages, expression tends to be not bare but rich in images. What is sought is not an abstract datum that after rational adjustment to other data can be made to produce a meaning, but rather a percept in which image and meaning are so fused as to enter the consciousness simultaneously. The reason is to be found in the

---

28 Rudolf Arnheim, W. H. Auden, Karl Shapiro, and Donald A. Stauffer, *Poets at Work* (New York: Harcourt, Brace and Company, Inc., 1948), pp. 139–40.

reluctance, both in art and in primitive cognition, to inhibit one kind of psychic activity until another has run its full course. Awareness does not make a series of cautious swoops at an object but instead bolts it down whole.

The psychic tendencies which have been described are most pronounced at moments of excitement but continue at a lower intensity among savages even when there has been no tuning-up to concert pitch. Only when empirico-theoretical reflection has become habitual as the result of a long and rigorous educational process is there no temptation to merge subject with object, to intuit meanings simultaneously with the registering of percepts, and to react to affective tones with which the field of attention appears to be suffused; and even then, as has been noted, there is some readiness to revert to the earlier patterns at times of special absorption.

Examples of undifferentiated consciousness

That primitives tend to remain more consistently than educated white people on the level of undifferentiated consciousness will be illustrated by two examples, neither in any way extraordinary.

A NEXUS OF MEANING PERCEPTS: THE "ERATHIPA" STONE. The first is drawn from a classic anthropological work on the Arunta of Central Australia, a people whose culture is low on an evolutionary scale. The Arunta believe that dead spirits wait underground for a woman to pass by, then issue forth and enter her womb in order to be reborn. Coitus is thought to be merely preparatory to conception, not an efficient cause. The bridge between the underground world and the upper world is a rounded stone, called *erathipa,* which contains a small round hole above ground; through this, the spirit children are supposed to look out as they watch for a likely woman to pass by.

> If a young woman has to pass near to the stone and does not wish to have a child she will carefully disguise her youth, distorting her face and walking with the aid of a stick. She will bend herself

double like a very old woman, the tones of whose voice she will imitate, saying, "Don't come to me, I am an old woman." [29]

The belief is no more irrational than many to be found among primitives. I propose that we put ourselves into a frame of mind sufficiently noncritical to allow us momentarily to share it.

The suggestion is less hazardous than it may at first seem and is unavoidable if we seriously wish to understand either the mental processes of savages or the affective elements in literary form. Like a physician who innoculates himself deliberately with the organism whose effects he wishes to study, we must try not only to note the outward manifestations of the phenomena with which we are concerned but also to *sense* them in process. Fortunately, in order to do so, we need not—indeed, we must not—fall into irrresponsible reverie. To be sure, the practice involves, on the one hand, a kind of release rather than intellectual stiffening, since it demands the recapture of habits long ago abandoned as mentally disreputable. On the other hand, it requires self-discipline, since it demands also the exclusion of irrelevant associations and the sharp focusing of attention on a given object. Fortunately, we can be assured that the psychic attitudes to be attained are dormant within us and instead of needing creation can merely be recaptured. It is a fundamental postulate of Freudian psychology that forgotten stages of an individual past, in which nonrational elements dominated rational elements, can be raised into consciousness; and Jungian psychology rests on the more far-reaching assumption that the racial past is not wholly dead in the most "advanced" Western mind. Whichever theory is to be preferred, an effort must be made to *share,* before we analyze them, some of the curious attitudes documented by anthropologists. Unless we can believe, for a few minutes, that the sun is angry at the moon and now and then takes a bite of her, as do the Mintira of the Malayan peninsula, or that all the waters of the earth were once contained in the body of a

---

[29] Baldwin Spencer and F. J. Gillen, *The Native Tribes of Central Australia* (London: Macmillan & Co., Ltd., 1898), pp. 336–37.

huge frog,[30] we are in no position to do more than record the phenomena. Sensitive analysis requires more than this.

Appreciation of the Australian belief is comparatively simple. Once we have succeeded in imagining that after death the soul goes underground and awaits an opportunity to become reattached to a human body, everything else follows without difficulty. The *erathipa* stone forms a credible bridge between the upper and lower worlds because it is partly buried but also projects above the soil. Besides this character, which it shares with other stones, it is provided with an orifice through which what exists in the lower world can effect a transition to the upper. The orifice is rounded, that is to say, invites penetration; because the solid body of the stone has retracted itself smoothly in all directions, the passage of something through it seems to be not only facilitated but offered, solicited, desired. Beneath the stone are the souls of the dead, submitted to the pressure of a yearning for renewed embodiment above ground. What wonder if they are forced by the pressure to the extreme limit of their "underground" habitat and watch through the opening for the passage of a human figure susceptible of invasion? The Arunta women wear no clothing, hence are easily vulnerable if they pass nearby (but no doubt would remain so even if fully dressed). In this half-world of inseparable meaning percepts, however, the assumption of a stooping posture, a shaky step, and a quavering voice suffices to destroy the *Gestalt* necessary for the completion of the re-embodiment cycle. It is unnecessary to draw Freudian inferences from the shape of the hole (and perhaps also from that of the rock?) or, indeed, to press the analysis further in any direction. Already, for the mind able to relax into prerational habits, the sensory complex is permeated with meaning —a meaning consistent with, and itself partly constitutive of, the total meaning configuration of Arunta society, but appreciable also in isolation from all the elements of that configuration except the reluctant underground existence of disembodied souls.

---

[30] Both beliefs are recorded in Andrew Lang, *Myth, Ritual and Religion*, Vol. I (London: Longmans, Green & Co., Ltd., 1913), pp. 132 and 43.

How consistent such a pattern of meaning percepts is with patterns common in literature can be seen if we convert the belief into story. For example: One day it happened that a chief's daughter, who passed near the stone while deeply preoccupied, became pregnant. Now the spirit which just then was waiting at the orifice chanced to be that of the chief's bitterest enemy, who had recently been killed in furious battle along with eight of his followers; so the child, when born . . . Already the spell of fictive adventure begins to fall upon us. The "impossible" assumptions cease to trouble us as they enter into combination with other elements that can be projected from them. In its living context, the superstition was credible because it formed part of a huge nexus of mutually supporting beliefs. In the literary version, a nexus, all the parts of which are conditioned by it, can be created around the superstition in such a way as to suspend the entire complex in a "virtual" world which we can enter imaginatively by choice. The *quality* of the primitive nexus and of the literary nexus is similar, for in both what feels right is convincing and acceptable, regardless of whether it is immediately justifiable to the reason.

THE ADAPTATION OF NATURE TO MAN: ILLUSTRATION OF THE WATER HOLE. The second example is both simpler, because it involves no particular background of mythological belief, and emotionally fairly cool. The story is told by Augustus Oldfield, again of Australian aborigines. A party of natives and whites needed water badly in western Australia, and after a while succeeded, at an apparently dry water hole, in digging through to a small patch of wet sand inside a large excavation. Thereupon a question arose among the natives: in what part of the excavation should digging be continued? Toward the west, said one, because the sea is there. No, said others; there the water will be salty. To the east, said a second, because the Angaardies, who live on that side, are great magicians and can cause rains when they wish. No, said an old man, the Angaardies may become angry if we trespass on their rights and turn their magic against us. At length it was decided that digging should be done on the south, since the whites had come from that direction and had found ample water hitherto.[31]

We may assume (I think) that, once wet sand had been found, the blacks had virtual assurance of water and that therefore whatever mental and physical distress they had felt no longer put heavy pressure on them. At least there is no suggestion in the published description of the incident that the discussion was violent or bitter. Yet how different the behavior of the blacks from that of white men in a similar situation! If discussion had been necessary at all among whites, it would have turned on comparative dampness and the obstructions offered by such features of the terrain as rocks or the roots of shrubs. Among the blacks the sole object of consideration was what would seem to the empirico-theoretical consciousness to be metaphorical fitness. The realities of the situation appeared to them to be governed by the adaptation of physical forces to conscious human activities—as when, in literature, a bright dawn signalizes the resolution of human tensions. Whether, as Edward B. Tylor believed, the primitive thought patterns which express themselves in situations of this kind are animistic, or whether some other analytic formulation is preferable, it is at least apparent that the traditional tendency of literature to have traffic with omens, symbols, and physical reciprocations—in a word, to bring into active participation whatever elements of the nonhuman environment are admitted to the fictive universe—has here a primitive parallel of sorts. A phrase of Wilhelm Wundt's is convenient: one of the processes active in mythical thought consists "in the assimilative combination of psychic elements which have different sources." The process is determined, he adds, by accompanying feelings.[32] Or in Cassirer's formulation (since Wundt is no longer an "authority"): in the mythical world view of primitive societies "there are not ideal forms of relationships which give the objective

---

[31] Augustus Oldfield, "On the Aborigines of Australia," in *Transactions of the Ethnological Society of London,* New Series, Vol. III (London: John Murray, 1865), pp. 282–83.

[32] Wilhelm Wundt, *Elemente der Völkerpsychologie* (Leipzig: Alfred Kröner Verlag, 1913), p. 355.

world the structure of a world determined and permeated by law; instead all being dissolves into the unity of concrete images." [33]

Summary

We have come far enough to draw together a few of the strands that have been implicit in the discussion. For the primitive consciousness, as for the sensitive modern reader of literature, perceptions are instantly *meaningful*. One thing *implies* or *is a sign of* another with which it stands in no causal relationship. Natural forces are *aware of* human designs and purposes. Feeling and reflection are mutually interfused, not dissociated. Thought tends to be material (*dinghaft*). The psyche works as a unit; cognition is not merely cerebral. As in dreams, so in aesthetic contemplation

> one might speculate . . . whether . . . imagination does not regress to the primitive perceptual world, to that "universe wherein quality leaps to cohere with quality across the abysms of classification that divide and categorize the universe of intellectual apprehension.[34]

In the following chapters, such speculation will be undertaken. As yet little more has been done than to indicate a possibility that, since there is psychic absorption of a special kind in much literary experience and psychic absorption of an apparently comparable kind in the mental experiences of primitives, the literary transaction can be illuminated by a study of the psychic tendencies of primitives. There is an antecedent likelihood that the psychic states produced by literature—an immemorial human institution with durable conventions of its own—will in some degree be archaic. Whether the habits of consciousness active in aesthetic creation and induced, at some remove, in empathetic observers of art works are *sufficiently* archaic to be continuous with psychic patterns still observable, or until recently observable, in primitive societies re-

---

[33] Ernst Cassirer, *Philosophie der Symbolischen Formen,* Vol. II (Berlin: Bruno Cassirer Verlag, 1925), p. 81.
[34] Arnheim, *Poets at Work,* p. 157 n. I have corrected a misprint.

mains to be discovered and can only be discovered by an investigation of details.

In the course of the investigation we may henceforth assume (I think) that primitive thought patterns tend always to be affectively toned. We need not, therefore, confine our observations to such savage activities as religious dances or hunting but can study the primitive mind in all its accessible manifestations. The other pole of the analysis will be the varieties of consciousness apparent in literary experience. I have spoken more than once of the absorbed *reader* of literature; but, in fact, the empathetic reader merely relives, more or less intensely, the effective moments of a creative process, and that process can best be seen in literature itself. We can avoid speculating constantly about what a good reader ought to be feeling by concentrating our attention upon psychic processes directly evident in creative works.

A note of warning may be added: an interest in feelings is not necessarily anti-intellectual, and the discovery that the basic material of literary cognition is affective would by no means prejudice the claim of literature to importance. As Cassirer has remarked, "Not only science, but language, myth, art and religion as well, provide the building stones from which the world of 'reality' is constructed for us, as well as that of the human spirit, in sum the World-of-the-I." [35]

---

[35] Ernst Cassirer, *The Philosophy of Symbolic Forms,* Vol. I, *Language,* trans. Ralph Manheim (New Haven, Conn.: Yale University Press, 1953), p. 91.

3

The Language of Literature (1)

No better beginning can be made than by comparing the language of literature, in so far as it differs from nonliterary language, with the speech of primitives. If there should appear to be a significant likeness, we may infer tentatively, as a hypothesis to be checked and rechecked later from other points of view, that during literary composition writers tend, under the influence of strong feeling, to regress in some degree toward primitive thought ways; for linguistic patterns are obviously and necessarily related to psychic patterns. It is unthinkable that a person who expresses himself in pattern Y should at that instant be perceiving, feeling, and thinking in a pattern *A* which includes no elements of *Y*. This would seem to be possible only if the expression were quite automatic and unconscious; but in that event it would have been prepared in the past and would accord with a pattern still existent and operative in the subconscious.

Objection to generalizing about primitive languages

Again we are confronted by a difficulty so enormous that it threatens to halt the investigation before it has begun. Is there, or was there ever, such a thing as "the" speech of primitives? A few generations ago, under Darwinian influence, it was assumed that there had been, and that the nature of primordial language could be discovered by extrapolating backward from the shared characteristics of existent primitive languages. At present, the second assumption is denied with such vigor as to destroy meaning in the first. The attitude of modern linguistics toward such speculation as was undertaken, for example, by Wilhelm Wundt is suggested by a comment of Edward Sapir:

> Many attempts have been made to unravel the origin of language, but most of these are hardly more than exercises of the speculative imagination. Linguists as a whole have lost interest in the problem, and this for two reasons. In the first place, it has come to be realized that we have no truly primitive languages in a psychological sense, that modern researches in archaeology have indefinitely extended the time of man's cultural past and that it is therefore vain to go much beyond the perspective opened up by the study of actual languages. In the second place, our knowledge of psychology, particularly of the symbolic processes in general, is not felt to be sound enough or far-reaching enough to help materially with the problem of the emergence of speech.[1]

The attention of linguists has therefore been diverted to other problems. It is no longer thought that the speech of very "low" savages,

---

[1] *Selected Writings of Edward Sapir*, ed. David G. Mandelbaum (Berkeley, Calif.: University of California Press, 1949), p. 13.

like the Veddas of Ceylon, the Bushmen of Africa, and the Negritos of the Philippines, yields better evidence than the speech of tribes in a higher state of culture for findings about primordial language. Every language has roughly as long a history as every other; and the fact that the "low" savage makes no pottery, uses simple weapons, and has no fixed residence does not imply that his speech has been relatively unchanged since the beginning. The works of "ready generalizers on social origins" [2] now carry little authority, and the gathering of specific data is preferred to attempts at large-scale synthesis.

All this has a strong ring of common sense and must make a deep impression on anyone who stands at the threshold of such an analysis as has been proposed. Moreover, the student of literature who attempts to "read up on" primitive languages is struck very early by their great diversity. The high-school pupil recognizes oddity in the unfamiliar syntax of Latin, and the student of such a non-Indo European language as Japanese must perceive an unexpectedly wide range of possible speech forms; but only a little reading in descriptions of American Indian languages destroys finally all illusions about the necessity of particular linguistic habits. For example, Europeans are unlikely to recognize any similarity in the two sentences, "I pull the branch aside" and "I have an extra toe on my foot"; but Benjamin Lee Whorf has explained that in Shawnee the apparently disparate ideas are expressed in nearly the same way, the root notion in both sentences being that of a forked or branching object. Again, also in Shawnee, the expressions for "I push his head back" and "I drop it in water and it floats" differ only a little: the resistance of the neck to pressure on the head is sensed as analogous to the resistance of water to a light object dropped into it. [3] If the perceptual and conceptual habits which underlie speech forms show such surprising variation, can there be much likelihood that study of many primitive languages will reveal significant common features?

---

2 *Ibid.*, p. 387.
3 Benjamin Lee Whorf, *Four Articles on Metalinguistics* (Washington, D.C.: Foreign Service Institute, Department of State, 1950), pp. 18–19.

A *reply*

Undoubtedly the project is hazardous. If it lies so directly in our path that it cannot be avoided, we must at least conceive of our objective in as modest and limited a way as possible; and even so we may expose ourselves to the charge of borrowing from ready generalizers. Yet four considerations, at least, offer comfort.

The first is that primitive cultures must have at least one common element which permits them to be classed as primitive. The element may be negative; but in that event it may appear that primitive languages also share a common deficiency. Or, in spite of great differences, common positive traits may be found.

Secondly, the very linguist whose illustrations of vast speech disparities were cited above encourages us to hope that beneath language, but dimly discernible through it, is something more basic and less variable. Contrasts which appear to be fundamental may sometimes be resolved in a common ground.

> My own studies suggest, to me, that language, for all of its kingly role, is in some sense a superficial embroidery upon deeper processes of consciousness which are necessary before any communication, signaling, or symbolism whatsoever can occur . . . The different tongues . . . may generalize down not to any such universal as "Language," but to something better—called "sublinguistic" or "superlinguistic"—and *not altogether* unlike, even if much unlike, what we now call "mental." [4]

For this reason, perhaps, Whorf thinks it possible to compare various Indian languages with what he calls Standard Average European, or SAE—a group which includes all European languages "with the *possible* (but doubtful) exception of Balto-Slavic and non-Indo-European." In the same way, one may hope, primitive languages can be found which do not differ essentially "with respect to the traits compared." [5]

Thirdly, many data have already been collected by generalizers who seem not to have been stigmatized as overly "ready." The first volume, *Language,* of Cassirer's *Philosophy of Symbolic Forms,*

---

[4] *Ibid.,* p. 21.
[5] The quoted phrases are taken from *ibid.,* p. 30.

although it is rich in anthropological data, appears not to have provoked scornful responses. This heavily documented and reflective
work will be immensely useful, as will several volumes by Werner,
also crammed with specific information. Even the writings of Lévy-
Bruhl, which arrive at dubious conclusions, include bodies of
linguistic data that appear not to have been condemned as inaccurate.

Finally, and most important, the real gist of Sapir's objection can
be evaded. We shall not "go much beyond the perspective opened
up by the study of actual languages," and no generalization will be
meant to be unexceptionable. Neither here nor elsewhere is it my
purpose to assert that literature uses *primordial* modes of expression. The hypothesis is that the perceptual and conceptual patterns
embodied in literature are archaic, not that they resemble those of
"first men." The aim will be accomplished if it can be shown that
the expressive patterns of literary art are very old. On what is, I
think, the necessary and incontrovertible assumption that the societies in which our remote ancestors lived were also primitive—
that is, that they shared whatever qualities are denoted by the class
concept "primitive"—this can be achieved by a demonstration that
the literary patterns coincide with those of a number of primitive
groups still accessible, or until recently accessible, to observation.
Nothing hinges on the universality of the patterns among *all* primitive peoples. Further, no necessity will arise that we extrapolate
often or seriously from existent primitive speech to the speech of
primordial men. Only two suggestions about primordial speech
will be offered, and both will be rejected as interesting but merely
hypothetical.

We come thus to the business itself. It will be well if the nature
of possible doubts is indicated in connection with the first point
to be made, but it is not essential, and would be prohibitively ex-
pensive of space, to refute anticipated objections in every part of the
discussion.

Concreteness of primitive speech

The first observation is that the language both of literature and of
primitive men tends strongly to be concrete, specific, sensory. So

far as literature is concerned, it will suffice for the moment to re-call the advice regularly given young authors in textbooks on how to write to say, not *tree*, but *oak* or *cottonwood;* not *ship*, but *freighter, bark, sloop,* or *tanker;* not *walk*, but *hasten, stroll, lurch, dawdle, stagger, saunter,* or *trip.* Neither is the urge toward speci-ficity a recent development. The student of Latin poetry is at first annoyed to find not *vinum* but *Falernum* or *Mereoticum,* the reader of Greek poetry to find gods and heroes referred to by epithets which attach them to specific places or incidents. Much of the annotation of old texts is in fact necessitated by the fondness of writers for what Henry James called "solidity of specification." The preference of neoclassical writers for general terms was temporary and atypical. And the concreteness urged upon young writers by precept is practiced spontaneously by savages.

That this is widely, if not universally, true can be suggested by examples. According to J. H. Trumbull, an early scientific linguist, in no American Indian language is there a term so general as our verb "to eat." The word differs according to whether—for example —the food is animal or vegetable, the meal that of an individual or of a group, and the like.[6] Most previous study of the American languages had gone wildly astray, Trumbull argued, by assuming that "equivalents of English *generic* names may be found among Indian *specific* and *individual* names." [7] The Indian verb, however, "is almost always *holophrastic*. It affirms—not action or existence *generally,* but—some special and limited act or conditioned ex-istence." [8] The same trait marks much primitive speech; for ex-ample, the Tasmanian aborigines had no generic word for tree but special names even for different varieties of the same species of tree.[9] Among savages, it would appear that words often attach themselves to objects as they present themselves directly to the senses, and that only much later are the objects classified into groups

---

6 J. Hammond Trumbull, "On the Best Method of Studying the North American Languages," in *Transactions of the American Philological Association, 1869–70* (Hartford: Case, Lockwood & Brainard, 1871), pp. 61–62.

7 *Ibid.,* p. 63.

8 *Ibid.,* p. 68.

9 A. H. Sayce, *Introduction to the Science of Language,* Vol. II (4th ed.; Lon-don: Kegan Paul, Trench, Trübner & Co., 1900), pp. 5–6.

containing recognizable common elements describable by low-level abstractions. Even in highly developed languages of non-European stocks—especially those of markedly conservative peoples like the Japanese and Arabs—a tendency is apparent to keep linguistic reference narrow. In Japanese, for instance, the verb meaning "to put on" differs according to the physical motions involved: *kaburu* is used of an article of clothing placed on the head, *kiru* of something wrapped about the body, and *haku* of something drawn upon the feet. In Arabic, according to an old (1855–1856) monograph by Hammer-Purgstall, there are no fewer than 5,744 words relating in some way to "camel" and suggesting every possible variation of sex, age, physical traits, and the like.[10]

The principle extends to words of all sorts and classes. In the Kwakiutl language, spoken on Vancouver Island, the idea expressed in English by "that house" cannot be stated so generally but must be made more specific, as follows:

> *The (singular or plural) house visible near me*
> *invisible near me*
> *visible near thee*
> *invisible near thee*
> *visible near him*
> *invisible near him*

Among Eskimos, directional implications are still more specialized. "That man" becomes

> *That man near me*
> *near thee*
> *near him*
> *behind me*
> *in front of me*
> *to the right of me*
> *to the left of me*
> *above me*
> *below me, etc.*

---

[10] Freiherr Hammer-Purgstall, *Das Kamel*, in *Denkschriften der Kaiserlichen Akademie der Wissenschaften*, Phil.-Hist. Klasse, Vols. VI and VII (Vienna, 1855-56).

The simple demonstrative pronoun, which to an American or Englishman appears already specific, thus has twenty-one subdivisions among the Eskimos.[11] Again, motor concepts are often remarkably specialized. A Ponca Indian cannot say, "A man killed a rabbit." He must say instead something like, "The man, he, one, animate, standing . . . , purposely killed, by shooting an arrow, the rabbit, he (*sic*), the one, animate, sitting." [12] Inflectional changes in the verb or the incorporation of particles results in designation of the person, the number, the gender (animate or inanimate), and position (standing, sitting, lying). In Kaffir, "Climb the hill" must become, "Change what you are doing and climb the hill," "Begin to climb the hill," "Stop dallying and climb the hill," "Walk to the hill and climb it," or "Climb the hill when you can." Among the Abipones of South America, the choice of a pronoun indicates posture. *Hiniha* means "he, seated"; *hiriha* means "he, lying down"; *eneha* means "he, walking and visible"; and still another form, *ekaha*, is used when the third person is invisible.[13] Still more significant is the attaching of sensory qualities to the categories of number, than which nothing seems to the Westerner more abstract. In many primitive languages (and again in Japanese), the choice of a numeral depends on visual characteristics. The use in Tsimshian, spoken in British Columbia, of different sets of numerals for flat objects, round objects, long objects, human beings, canoes, and measures [14] is in no way extraordinary.

So deep-seated a linguistic trait as this can best be considered not in terms of dozens, or hundreds, of examples but synoptically, as Cassirer has treated it in volume one, *Language*, of his immense work on symbolical forms. Hermann Osthoff (he says), in investigating the "irregular" comparisons of adjectives and conjugations of verbs in Indo-European languages (*bonus, melior, optimus; fero,*

---

[11] For the examples see Franz Boas, *Handbook of American Indian Languages* (Washington, D.C.: Smithsonian Institution Bureau of American Ethnology, Bulletin 40, Part I, 1911), pp. 40–41.

[12] J. W. Powell, *Introduction to the Study of Indian Languages* (Washington, D.C.: Government Printing Office, 1880), p. 74.

[13] For the last two examples, see L[ucien] Lévy-Bruhl, *Les Fonctions mentales dans les sociétés inférieures* (Paris: Librairie Félix Alcan, 1922), pp. 160 and 167.

[14] Cf. Boas, *Handbook*, I, 396.

tuli, latus), was led to the conclusion that the anomalies were re-sidual from "an older stratum of language formation, in which an 'individualizing' trend still outweighed the 'grouping' tendency." Among verbs, the older stratum persisted especially in words which expressed motion (*to go, to come, to run*); but it persisted also in others having to do with such activities as eating, striking, seeing, and speaking. These results have been confirmed by Ernst Curtius, who showed that

> ur-Indo-Germanic, for example, differentiated the *varieties* of "going" before it arrived at the general *concept* of going. He dem-onstrated that such varieties as peering, spying, looking, watch-ing, etc., must have been designated earlier than seeing as such, and the same for the other sensory activities, hearing, feeling, etc. And such verbs as the post-Homeric αἰσθάνεσθαι, *sentire,* des-ignating sense perception in general, developed last of all.[15]

Since the same phenomena are observable in other language fami-lies, such as Semitic, in Cassirer's opinion "We must conclude that word formation here reflects a general trend in the development of linguistic concepts."[16]

The foregoing remarks, which will seem commonplace to stu-dents of general linguistics, may evoke surprise among literary critics. The typical Westerner will assume that peering, spying, look-ing, and watching are refinements of an earlier, more general, con-cept of seeing. Linguistic simplicity, however, is not always given but must be achieved. Conceptualization may come not immediately with the development of psychic awareness but much later, when specific activities are discovered to have common elements which permit categorical grouping. The fondness of writers for concrete-ness—which of course is aesthetically "right"—is thus not antici-patory of an advanced linguistic development but regressive.

Configurational perception

The tendency toward concretion in primitive languages is bound up, perhaps necessarily, with what may be called configurational

---

15 Ernst Cassirer, *The Philosophy of Symbolic Forms,* Vol. I, *Language,* trans. Ralph Manheim (New Haven, Conn.: Yale University Press, 1953), p. 291.
16 *Ibid.*

rather than isolating perception. What differentiates *peering* from *seeing,* for example, is that, whereas in the latter visual awareness is stripped of qualifications, in the former it is accompanied by difficulty; the observer is seeing from behind a bush, against the sun, into darkness, and so forth. The condition under which the percept is registered is absorbed into the verbal description.

The inclusion in cardinal numerals of an element suggestive of visual quality is particularly instructive in this connection. Often, however, the primitive avoids numbers altogether in situations in which the use of them would seem natural to us. The Abipones of South America do not count their dogs before leaving on a hunt, but nevertheless they know at once whether any are missing, "because they experience the individuality of all domestic animals in a characteristically concrete manner." [17] Again, in the South Seas, the arrival of a party of visitors will be reported not as "five people have come" but in the form, "A man with a large nose, an old man, a child, a man with a skin disease, and a little fellow are waiting outside." [18] The category of number is rendered contextually, so that unity is attached to an object. Franz Boas reminds us that "counting does not become necessary until objects are considered in such generalized form that their individualities are entirely lost sight of." Primitive man, however,

> is not in the habit of discussing abstract ideas. . . . Discourses on qualities without connection with the object to which the qualities belong, or of activities or states disconnected from the idea of the actor or the subject being in a certain state, will hardly occur in primitive speech.[19]

What seems to the modern Westerner to be a single percept (twoness or threeness) tends for the primitive to be tied into a sensory background.

INABILITY OF PRIMITIVES TO THINK ABSTRACTLY.   An interesting verification of this hypothesis is afforded by the difficulty some-

---

[17] Heinz Werner, *Comparative Psychology of Mental Development* (rev. ed.; Chicago: Follett Publishing Co., 1948), p. 288.

[18] *Ibid.*

[19] Boas, *Handbook,* I, 66 and 64–65.

times felt by primitives when called on by whites to think on a high level of abstraction. Karl von den Steinen remarks that the Central Brazilians fell silent for a long time whenever he spoke a generalization. The sentence, "All men must die," caused an interpreter much trouble; apparently the natives not only could not express such an idea but did not themselves have it.[20] A still more significant report has been noted by Werner.

> An Indian was asked to translate the following sentence: "The white man shot six bears today." He was unable to do this, and explained that a white man could not possibly shoot six bears in one day.[21]

Here it is evident that the interpreter's effort to conceptualize the assertion abstractly failed. The sentence refused to compose itself against a concrete background which the white interrogator could easily hold in abeyance.[22]

EXCEPTIONS AND QUALIFICATIONS. All this is by no means to say that primitive languages are wholly incapable of abstraction. As has already been acknowledged, neither this tendency nor any other that will be noted is unexceptionable. The English translation of a Maori myth begins like a passage from T. S. Eliot's *Four Quartets:*

> From the conception the increase,
> From the increase the swelling,
> From the swelling the thought,
> From the thought the remembrance,
> From the remembrance the consciousness, the desire.[23]

The translation may, of course, have been sophisticated; the words may have had much more concrete reference in the original, so

---

[20] Karl von den Steinen, *Unter den Naturvölkern Zentral-Brasiliens* (2d ed.; Berlin: Dietrich Reimer, 1897), p. 303.

[21] Werner, *Comparative Psychology,* p. 251.

[22] Patients suffering from aphasia are similarly unable to imagine hypothetical or "unreal" situations, and Laura Bridgman, who was born deaf, dumb, and blind, accepted as "true" the situations described in arithmetical "story problems." See Ernst Cassirer, *An Essay on Man* (New Haven, Conn.: Yale University Press, 1944), p. 58 n. We seem here to glimpse an archaic mental state reproduced in abnormal modern persons.

[23] Richard Taylor, *Te Ika A Maui; Or, New Zealand and Its Inhabitants* (London: William MacIntosh, 1870), p. 109.

that the impression of abstractness is magnified.[24] Nevertheless, the excerpt is remarkable. Account must be taken also of Whorf's observation that specificity along one axis may be balanced by abstraction along another. In Hopi, the nouns are highly concrete, but words generically called "tensors" are "abstract almost beyond our power to follow." [25] Again, Franz Boas asserts that, although the concepts of Western science would be difficult to express in many primitive languages, "it is not true that primitive languages are unable to form generalized concepts"; [26] and Sapir has pointed out that environmental objects which are culturally indifferent tend to "be embraced in a single term of general application." Thus an Indian tribe which has separate words for each of the plants referred to collectively by white men as "weeds" may designate the sun and the moon by a single term.[27] It is necessary, accordingly, to consider whether real meaning attaches to our findings. As has already been indicated, the problem will serve as a test case. Objections of a roughly similar kind might be offered to any one of the sets of remarks which follow.

With regard to the Maori poem, I must satisfy myself with the claim that, so far as my knowledge goes, it is unparalleled (a fact which has led me to suggest inaccuracy in the rendering). My attention was first directed to it by Joseph Campbell's *The Hero with a Thousand Faces,* in which, among scores or hundreds of translated excerpts, it stood out as glaringly atypical. No one, I think, who has browsed for a long time among anthropological reports could fail to have a similar reaction. Indeed, the presence of the passage might well have led me to a first recognition that the other translations shared a quality absent from this one. Another comment by Whorf is relevant here. The popular understanding of the phrase, "The exception proves the rule," is, he argues, more pro-

---

[24] Trumbull, *op. cit.,* p. 68, notes that the numeral translated as "one" may actually mean something much more concrete—"a small thing," "a beginning," "the little one" (i.e., finger), etc. Taylor's chapters on the Maori language (*Te Ika A Maui,* pp. 373–413) certainly suggest no very sophisticated linguistic awareness.

[25] Whorf, *Four Articles,* p. 35.

[26] Franz Boas (ed.), *General Anthropology* (Boston: D. C. Heath and Company, 1938), p. 141.

[27] *Selected Writings of Edward Sapir,* p. 92.

found than the historical sense, since a rule with no exceptions "is not recognized as a rule or as anything else; it is then part of the background of experience of which we tend to remain unconscious." A race of people who saw only blue would have no word for "blue" but only for different intensities of light.[28] Such texts as the Maori one, if it is really as abstract as it seems, and if it can be matched by others equally abstract in other primitive tongues, at first intensify what may previously have been only a half-focused perception and later dictate a wholesome avoidance of dogmatism, but they would have to exist in considerable numbers to motivate the total abandonment of the argument for primitive specificity advanced by Cassirer and many other scholars in the separate but overlapping areas of linguistics, anthropology, and philosophy.

The other considerations have a more or less equivalent relevance: that is, they suggest temperate qualifications but do not invalidate the large quantities of available evidence. Boas himself says, "Generalized terms are not by any means the rule"; [29] and in a continuation of the passage quoted earlier he remarks:

> In primitive culture people speak only about actual experiences. They do not discuss what is virtue, good, evil, beauty; the demands of their daily life, like those of our uneducated classes, do not extend beyond the virtues shown on definite occasions by definite people.[30]

This observation may lead us to recognize the very limited drift of Sapir's remark about the failure of primitives to discriminate *objects* that are culturally indifferent. The use of a single term to designate two or more objects which differ to perception does not constitute abstraction of a very high level. As used here, in fact, "abstraction" does not refer primarily to objects at all but to qualities and concepts separated from objects—precisely the goodness, evil, and beauty which Boas informs us tend not to be specified by primitives. In conclusion, the tensors which are so important in Hopi, although worthy of notice, again cut across the present discussion at

---

28 Whorf, *Four Articles,* pp. 3 and 4.
29 Boas, *General Anthropology,* p. 130.
30 *Ibid.,* p. 141.

an angle. They "convey distinctions of degree" (like the German prefix *ver-* in certain uses) or of "rate, constancy, repetition, increase and decrease of intensity, immediate sequence," and the like.[31] They have to do, it appears, rather with *felt* than with *conceptualized* differences. Although by no means negligible, they tend, apparently, as much to differentiate similar processes as to classify them and therefore add specificity in one direction while suggesting generality in another.

The objections which might be offered to following parts of the discussion are roughly similar to these and could be answered in analogous ways. In the future, therefore, I will leave to the reader both the raising of questions and—if he is willing to co-operate so far—the answering of them.

THE SAME TRAITS IN LITERARY LANGUAGE.   That the language of literature resembles primitive language not only in being extremely concrete but also in tending to register percepts in *Gestalten* will require little demonstration. The writer's eye tends instinctively to see objects in groups or against backgrounds. Thus, in "The End of the World," Archibald MacLeish chooses to image human life as a circus. The gist of the poem is that some of us do showy but pointless things while others watch passively; but the picture has a specificity which is conceptually unnecessary.

> Quite unexpectedly as Vasserot
> The armless ambidextrian was lighting
> A match between his great and second toe
> And Ralph the lion was engaged in biting
> The neck of Madame Sossman while the drum
> Pointed, and Teeny was about to cough
> In waltz-time swinging Jocko by the thumb . . .

Concretion has gone so far that not only the human performers but also the animals have been provided with personal names. More important, a great deal is seen at once, or as nearly at one instant as the temporal nature of language permits. The sensory field is very wide. John Crowe Ransom was perhaps thinking of just such breadth when he praised poetry for textural irrelevancies, which he

---

[31] Whorf, *Four Articles,* p. 36.

believes give it more "reality" than can be claimed for other forms of discourse.[32]

Association of contiguities in primitive thought

The tendency in primitive thought for sensory phenomena to be registered in clusters, without an immediate and quasi-automatic segregation of some elements considered causally interrelated from other elements considered accidentally contiguous, leads to the acceptance of cognitive associations which to the philosophical consciousness appear naïve. It is well known that animals draw curious inferences; for example, a dog may think it impossible that his master should take his daily walk unless a cover has first been placed over the typewriter. The dog does not, of course, conceptualize his understanding of relationships, but, if a part of the routine preparation is omitted, he may show perplexity when invited to leave the house. Similarly, it is conceivable that a very young child might believe the serving of dinner to bring his father home from the office. In the cognition of primitives, such alogical conjunctions appear to play an important role. Cassirer, who, in Volume II, *Das Mythische Denken,* of his *Philosophie der Symbolischen Formen,* has considered enormous masses of anthropological evidence, believes associations of this kind sufficiently common to justify the laying down of the principle *juxta hoc, ergo propter hoc* as operative in primitive cognition.[33]

Cassirer's favorite example is that of the association of specific animals, plants, and the like, with the seasons: "It is a current view, in this thought, that the animals which appear in a certain season are the bringers, the originators, of the same; in the mythical view

---

[32] See John Crowe Ransom, "Criticism as Pure Speculation," in *The Intent of the Critic,* ed. Donald A. Stauffer (Princeton, N.J.: Princeton University Press, 1941). In a similar way, he says, music is "more realistic" than mathematics, and "less naive" (p. 117). The foregoing excerpt of poetry is from Archibald MacLeish, *Streets in the Moon* (Boston: Houghton Mifflin Company, 1926), p. 101.

[33] The idea goes back at least as far as Andrew Lang, who, in *Myth, Ritual and Religion,* Vol. I (London: Longmans, Green & Co., Ltd., 1913), p. 94, said that primitive philosophy "takes resemblance, or contiguity in space, or nearness in time as a sufficient reason for predicating the relations of cause and effect." The observation has since been often repeated.

it is actually the swallow which makes the summer." [34] The association is that of contact (*Berührung*); phenomena which come together in experience "flow into each other, are interwoven, paired
together. . . . One might believe that when two images have once
occurred in a certain mutual propinquity the separation of the two
will never be accomplished." [35] Other speculators have offered different analyses of the same cognitive tendency. Lévy-Bruhl argued
in favor of a mystical "participation" of essences. Werner, in
Ursprünge der Metapher, suggested that power is conceived by
savages in the form of *pneuma,* and that the *pneuma* is transferable
by contact.[36] What is important in the present context, however, is
not the cause of the tendency but rather the tendency itself; and for
this many additional illustrations are accessible.

A very clear instance is reported by Von den Steinen. The
Bakairí of Central Brazil, distressed that communication with the
Europeans was difficult and "confusing hearing with understanding," begged him to take some spittle on his finger and rub it into
their ears.[37] Here an intellectual process is thought to be caused by
a purely sensory process which is qualitatively different but tem-
porally and spatially adjacent. An Osage legend registered by Ruth
Benedict reverses the causality appreciated by Westerners. An ancestral mussel speaks as follows to the first members of what was
to become the mussel clan:

> You say the little ones have nothing of which to make their bodies.
> Let the little ones make of me their bodies.
> When the little ones make of me their bodies,
> They shall always live to see old age.
> Behold the wrinkles upon my skin [shell]
> Which I have made to be the means of reaching old age.[38]

---

[34] Ernst Cassirer, *Philosophie der Symbolischen Formen,* Vol. II (Berlin: Bruno
Cassirer Verlag, 1925), p. 60.

[35] *Ibid.,* pp. 60–61.

[36] Heinz Werner, *Die Ursprünge der Metapher* (Leipzig: Wilhelm Englemann,
1919), p. 39.

[37] Von den Steinen, *Unter den Naturvölkern,* p. 83.

[38] Ruth Benedict, *Patterns of Culture* (Boston: Houghton Mifflin Company,
1934), pp. 40–41.

If the translation is accurate, the wrinkles are thought to be not the effect of old age but its cause. In a somewhat analogous way, but less oddly, the Hupa Indians of California believed the symptoms of a disease to be its cause.[39] Other primitive associations are harder to appreciate. The restrictions put upon fathers during their wives' pregnancies in the institution known as the "couvade"[40] seem to us merely ridiculous, as does the widespread belief that a good harvest is dependent upon the success of some other tribal activity undertaken at the same time of year, such as a deer hunt. Yet it is doubtful whether the description of such connections as "mystical" is accurate. The associations are of course irrational; but so too are many made even by modern Westerners as children, and these also may depend rather on mental contiguity than on a distinct belief in disembodied forces.[41] Jean Piaget gives an interesting example: a five-year-old explained that the moon didn't fall down *"because it is very high up, because there isn't any sun, because it is very high up."* Since the moon's height in the sky, its shining when the sun is hidden, and the fact that it doesn't fall down form a unitary percept, "the child explains one of these features simply by an enumeration of the others."[42]

IN LITERATURE. The tracing in literature of irrational conjunctions similar to those just discussed is very difficult for several reasons, of which two are especially important. First, the skillful writer tends so to tighten the contextural relationships in his work that

39 See Pliny Earle Goddard, *Life and Culture of the Hupa*, University of California Publications in American Archaeology and Ethnology, Vol. I, No. 1 (Berkeley, Calif.: University of California Press, 1903), p. 63.

40 The couvade, at its fullest development, requires the father to take to bed when his wife is to bear a child, but there are many analogous practices. For interesting examples, see Basil Thomson, *The Fijians: A Study of the Decay of Custom* (London: William Heinemann, Ltd., 1908), pp. 179–80.

41 I myself recall having made such associations as a boy of twelve or thirteen; for instance, one day as I delivered newspapers on a bicycle: "If I can ride no-handed as far as Twenty-fifth Street, folding newspapers all the time, I will win my first-round match in the tennis tournament." Of course I did not really *believe* in the connection (for which reason I am dubious about *"propter"* in Cassirer's formula); but I arbitrarily brought the success of one activity into association with the success of another.

42 Jean Piaget, *The Language and Thought of the Child*, trans. Marjorie Gabain (New York: Meridian Books, Inc., 1955), p. 147.

associations which in their basic nature rest on mere contiguity are made to appear probable. Secondly, in so far as *any* cognition is not articulated in terms of meticulously scrutinized cause-and-effect relationships, it must accept contiguity as evidence of involvement. Accordingly, a thorough examination of the subject would require the investigation of much more than would be appropriate to a discussion of literary language.

Let us take as a first example the association, in the cycle of stories about King Arthur, of Guinevere's adultery and the downfall of the Celtic kingdom. In its origin, the connection of moral rottenness in the court with military defeat in the field may have been at least partly irrational. To borrow Lévy-Bruhl's doubtful term, the realm "participated" in the Queen's guilt and therefore was implicated in her punishment. In the stories as they exist, however, the connection has been more or less rationalized. Moral contagion spreads from royalty to the court, from the court to the army, and from the army to the nation, so that in late versions—for example, Tennyson's—a persuasive causality is established. We are satisfied with the particularities given and do not reflect that in fact many morally tainted rulers have reigned successfully (Kings Henry IV and VIII of England). And so with many other basically irrational associations. We must expect, therefore, some rationality in the literary context and not, unless exceptionally or in very early writings, conjunctions that are transparently absurd.

Once the necessity of broad constructionism has been accepted, literary examples spring to the mind. Persephone is permitted to return to earth during only six months of the year because in Hades she ate six pomegranate seeds. The killing of a stag by Agamemnon causes the Greek host, assembled at Aulis, to be delayed by contrary winds. Caesar dies, and ghosts squeak and gibber in the Roman streets. At the nativity of Owen Glendower, in *Henry IV, Part I,*

> The front of heaven was full of fiery shapes,
> Of burning cressets, and at my birth
> The frame and huge foundation of the earth
> Shak'd like a coward.

Oscar Wilde's Dorian Gray dissipates, and his painted portrait looks more haggard and evil. D. G. Rossetti's Sister Helen melts a waxen figure, and in another place the lover who has rejected her weakens. In an ancient Egyptian tale reported by Andrew Lang, a flower is cut from a tree, and the hero dies.[43] In the widely disseminated story of the Fisher King, an injury to the King's genitals causes the sterility of an entire country. In some of these examples, the relevance of the primitive thought tendency to literature is patent; in others, it is more or less skillfully disguised. In all, however, at the root of a fictive situation is a conjunction between objects or phenomena that to the scientific or philosophical consciousness would appear unrelated.

So far, the discussion has turned less on the use of language than on the fabrication of incident; but a connection with language is easy to establish. Many uses of metaphor, simile, synecdoche, and even symbols can be traced to the association of contiguities. The red rose to which Robert Burns likened his sweetheart was beautiful, like the sweetheart; but beauty alone would provide an insufficient basis for comparison. A golden trout or a tropical clam is also beautiful, and except in respect of texture a red cabbage would do every bit as well as the rose. If poets do not liken their sweethearts to cabbages or clams, the reason is at least partly that flowers are *nearer* to courtship both in space and in time; young couples often walk in gardens, and flowers are conventionally given to young women by their suitors. When the terms of a poetic comparison are distant in the reader's culture, as when a city dweller comes upon the pastoral phrase, "Thy two breasts are like two young roes that are twins," [44] the reader is momentarily jarred.

Another kind of contiguity is *affective*. Gloomy weather is affectively adjacent to death because the induced feelings lie near to each other in the psyche; the thought of one easily becomes involved with the thought of the other. Ruskin's "pathetic fallacy" is indeed logically fallacious, but not therefore aesthetically improper. An extended discussion of metaphor, simile, and synecdoche must be

---

[43] See *The Two Brothers,* given at length by Lang in *Myth, Ritual and Religion,* II, 318–20. In this very old tale primitive thought ways appear starkly.

[44] Song of Solomon 4:5.

postponed, however, to another context. It is sufficient here to indicate that figurative speech is encouraged by the primitive tendency, reverted to in the excitement of literary composition, to perceive concretely and with sufficient breadth of focus to permit the sensing of data not discretely but in clusters—and this, of course, whether the data are physically present or called up to the mind's eye by imagination.

Parataxis in primitive speech

Up to this point, we have considered language from the point of view of diction and content but not of syntax. Syntactically, the equivalent of the associating of contiguities is parataxis: grammatical elements are laid end to end without an indication of logical relationships, mere contiguity sufficing to establish the connections.

That primitive syntax tends strongly toward parataxis has often been asserted. Cassirer, in his volume on language, remarks, "Language takes up the pure category of relation hesitantly, as it were, and learns to apprehend it only deviously, through other categories, particularly those of substance and attribute." Even the relative pronoun "appears to be a late development and, if we consider language as a whole, rather rare." [45] Hypotaxis—the grammatical subordination of some syntactical elements to others—is in his opinion the "highest product of language." [46] It is also, however, an "ultimate" product; for the typical primitive language, whether or not it forms words and even whole sentences by agglutination, appears to indicate relationships by mere contiguity. What for the modern Western intelligence would be a single complex notion is often laid apart into a whole series of syntactically co-ordinate elements which describe as process what would be formulated by us as a qualified generalization.

How this is done will be indicated by an example. The dissatisfaction of the African Bushman with the way he has been treated by the whites might be expressed, in our terms, as follows: "If the whites, at first, treat the Bushmen fairly well, the reasons are selfish;

---

[45] Cassirer, *Symbolical Forms,* I, 312 and 311.
[46] *Ibid.,* p. 310.

the treatment soon becomes so severe that the Bushmen have to save themselves by flight." An actual complaint by a Bushman ran, however, as follows:

> Bushman-there-go, here-run-to-white-man, white-man-give-tobacco, Bushman-go-smoke, go-fill-tobacco-pouch, white-man-give-meat-Bushman, Bushman-go-eat-meat, stand-up-go-home, go-happy, go-sit, graze-sheep-white-man, white-man-go-beat-Bushman, Bushman-cry-very-painful, Bushman-go-run-away-white-man, white-man-run-after-Bushman, Bushman-there-another-one [i.e., another Bushman is found to replace the first], this-one-graze-sheep, Bushman-entirely-away.[47]

Wundt, whose German version I have turned into English, was especially impressed by the concreteness of the description. "Everything is concrete, visual; it is not said, 'The Bushman at first is well received by the white man,' but 'The white man gives him tobacco, he fills his pouch and smokes, the white man gives him meat, he eats.' "[48] This is true, but our present interest is in the total lack of grammatical subordination. Every predication stands on exactly the same level as every other; there is not, apparently, the slightest suggestion of clausal relationship. The pidgin English spoken by blacks in many parts of the world has the same syntactical peculiarity. So also have the English speeches of American Indians in fiction, and even in cheap moving-picture and television drama.

IN CHILDISH SPEECH. The same thing is true of children. In the speech of six-year-olds, says Jean Piaget in *The Language and Thought of the Child,* "causal relations are rarely expressed, but are generally indicated by a simple juxtaposition of the related terms." Storytelling or the giving of an explanation proceeds by the mere lining up of elements; like the savage, "the child prefers factual description to causal explanation."[49]

IN LITERATURE. Whether, or to what extent, the primitive tendency toward parataxis is reflected by a similar tendency in the language of literature cannot be established without investigations

---

[47] Wilhelm Wundt, *Elemente der Völkerpsychologie* (Leipzig: Alfred Kröner Verlag, 1913), p. 72.
[48] *Ibid.*
[49] Piaget, *Language and Thought of the Child,* pp. 121 and 131.

which lie beyond the scope of the present study. There is a strong possibility, however, that the syntax of poems, plays, and novels would be found markedly more paratactic than that of other educated language. One remembers paratactic patterns in the beginnings of Western literature—for example, in Homer:

> *And* Hera of the golden throne stood on the peak of Olympus, *and* saw with her eyes, *and* anon knew him that was her brother and her lord's going to and fro through the glorious fight, *and* she rejoiced in her heart. *And* she beheld Zeus sitting on the topmost crest of many-fountained Ida, *and* to her heart he was hateful. *And* she took thought, the ox-eyed lady Hera, how she might beguile the mind of aegis-bearing Zeus. *And* this seemed to her in her heart to be the best counsel . . .[50]

The steady rain of clauses seems right for epic. The *Aeneid,* which is more hypotactic than the *Iliad,* in spite of many striking excellencies grips modern readers less and in its own country had a less broadly based popularity. The *Chanson de Roland,* a cruder and lesser poem than the *Aeneid,* nevertheless has greater narrative momentum and uses parataxis more.[51] Whether in other forms of creative literature than epic there is a correlation between parataxis and the power of inducing absorption is a question that could be answered only after long and intricate researches. In so far, however, as literature is sensory rather than abstract, color and shape and motion rather than philosophical analysis, it tends almost necessarily toward the indication of relationships in terms not of static categories but of process. "He said, and Hera the ox-eyed queen was afraid" sounds more literary, although less accurately conceptualized, than "Hera the ox-eyed queen was afraid because of what he said." In aroused contemplation, significance appears *in* the

---

[50] *Iliad* xiv. 153–61. The translation given in the text is fairly literal; but I have changed one "now" and one "then" to "and," since the word δέ is the same as that elsewhere translated "and." The translation is by Andrew Lang, Walter Leaf, and Ernest Myers and is now published by Random House, Inc.

[51] For comments on parataxis in the *Chanson de Roland,* see Erich Auerbach, *Mimesis: The Representation of Reality in Western Literature,* trans. Willard Trask (Princeton, N.J.: Princeton University Press, 1953), p. 103. Auerbach has noted also the parataxis of the Biblical style (*ibid.,* p. 75), the style of early Germanic epic (pp. 110–11), and that of the French *Chanson d'Alexis* (p. 111) and its Latin source (p. 117).

sensory datum and need not be hypotactically pointed. The field of attention is wide enough to allow the immediate perception of relationships that are not explicitly indicated.

The part for the whole
in primitive thought

Up to this point, we have considered contiguity in terms of more than one object or activity. When attention is attracted to a peripheral segment of a rather diffuse sensory field, the cognitive association of adjacent data may be said to move outward from a center. It is possible, however, for the observer, by narrowing the field of awareness, to become sensitive to adjacencies within a unitary process or object. When this is done, the primitive appears to cognize the relationship of the parts to the whole differently from educated Westerners. Beside the principle *juxta hoc, ergo propter hoc* may be set another: the rule of *pars pro toto*.

This second principle, which has also been frequently commented on, is described by Cassirer as follows:

> For our empirical understanding the whole "arises" from the parts; for the logic of the natural sciences and for that of the philosophically analytical conception of causality the whole "results" from the parts. For the mythical understanding, however, at bottom the one holds as little as the other. Instead, there still prevails here an actual lack of disjunction, a reflective and real "indifference" of the whole and the parts. The whole does not "have" parts and fall away into them, but the part here is directly the whole and works and functions as such. This relationship also, this principle of the *pars pro toto,* has been indicated flatly as a basic principle of "primitive logic." [52]

No mental habit of primitives has been more profusely documented or seems to be more widespread. As yet, an explanation of the tendency is not agreed on; but the tendency itself is well known to anthropologists and need be illustrated here by only a single example.

---

[52] Cassirer, *Philosophie der Symbolischen Formen,* II, 66.

Of the Gazelle Peninsula of New Pomerania, Richard H. R. Parkinson reports:

> As a rule the effectiveness of magical practices requires that the latter include an object which forms a part of the person to be bewitched (for example, his hair, a piece of his clothing) or which stands in some kind of relationship to him (for example, his excrement, scraps from the refuse of his meals, his spittle, his footprints, and so on). All such objects can be used as *panait,* that is, as a medium for *panait* or magic, consisting in an incantation or muttering of a certain formula, together with the blowing into the air of a bit of burned lime held in the hand.[53]

What is done to the part is done to the whole; the bewitching of a hair accomplishes the bewitching of the person to whom the hair had belonged. Similar reports have come from every part of the world in which low cultures exist, or existed until recently. It is unimportant to decide whether the part participates mystically in the whole, or is connected with it by means not only of contiguity but of an identity of *pneuma* or *mana,* or is simply not disjoined cognitively from it because of a tendency to keep the sensory span wide. In magical practices the world over, the enchanter *acts as if* the whole and the part were indissolubly one.[54]

This is the clearest and most easily accessible illustration; but an analogous association appears in many fertility rites, in which powers conferred upon a few ears of Indian corn or some other agricultural product are assumed to communicate themselves to the whole crop. The reason for the primitive reluctance to change the shape or ornamentation of any object either of daily or of cult use is, again, an unanalyzed feeling that a change in any part will transform the whole. The relationship of a house post to a house is construed similarly to that of a nail paring or a shadow to a man.

Like many other primitive thought ways, the principle of *pars*

---

[53] R[ichard] H. R. Parkinson, *Dreissig Jahre in der Südsee* (Stuttgart: Strecker & Schröder, 1907), p. 118.

[54] If an explanation were necessary, I should myself prefer Von den Steinen's, written of the Brazilian Bakairí: "As soon as feeling is aroused, the part in fact calls forth the entire group of associations; one can sense from a picture or a piece everything he can sense from the original or the whole."—*Unter den Naturvölkern,* p. 296.

pro toto seems to represent a permanent cognitive possibility for human beings. Werner believes that for young children also the part is the same as the whole. A child who is fearful of spiders is fearful also of the single remaining strand of a broken spider web; a mother may be urged to close the window on a ray of sunshine in order that the sun may be caught. "Children accordingly conceive objects as much less structured, more totally than we adults"; "What among primitives sounded much more hypothetical, first becomes clear to us in the realm of child psychology." [55] In the course of time, in our society, the child learns to discriminate more sharply; but in a culture in which no sophisticated understanding of the relation of parts to the whole had arisen, the early confusion might easily persist through adulthood.

IN LITERATURE. When we inquire whether in literature, too, the part tends to be equated with the whole, we are reminded at once of the figure of speech called "synecdoche." The analysis of rhetorical figures is no longer a popular method of literary analysis; but for many centuries it was thought sufficiently important to deserve extended consideration in rhetorical treatises. In nearly all such works, from Aristotle's *Poetics* to Alexander Bain's *English Composition and Rhetoric* (1887), synecdoche, or "the use of the part for the whole" (alternatively, of the whole for the part), occupied an honorable place alongside such other figures as personification, metonymy, and prosopopoeia. It appears to have been assumed—and this for many hundreds of years, by men of a reflective temperament—that in literary speech, which perhaps grew out of excitement and certainly had the power to sway men's emotions, the mind tended to function less rationally than in other speech: to imagine inanimate objects as living, to accept the container for the thing contained, to address absent persons and objects as though present, and so on. Such illogicality was not, of course, condemned. On the contrary, it was admired; for did it not illustrate the force of the writer's passion? Thus the tendency of good writers sometimes to say *roof* for *house, poop* or *sail* for *ship,* and *Croesus* for *all*

---

[55] Heinz Werner, *Einführung in die Entwicklungspsychologie,* (3d ed.; Munich: Johann Ambrosius Barth, 1953), pp. 86–87. Here again the English edition (see Note 17, above) lacks details present in the later German edition.

rich men, although rationally incorrect, was aesthetically unexceptionable. Although it would not have occurred to rhetoricians to say that in literary creation the mind *regressed* to earlier thought patterns, the classical aesthetic thus included in a different idiom, as one of its basic postulates, a view analogous to that recommended here.

More generally considered, synecdoche is a fundamental element both in literature and in all reflection. In scientific polls of public opinion, as in much empirical research of other kinds, a part is studied instead of an unmanipulable whole. Yet there is a significant difference between responsible sampling techniques and the use of "types" or "test cases" by the literary artist. The scientific thinker is aware that the extension of his experimental findings by generalization involves extrapolation and that in all extrapolation there is an element of risk. The literary artist, in contrast, often appears to believe that by playing out the fates of a few imaginary personages he has arrived at general truths about all mankind. His "themes" can be established only in so far as the social microcosm he portrays can be assumed to "participate in" a social macrocosm whose total nature it is impossible for him to describe or, indeed, to understand.

Shakespeare's *Macbeth* will provide an example. The theme of this tragedy is usually said to lie in the demonstration that vaulting ambition o'erleaps itself and falls on the other side. Undoubtedly, this is what happens to Macbeth's ambition; and the play is so contrived as to persuade us that his defeat is causally connected with his aspirations. No one in his senses would argue, however, that the play has "proved" all tyrants will come to a bad end. History offers ample evidence to the contrary. If we rise from a reading of the tragedy with a profound conviction that Macbeth's fate is typical, the reason is that we have been sufficiently stirred to fall back into a cognitive habit characteristic of primitive reflection.

It would be improper at this point to develop further a matter which has to do rather with plot than with language. It is appropriate, however, to suggest that the use of synecdoche in literature is not limited to the occasional use of rhetorical tropes but permeates whole works as an important element in their structure. Kenneth

Burke's assertion in *The Philosophy of Literary Form* that synecdoche is the basic figure of speech and, again, that synecdoche is the "basic" process of representation,[56] has much to recommend it; but the similarity between synecdoche and the tendency of savages not to make cognitive distinctions between a part and the whole has not, I think, hitherto been distinctly asserted.

Sensory and motor emphasis

One more consequence must be drawn from the tendency of primitives to sense complexes of data simultaneously. When the visual field is comparatively broad, movements within it attract attention because they produce modifications of contour and relationship. If the movement is lateral, there is a change in the left-to-right structure of the field; if it is in the same direction as the line of sight, the relationship of foreground to background is altered. Similarly, dynamic posture is an element in the configuration because it implies the possibility of future movement. Hence, in part, the tendency of primitive languages to describe with astonishing accuracy forms, contours, movements, and positions in space. From this point of view, what was discussed earlier as the concreteness of primitive speech appears as precision in the denotation of contour, whether static or fluid.

Since comments have already been offered about the use in primitive languages of variant forms to indicate differences of posture (*hiniha,* "he, seated"; *hiriha,* "he, lying down"; *eneha,* "he, walking and visible"; and so on), it will be sufficient at this point to cite examples of motor images. In the Klamath Indian language, for instance, there are twelve suffixes which differentiate movements as occurring in a straight line, toward the sun, toward some other object or toward the subject of the verb, far from, above, on a horizontal plane, in a circle, and so on—these in addition to nine other suffixes which indicate states of rest or repose. Many other primitive languages have a similar characteristic.

---

[56] See Kenneth Burke, *The Philosophy of Literary Form: Studies in Symbolic Action* (Baton Rouge, La.: Louisiana State University Press, 1941), esp. pp. 26 and 27.

In the Huron language, "to describe a trip, the expressions differ for travel by land and by water. . . ." Among the Nez-Percés, the verbs take different forms depending on whether it is considered that the movement is toward or away from the subject or the object. In the Yahgan language, [there are] "ten thousand verbs . . . , whose number is still further augmented by the way in which they add numerous prefixes and suffixes . . . indicating that one is coming from a certain direction, or is going there, toward the north, the south, the east, or the west, up, down, out, in . . . an almost incalculable number, without counting a mass of adverbs which indicate position." . . . In South Africa, Livingstone found the same richness of nuance expressed by verbs. . . . "I have heard nearly twenty terms to designate different ways of walking. One walks leaning forward, or back, with a swing, lazily or vigorously, with importance, swinging both arms or only one arm, with head lowered, or raised, or otherwise leaning: each of these ways of walking was expressed by a special verb." [57]

The limits of the sensory field can evidently be adjusted at will. A man moving across a background of trees may be perceived as moving in relation to the trees, or, alternatively, parts of his body may be perceived in relation to his body as a whole. Whichever configuration is implied by a verbal description, however, the motor impulses are given value and are not devitalized, as happens so often in European speech. The separation, in "advanced" tongues, of elements which in many primitive languages are inseparable permits an abstract utterance denied to the typical savage. The primitive, however, tends to speak a language rich in motor imagery and therefore more precise in the delineation of shifting contours.

LAUTBILDER.   We may follow Lévy-Bruhl, whose collections of empirical data are often convenient, into a brief consideration also of *Lautbilder*. The *Lautbild,* or sound image, is not confined to the imitation of noises but attempts often to provide an auditory equivalent of appearances, odors, tactile sensations, tastes, and, especially, movements. The resemblance between the sound image and the phenomenon it attempts to imitate is often difficult or impossible to analyze. Why, for instance, it should appear to the Japanese that

---

[57] Lévy-Bruhl, *Fonctions mentales,* pp. 173–74.

the act of smiling is represented by the reduplicating sounds *niko-niko* is mysterious, since the lateral spreading of the lips motivated by the *ee* sound is at once compromised by the slight rounding which accompanies the *o*. Yet such *Lautbilder,* often reduplicated, occur in primitive languages all over the globe; and they seem to be applied with astonishing frequency to movements.

Two examples must serve for many. In the Ewe language of western Afria the verb *zo,* meaning to "walk," is qualified by adverbial modifiers descriptive of varieties of movement but used with no other verb. *Zo bafobafo* is used of a small man whose limbs move briskly as he walks; *zo biabia* of a man who throws long legs forward; *zo kondzrakondzra* of a person who takes long steps while pulling in his stomach; *zo hloyihloyi* of one who carries many objects or has many bits of clothing floating about him; and so on. Lévy-Bruhl cites thirty-three such reduplicating adverbs, all attached only to *zo,* from Diedrich Westermann's *Grammatik der Ewe-Sprache* [58] without exhausting the list.[59] There are similar *Lautbilder* to specify ways of running, climbing, swimming, riding on horseback or in a carriage, and the like. In the Ronga language of Africa, again, there are words

> which the Bantu grammarians view generally as interjections, onomatopoeic words. They are usually vocables of a single syllable, by means of which the natives express a sudden or immediate impression made on them by a spectacle, a sound, an idea, or describe a movement, an appearance, a noise. It is necessary only to have been present at a few conversations of the blacks in the freedom of nature . . . to have noticed what a prodigious number of expressions of this kind they have at their command.[60]

All such particles tend, in the degree of their expressiveness, to make language more graphic; and an element in the sensory fullness of the design is the oral imitation of motor impulses which modify or color the visual field.

THE RELATION OF PRIMITIVE SPEECH TO GESTURE. The rich-

---

[58] *Ibid.,* pp. 183–85.
[59] For the list see Diedrich Westermann, *Grammatik der Ewe-Sprache* (Berlin: Dietrich Riemer, 1907), pp. 83–84.
[60] Lévy-Bruhl, *Fonctions mentales,* pp. 186–87.

ness of primitive languages in sensory percepts of all kinds, but especially in visual and motor data, has more than once suggested to thoughtful scholars the possibility that the origin of language may be sought in gesture. Giambattista Vico expressed this view in his *Scienza Nuova* at least as early as 1744.[61] Wilhelm Wundt, in *Elemente der Völkerpsychologie* (1913), proposed it again after checking it by a study of the spontaneous rise of gesture language among uninstructed deaf-and-dumb people.[62] More recently, at the International Symposium on Anthropology held in New York in 1951, the discredited theory of Wundt was revived by Kenneth P. Oakley. Oakley cited Sir Richard Paget, who some years ago urged that "speech as we understand it now is very different from the original communicating system, which may have consisted much more of manual gesture and vocalized copying of manual gesture by the tongue and mouth." This theory, he added, was substantiated by Alexander Johannsson, who had recently

> reached the same conclusion by an entirely different route—the comparison of six unrelated families of languages. . . . He reached the conclusion that modern language families are of comparatively recent origin and have a number of roots in common, all with a probable origin of gesture.[63]

The suggestion was not well received, and the existence of a connection remains doubtful. Yet it is interesting to note that the importance of visual and motor imagery in primitive speech is sufficiently marked to have provoked more than once an argument that manual description, which almost necessarily emphasizes contour and movement, preceded oral utterance and is its ancestor.

VISUAL AND MOTOR EMPHASIS IN LITERATURE. Is the visual and motor emphasis of primitive languages a characteristic also of the language of literature? Enough has been said in a different context to indicate that literature may be granted a special concreteness;

---

[61] See Giambattista Vico, *La Scienza nuova, e opere scelte*, ed. Nicola Abbagnano (Torino: Unione Tipografico-Editrice Torinese, 1952), p. 330.

[62] Wundt, *Völkerpsychologie*, pp. 60–65.

[63] See *An Appraisal of Anthropology Today*, ed. Sol Tax, Loren C. Eiseley, Irving Rouse, and Carl F. Voegelin (© 1953 by the University of Chicago Press), p. 265.

and the concreteness is so dependent upon sensory qualities that without visual and motor imagery it would be inconceivable. The difficulty, here as elsewhere, is not merely in representing "literature" by a few extracts but also in finding extracts which will illustrate only whatever characteristics are intended to be put into focus.

Even so, the chief source of perplexity is an overabundance of materials. In general, literature supports easily the proposition that good writers tend to be sensitive to visual contours and quick to note modifications produced by motor impulses—and this whether the sensory images come directly from physical objects, are remembered after the lapse of time, or are invented by the creative imagination. If there are exceptions, they may be expected to appear especially in the eighteenth century, when the official aesthetic emphasized generality, or after the romantic movement, when an interest, later to be encouraged by the development of modern psychology, had been awakened in private mental states as opposed to "objective" happenings. Perhaps Samuel Johnson's *Rasselas* and a late novel by Henry James will serve as test cases.

The first chapter of *Rasselas* is entitled "Description of a Palace in a Valley" and is therefore committed to some observation of physical setting. The second, which is called "The Discontent of Rasselas in the Happy Valley," will serve our purpose admirably. We skip over three introductory paragraphs and settle upon the fourth, in which the analysis of Rasselas' dissatisfaction properly begins.

Thus they rose in the morning and lay down at night, pleased with each other and with themselves, all but Rasselas, who, in the twenty-sixth year of his age began to withdraw himself from their pastimes and assemblies, and to delight in solitary walks and silent meditation. He often sat before tables covered with luxury, and forgot to taste the dainties that were placed before him: he rose abruptly in the midst of the song, and hastily retired beyond the sound of music. His attendants observed the change, and endeavoured to renew his love of pleasure; he neglected their officiousness, repulsed their invitations, and spent day after day, on the banks of rivulets sheltered with trees, where he sometimes listened to the birds in the branches, sometimes observed the fish playing in the stream, and anon cast his eyes upon the pastures and mountains filled with animals, of which some were biting the herbage, and some sleeping among the bushes.

It is true that in this paragraph the imagery, in keeping with Johnson's theory of art, is nowhere tied down to particulars. "Luxury," "dainties," and "pleasure" stand for concepts too general to be sharply visualized. Yet a reader whose senses are active is conscious of loaded tables, vocal and probably also instrumental music, birds singing in trees, and so on. More significantly in the present context, the passage is full of motor imagery. Rasselas "withdrew" himself from court pastimes, took "solitary walks," "sat" before tables only to "rise abruptly" from them, "repulsed" the invitations of his attendants, spent many days on stream banks observing the "fish playing," "cast" his eyes upon pastures and mountains, where he saw some animals "biting the herbage" and others "sleeping among the bushes." The motor energy suggested by the description, although never abrupt and perhaps not even vigorous, is sufficient to make the little scene dynamic. In a century of elegance and deliberate movement, language is not yet infinitely distant from physical gesture. In a good oral reading of the passage, hand and body might find much to do.

The prose of Henry James has different characteristics, and in *The Wings of the Dove* whole pages might perhaps be found in which there were few visual objects and little motor energy. More typically, however, the descriptions are in some degree vitalized. For example, a passage chosen at random:

It was by her personality that Aunt Maud was prodigious, and the great mass of it loomed because, in the thick, the foglike air of her arranged existence, there were parts doubtless magnified and parts certainly vague. They represented at all events alike, the dim and the distinct, a strong will and a high hand. It was perfectly present to Kate that she might be devoured, and she likened herself to a trembling kid, kept apart a day or two till her turn should come, but sure sooner or later to be introduced into the cage of the lioness. (From Chapter II.) [64]

---

[64] Henry James, *The Wings of the Dove* (New York: Charles Scribner's Sons, 1902), I, 33.

In the "looming" of the massive personality, the threat that Kate might be "devoured," the "trembling" of the doomed kid, and the potential "introducing" of the victim into the lioness' cage there are still hints for descriptive gesture—as also, perhaps, in the "thick, foglike air" of a mode of living, the "magnifying" of certain experiences, and elsewhere. Visually, the passage is hazy but not blank. At the furthest possible remove from primitive diction and syntax, the language of literature preserves some of the sensory qualities of primitive speech.

Linguistic regression—deliberate or spontaneous?

Up to the present point, it has been found that primitive languages are remarkable for concreteness and that they reflect in several ways perceptual habits different from those which accompany the analytic reflection of educated Westerners. Sensory *Gestalten* are not laid apart into discrete elements, as in scientific or philosophical thought, but are perceived *as Gestalten*. Adjacent perceptual items are assumed to be mutually involved; a part is often assumed to act as or be equivalent to the whole; and visual contours are so delicately registered that motor impulses which affect them are absorbed into the descriptive locutions. The language of literature, as distinct from the language of philosophy or science, shares all these primitive traits, if not in every sentence, yet consistently enough to appear psychically regressive.

Is this appearance, however, misleading? We must consider briefly whether the literary artist may not imitate archaic linguistic patterns deliberately, instead of falling into them as the result of perceptual tendencies inseparable from the creative process. Quintilian and other rhetoricians who have discussed such figures as synecdoche seem to imply that the figures can be manufactured at will, for the ornamentation of discourse.

Certainly it must be granted that the role of tradition in literature is very powerful and that the linguistic patterns which have been noticed may owe something to imitation. The synecdoches and other figures of speech in Virgil derive partly from those in Homer, and those in Milton partly from those in both Virgil and Homer. To assert, however, that literary language resembles primitive language *merely* because writers tend to imitate one another consciously would be to argue that aesthetic creation is a purely mechanical process; and this proposition modern aestheticians will not tolerate for a minute. If at times, during the composition of *Paradise Lost,* Milton said to himself *sotto voce,* "Time for a Homeric simile," he did not cease working over the simile until it had become not only a particular kind of syntactical pattern but also a particular kind of perceptual *Gestalt.* This is to say that, in seeking to write, for the moment, as Homer wrote, Milton was forced to sense as Homer had sensed; and in doing so he fell back into psychic habits which were already more than two thousand years old. The imitation was psychological as well as linguistic. Moreover, the process, when successful, must have been accompanied by some degree of excitement. Through an image like that describing the sea beast Leviathan in Book I, feeling surges in energetic swells.

I suggest that excitement not only accompanies the linguistically regressive turns of speech but is in large part their source. When creative absorption is intense, the mind sinks through layers of superficial habit to the bedrock of biological tendency. At such times, as dozens of artists have testified, the aesthetic medium seems to work by itself, and control is only partly conscious. Discursive reflection is not "natural"; it is an acquired habit, superimposed by education upon other habits which tend to reassert themselves when strong feelings are aroused. At bottom we are all primitive still. At his best moments, the good artist reaches a long way toward the bottom; and even at moments not his best he writes from a depth not easily attained by men who are not artists.

4

The Language of Literature (2)

Primitive animism

Of all the psychic habits of primitive men, none has been more richly documented than that which Edward Tylor, in an ephocal anthropological work, called "animism." The savage appears to recognize not only consciousness but also a power resembling will in objects and processes which seem to the educated Westerner to be controlled by mechanical or biological law.

A familiar illustration of the habit can be found in Greek mythology, in which the principle of fire is personified as Hephaestus, that of thunder as Zeus, that of the wind as Aeolus, that of the rainbow as Iris, and that of war as Ares—names for which the Romans had equivalents. Trees were personified as dryads, streams as naiads, mountains as oreads. In Homer rivers speak; in Virgil branches bleed. Nature was more fully alive for our cultural ancestors than it is for us. Men did not yet move through a universe in which human beings were pre-eminently aware and pre-eminently capable of initiating actions by will.

On more primitive levels of human consciousness, the animizing tendency expressed, and still expresses, itself somewhat differently. In savage communities which have developed no gods *of* fire, *of* thunder, and *of* the wind, it appears often to be assumed that everything which exists has consciousness and the power of choice. Animals are entreated to allow themselves to be killed; arrows and other missiles are urged to find their marks; endearing speeches are addressed to shell armlets and other articles of economic value. Even objects made by human hands are often personified.

> There was an amazing degree of individualization of objects among the Marquesans, everything being personified. Just as each individual was a distinct entity in his tribe, so every axe or food bowl or canoe was also a distinct entity and had a name. . . . A house not only went through the process of creation, but was hung with a loin cloth so that it would be decently clad.[1]

The Zuñi Indians, "no less than primitive peoples generally, conceive of everything made, whether structure, utensil, or weapon, as animistic, as living." [2] The illustrations are typical: "The savage, it has been thought, attributes personality to everything without exception." Even stones are often believed to reproduce their species.[3] At present there is some disposition among anthropologists to question the appropriateness of "animism" as a descriptive name

---

[1] Ralph Linton, writing in Abram Kardiner, *The Individual and His Society*, with a Foreword and Two Ethnological Reports by Ralph Linton (New York: Columbia University Press, 1939), p. 148.

[2] Frank Hamilton Cushing, "Outlines of Zuñi Creation Myths," in J. W. Powell, *Thirteenth Annual Report of the Bureau of Ethnology to the Secretary of the Smithsonian Institution, 1891–92* (Washington, D.C.: Government Printing Office, 1896), pp. 361–62.

[3] Andrew Lang, *Myth, Ritual and Religion* (London: Longmans, Green & Co., Ltd., 1913), II, 198, and I, 98.

for the tendency; but as recently as 1934 Ruth Benedict was able to call animism one of "those few traits that are universal or near-universal in human society." [4] Under this or some other name, the tendency is undoubtedly real.

IN STORIES. Nowhere does the primitive tendency to personalize, to impute will and the power of self-direction to lifeless objects, appear more clearly than in crude myths. The role of animizing metaphors in primitive speech is difficult to assess because metaphors are recognized as such only when the language is very thoroughly known and attention has been focused specifically upon them. In translation, the "head" of a stream might be called its "source" and one of its "arms" a "tributary." [5] In myths, however, the imputing of life to inert objects is often inseparably fused with the plot. I quote a representative excerpt about Yimantuwinyai, a culture hero of the Hupa Indians.

> When he came to Orleans Bar he found two women had come into existence there. These women were well behaved and always stayed in the house. Yimantuwinyai wanted in someway to meet them. Picking up a stick he wished it would become a canoe and it did. Then he wished for a lake and the lake was there. Putting the canoe in the water he transformed himself into a child and seated himself in it. At earliest dawn the women came along and saw him there. They started to catch the canoe and secure the baby, but the boat avoided them. They made the circuit of the lake wading or swimming after it. When they were about to catch it, the water broke out of the banks and they failed.[6]

The stick responds to a wish; the lake creates itself at a wish. More interesting, in this legend, is the malicious willfulness of the canoe and the water: things which at one minute are helpful at the next minute become deliberately recalcitrant. The world is too full of

---

[4] Ruth Benedict, *Patterns of Culture* (Boston: Houghton Mifflin Company, 1934), p. 19.

[5] "Tributary" is, of course, also an animizing metaphor, although less easily recognizable as such than "arm."

[6] Earle Pliny Goddard, *Hupa Texts,* University of California Publications in American Archaeology and Ethnology, Vol. I, No. 2 (Berkeley, Calif.: University of California Press, 1904), p. 125.

self-initiating energy to submit tamely to the control even of a culture hero.

The animism implicit in the legend continues, less obtrusively, into more sophisticated cultures and times. The swords of King Arthur and Roland possess intrinsic power; in folk tales animals regularly understand human speech and often are capable of it, birds serve as benevolent guides, boats obey verbal directions, tools work by themselves, and split trees close on victims. The innate human tendency to consider oneself as "a link in the chain of all life, within which every existence is magically bound with the whole," [7] is too powerful to yield quickly to changing philosophical assumptions.

AMONG CHILDREN.   The extent to which the animizing tendency is fundamental to human thought patterns can be seen in the recapitulation by children of the personifying habit of their racial ancestors. Alfred Biese, whose little nineteenth-century work on *Die Philosophie des Metaphorischen* has lost none of its cogency, reports the behavior of his own children at ages between two and five years. Dolls must drink, take bites out of rolls, catch the measles along with their owners, and be treated by the doctor. When the moon disappears from the sky, it has gone to visit Grandmother. A rain which prevents the child from playing out of doors is naughty and must be spanked. Anything hit by a falling object will feel the same pain the child would have felt had he been struck. A child who has not yet learned numbers, or who thinks they are too little perceptual to be interesting, may count a row of balls or apples by calling them Father, Mother, Brother, and Sister or by naming them, somewhat more abstractly, after the days of the week or the months.

> For the child the cleavage between living and lifeless has not yet arisen; if he assigns sensation and activity to the latter, his expression will appear metaphorical to the grown-up, although for the child it signifies merely the most accurate and trustworthy reality.[8]

[7] Ernst Cassirer, *Philosophie der Symbolischen Formen,* Vol. II (Berlin: Bruno Cassirer Verlag, 1925), p. 240.

[8] Alfred Biese, *Die Philosophie des Metaphorischen* (Hamburg and Leipzig: Leopold Voss, 1893), p. 18. The illustrations from childish behavior are taken from pp. 18–21 and 33.

The assumption that the child speaks animistically only because he does not yet have a linguistic competence equal to the task of expressing abstractly what exists in his mind as abstract thought is unwarranted. The power of abstract conception does not precede that of abstract expression but develops simultaneously with it.

IN ALL LANGUAGE. So persistent, and so general, has been the animizing habit in human consciousness that all language bears its traces. This fact was noted as early as 1744 by Giambattista Vico in his *Scienza Nuova.*

> It is noteworthy that in all languages the greater part of the expressions relating to inanimate things are formed by metaphor from the human body and its parts and from the human senses and passions. Thus, head for top or beginning; eyes for the looped heads of screws and for windows letting light into houses; mouth for any opening; lip for the rim of a vase or of anything else; the tooth of a plow, a rake, a saw, a comb; beard for rootlets; the mouth of a river; a neck of land; handful for a small number; heart for center (the Latins used *umbilicus,* "navel," in this sense); foot for end; the flesh of fruits; a vein of water, rock or mineral; the blood of grapes for wine; the bowels of the earth.[9]

Biese adds to Vico's examples many others of a similar kind: the weather is cheerful, severe, gloomy, the fire dances, the wind whispers in the flue, nature sleeps in the winter, the waterfall complains, earth is the mother, spring is a young, flower-crowned boy, and so on.[10] But the animizing tendency expresses itself in more subtle ways, some of which seem not to have been often observed.

Take, for example, the use of prepositions to express relationships. We say, quite without realization that a temporal concept is being expressed in terms of spatial proximity, *at* such-and-such a time, *nearly* two days later, not *far* from Christmas. By locating moments of time in space, we give them a quasi-physical objectivity. The Latin words *hic, hinc, ibi, ubi,* and *inde,* and the Greek words ἔνθα and ἔνθεν pass easily into temporal desig-

---

9 Giambattista Vico, *The New Science,* trans. from the 3d ed. (1744) by Thomas Goddard Bergin and Max Harold Fisch (Ithaca, N.Y.: Cornell University Press, 1948), pp. 116–17 (par. 405).

10 Biese, *Philosophie des Metaphorischen,* pp. 28–29.

nations: the Germans say *am* Tage, *um* Pfingsten, *bei* Nacht, *vom* Morgen, *bis* Abend.[11] That experiential time is not necessarily spatialized is not only clear to common sense but is indicated by the quite different treatment of temporal concepts in such a language as Hopi.[12] Again, grammatical gender, as it appears in the Indo-European and Semitic languages, thinks Biese, is "nothing but metaphor"—specifically, personification. Even the analysis of etymological roots yields evidence of animistic thought patterns.

> How much develops out of the Sanskrit root *mar,* which means the activity of grinding! Sickness and death and war are first of all decomposing and crumbling forces; and so arose *morbus* and *mort* [*sic*] and *Mars* in Latin, and *mare* as the uprooter.[13]

Language is so permeated with animism, sometimes easily apparent, sometimes disguised almost beyond recognition, that were we never to assign in speech some degree of animal vitality to objects and processes which we know in reality to lack it, we should hardly be able to construct a sentence. We could not speak of a *soft* tone or a *warm* color; [14] an argument could not be *weak,* a chasm *yawn,* or the sun *rise;* it would be improper to mention a chemical *reaction,* or to speak of the *resistance* of an electrical conductor. Fortunately, we can reassure ourselves that most of these expressions are "metaphorical." In the beginning, however, many of them were not metaphorical. Our ancestors lived, as in many parts of the world savages still live, in a *beseelte Welt;* and when a new experience had to be assimilated, the process usually involved the imputing of some degree of vitality to objects actually inert.

AN EXPLANATION.   When we inquire why animism was so deeply rooted in early thought patterns, an answer presents itself almost immediately. "Man in his ignorance," wrote Vico in a continuation of the passage quoted earlier, "makes himself the rule

---

[11] Cf. *ibid.,* p. 32.

[12] Cf. Benjamin Lee Whorf, *Four Articles on Metalinguistics* (Washington, D.C.: Foreign Service Institute, Department of State, 1950), pp. 33–34.

[13] Biese, *Philosophie des Metaphorischen,* pp. 29 and 25–26.

[14] Cf. *ibid.,* p. 29.

of the entire world." The idea is developed more philosophically by Biese. In discussing this very passage by Vico, Biese says aptly:

> His metaphysics rests, when we recast it in terms of contemporary thought-patterns, on the thought that the perception and understanding of a strange object is nothing else than assimilation of impressions offered us by the object with notions already present in us; that the mode of understanding depends merely upon the number of suppositions ready and at hand. It follows from this that everything which is not conceived is personified. In the earliest stage there can be no question of a comprehension of nature; hence the new object is identified at once with an already accessible notion.[15]

The mind, we observe again, is not passive in perception but brings to the interpretation of sensory data a limited range of intellectual categories. (This was the basic insight of Kant.) If we move far enough back into prehistory, we arrive eventually at a time when subjective knowledge—immediate and felt rather than conceptualized, and full of motor vitality—far predominated over objective knowledge, as it visibly still does in animals. At this level, the process of animizing or personifying was automatic.

As a result of this discovery, it becomes clear that among savages personification and other animizing turns of speech were by no means originally the linguistic "ornaments" admired by rhetoricians but rather the inevitable linguistic expression of instinctive psychic processes. When the Kai of New Guinea say that the grass of certain plains "is sticking in the sun's eye, so that the eye weeps (rain) and the sun hides its face (clouds)," they speak not metaphorically but animistically. Heinz Werner remarks:

> However strongly this and other mythological judgments give the impression of being comparisons drawn from natural happenings and forces, all experienced observers of primitive psychology are agreed that these colored soap-bubbles of an apparently excessive fancy are held originally to be true and actual.[16]

---

15 Ibid., pp. 8–9.
16 Heinz Werner, *Die Ursprünge der Lyrik* (Munich: Ernst Reinhardt, 1924), p. 45.

In interpreting them otherwise we read our own mental processes into the products of minds which are structured differently. Neither is it surprising that, in ages when minds were less thoroughly remade by a conceptualized education than at present, men fell back easily into animistic thought patterns: that Xerxes wished the Hellespont to be scourged; that inert objects which had slain men were judged at the Prytaneia in Athens; that in the Middle Ages animals were sometimes condemned like human malefactors.[17] Even now it is not unusual for a workman to become provoked at the misbehavior of a tool, an angry golfer to break one of his clubs, or a frustrated motorist to kick at a blown-out tire. At times of emotional stress, though the mind may not be wholly deceived, the feelings may drive us into physical behavior of a kind not repudiated by the reason in Western prehistory or among modern children.

IN LITERARY LANGUAGE.   Is the animizing tendency active in literature to such an extent that literary speech, like primitive thought, endows dead matter with living energy? It has already been shown that all language is saturated with personifying metaphors; hence the question reduces itself to an inquiry about the comparative density and vitality of such expressions in literary and nonliterary speech. But this inquiry is no sooner launched than a reply urges itself upon us irresistibly.

It is not only that the animism in nonliterary language is often unconscious and nonperceptual ("Morning has come"), whereas that in literature tends to be vigorously sensory ("Jocund morn/ Stands tiptoe on the misty mountain-top"), or that personification has been recognized for at least two thousand years as a peculiarly literary "ornament." The point is that good writers, in energizing their materials, instinctively endow them with life.

> All day I hear the noise of waters
>   Making moan,
> Sad as the sea-bird is, when going
>   Forth alone,

---

[17] For the foregoing examples, see Biese, *Philosophie des Metaphorischen*, p. 19.

He hears the winds cry to the waters'
Monotone.[18]

Not even for the twentieth-century poet is the ocean mere salt water, heaving or pounding because of meteorological pressures such as the moon's pull and the failure of the earth's gravity to hold the atmosphere motionless. It has moods, feelings, consciousness; and the winds which produce its movements do not simply blow (a verb which itself implies personification) but, more actively, "cry." "As the idea of personality grows more distinct," remarked Andrew Lang, "it necessarily becomes less extensive, till we withdraw it from all but intelligent human beings." [19] Yes, in discursive thought; but literary cognition is not basically discursive, and what is denied by the reason creeps in by way of the feelings. "The poet opens the shaft of hidden depths, and his magical key is analogy, is anthropomorphism, is metaphor." [20] Wordsworth recognized this truth in his poetic practice:

> To every natural form, rock, fruits or flower,
> Even the loose stones that cover the highway,
> I gave a moral life.[21]

Coleridge signalized it in his critical theory; one proof of original genius in the use of images appears, he said, when "a human and intellectual life is transferred to them from the poet's own spirit." [22] The practice, however, has always been common. Geoffrey Chaucer used it in *The Knight's Tale* when, after describing the felling of a grove of trees, he wrote:

> . . . The ground agast was of the light,
> That was nat wont to seen the sonne bright.[23]

Most poetry is pathetically fallacious; but pathetic fallacy reveals itself again to be poetic truth, for in aroused aesthetic contempla-

---

[18] From "All Day I Hear," in *Collected Poems,* by James Joyce, Compass edition. © 1918 by B. W. Huebsch, 1946 by Nora Joyce. Reprinted by permission of The Viking Press, Inc.
[19] Lang, *Myth, Ritual and Religion,* II, 193.
[20] Biese, *Philosophie des Metaphorischen,* p. 94.
[21] William Wordsworth, *The Prelude,* Book III, lines 127–29.
[22] S. T. Coleridge, *Biographia Literaria,* chap. xv.
[23] Geoffrey Chaucer, *Canterbury Tales,* A, 2931–32.

tion the feelings reanimate what the scientific intelligence has killed.[24]

Metonymy

Other figures of speech also derive from psychic habits which have deep roots in the past. Metonymy, for example, substitutes a single, especially prominent sense impression for the total perceptual image. The cry of a bird may be used as the bird's name (*cuckoo, whippoorwill;* in childish speech, *bow-wow* for *dog, moo-moo* for *cow,* and so on); or the most striking or affectively powerful visual characteristic may absorb sufficient attention to be given linguistic emphasis (*sail* for *ship, the crown* for *the King*). In neither usage need we always find figurative values; and to discover such values in comparable primitive locutions would be to read back our own reflective habits into peoples among whom consciousness was differently structured.

> Since words do not indicate the objects themselves, but only the images of these as they are engendered in our spirit, . . . it is clear that the roots become pictures, symbols for the most important activities of the phenomena in order to characterize the phenomena themselves. Thus the stone becomes the grinding eater, the tooth the cutting eater, the river the runner or the rustler or the plower, the wolf the tearer, the snake the creeper, the elephant the one-having-teeth, the moon the measurer, dawn the waker, thunder the roarer, etc.[25]

The very names which arise out of metonymical noun building sound "poetical"; but we are not to think of them as having been from the beginning consciously literary. They were created, like other words, by linguistic processes stimulated by a psychic need.

The primitive confusion of percept and imagination

Instead of dwelling longer on personification and related figures, we may observe next that for primitive consciousness the bound-

---

[24] Cf. with the whole course of the foregoing argument, Max Rieser, *Analyse des Poetischen Denkens* (Vienna: Verlag A. Sexl, 1954), p. 55.

[25] Biese, *Philosophie des Metaphorischen,* p. 25.

aries between external and internal are fluid. Perceptions and subjective states of mind often flow together in such a way as to be
indistinguishable. This fact is partly implicit in what has already
been said about animism—the internal vitality of the subject is
projected upon the outer phenomenon—but the notion may be
briefly developed, since in this respect also the aesthetic psyche
resembles the primitive.

A pertinent series of observations is made by Werner. On the
higher levels of discursive mental organization, an imagined object
is sharply distinguished from a perceived object. An imagined
object exists in the mind; a perceived object is "out there" and
has a reality independent of perception.[26] Among children and
savages, however, the part of an image which originates in the
psyche can be separated only with difficulty, or not at all, from
the part which originates in sensory impulses coming from the
perceived object.

Eidetic images as intermediary

One source of confusion is the ignorance of both child and
savage about the physics of perception; but another is the tendency
of both to have eidetic images which stand midway between percept and fantasy. The eidetic image is an after-image which owes
something of its character to perception but is susceptible, in
greater or less degree, to will and other psychological processes.
That it is not purely arbitrary is apparent from the surprise evoked
by some of its manifestations.

> An experiment in the mixing of colors will illustrate this: To a
> child who has this eidetic faculty there is presented a blue square
> on a white screen. Once the child's eidetic image has been estab-
> lished, a yellow screen is substituted for the white one. It may then
> happen that the eidetic image of the blue square on the screen will
> become gray, in accordance with the laws of spectral color mix-
> ture, because of a fusion with the yellow background. This remark-
> able change is not pure fancy suggested by any reflective process on

---

[26] Cf. Heinz Werner, *Comparative Psychology of Mental Development* (rev.
ed.; Chicago: Follett Publishing Co., 1948), p. 143.

the part of the child. Indeed, he himself is often astonished and bewildered by what has occurred.[27]

Yet the eidetic image is not completely subject to the laws governing sensory phenomena. It can be played with, reorganized; it has "susceptibility to imaginative influence, to creative fantasy." [28] Here is something which is neither mere percept nor mere imagination —a psychic activity which, in an aesthetically gifted man, might lead to the creation of an art work in which the perceptual world is restructured to satisfy psychological demands.

According to E. R. Jaensch, from 10 to 60 per cent of all children have the capacity to experience eidetic imagery, which may be considered "a normal developmental characteristic of the child, one that decreases with age." [29] No figures have been reported for savages; but in Werner's opinion it is highly probable that

a primordial functional unity exists in the sensory and imaginative fields, and that out of this undifferentiated function arise [*sic*] the true memory and fantasy image (the knowing of an inner world) in contradistinction to objective perception (the knowing of an outer world).[30]

It is noteworthy, for example, that more Mexican children were found to be capable of eidetic imagery than white children, and that 84 per cent of the Negro children studied had such images.[31] These findings point to a negative correlation between cultural sophistication and eidetic capability. Many other indications support the same hypothesis. Primitive men are far more subject to "visions" than white men—visions which may arise without external stimulus but are often suggested by the shapes of trees, rocks, clouds, etc.[32]

Again, it is possible that "the so-called naturalistic art of primitive hunters (Eskimos, Bushmen, etc.) is based on eidetic images which are actually seen as projected on the surface of the material on which the picture is to be drawn or painted." A Bushman, who

---

[27] *Ibid.,* p. 144.
[28] *Ibid.*
[29] Reported *ibid.,* p. 145.
[30] *Ibid.*
[31] See *ibid.,* note.
[32] Cf. Werner's comment on this phenomenon, *ibid.,* p. 146.

said he was working in the same way as all the other artists of his tribe, began a drawing by putting down a number of isolated dots, which to a white observer "appeared like a picture of the stars"; but when the dots had been joined by bold, free strokes, the form of an animal emerged.[33] When—as is usual—primitive paintings are distorted, the reason may be that the proportions have been made to accord with affective impact. In a Brazilian Indian picture of a fight between a jaguar and a tapir, the jaguar, as the more powerful animal, is enormously exaggerated. Something apparently analogous occurs in children's paintings: human figures are at first smaller than human faces, since it is primarily to faces that the child looks for affective meaning.[34] Finally, on the assumption that evolutionary development is generally in the direction of greater differentiation, it is probable that discrimination between perception and imagination is not an aboriginal *given* but emerges gradually, as a product of acculturation.[35]

If in this respect, as in the others already commented on, the psychic patterns of artists resemble those of primitive men and children, the language of literature must not be expected to be steadily responsible to perceptual fact. It will tend rather toward the restructuring of objective reality in terms of affective values. This is not, of course, to say that the artist is incapable of accurate observation, or even that his senses may not be notably keener than those of other men. In purely practical situations, savages too sometimes astonish white men by the accuracy of remembered images.[36] Yet the same savages, when aroused, as during a hunt or a religious ceremony, allow their perceptions to become mingled with the communally sanctioned images stored in their memories by cultural preconditioning. In the same way, the white artist, however sharp his senses, does not often attempt to reproduce an object exactly as it may have appeared to him at some moment of disinterested attention. The remembered image is adjusted to its

---

[33] Reported *ibid.,* pp. 147–48.

[34] Cf. *ibid.,* pp. 148–50.

[35] Every parent has observed the tendency of children, at certain ages, to "lie," i.e., to confuse truth and fantasy.

[36] See a comment of Sir Francis Galton's reported by Werner, *Comparative Psychology,* p. 147.

aesthetic context; and this process requires the heightening of certain sensory characteristics and the slurring or suppressing of others. In other words, the memory image becomes an eidetic image, which is manipulated until it serves a desired function.

If this were not so, creative literature would obviously not be creative, and judgment of it would depend in some degree on the verification of descriptions by reobservation of whatever described objects were publicly accessible. We do not ask, however, whether John of Gaunt's encomiastic description of England in *Richard II* corresponded exactly to the England accessible to everybody's senses in the fourteenth century, or even whether the Malabar Caves described in E. M. Forster's *A Passage to India* are in all respects identical with the real Indian caves as they would have appeared to a disinterested spectator about 1924. In both instances, the description is of something as it appeared to somebody of a particular character and in a particular psychic state, not of something as it appears to everybody who may wish to study it carefully. And so typically in literature. Although there exist rare works which profess literal truthfulness to specified data (and, by doing so, perhaps run the danger of becoming documents instead of art), states of mind usually color the perception of external objects. What counts is not so much the sensory stimuli that flow from an observed object as their impingement upon a human psyche. Even when the objects in a literary description are in their "real" physical positions and have their "real" colors and contours, they are usually endowed with mood and human meaning.

Process images as a substitute
for conceptualization

As feeling becomes mingled in much savage perception with the sensory stimulus, so what occurs within the psyche as process tends to be read back into external correlatives. Here, perhaps, is an explanation of much mythology: dynamic mental states are attached to series of imagined incidents. Process images are, in fact, an aboriginal substitute for conceptualization. The primitive mentality, when confronted by a puzzling phenomenon, seeks relief not in the discovery of a physical or biological principle but in the fabrication of an adequate explanatory plot.

Since plots must be reserved for discussion in a later chapter, at present we can observe the outward projection of dynamic mental states only on a small scale, as transitional to a consideration of metaphor. According to Werner, who in another book entitled *Die Ursprünge der Metapher* studied exhaustively the use of metaphor by primitive races, process images, which often take the form of "thing metaphors," are transitional to verbal metaphors and may precede them in time. The pouring or spitting of water to induce rainfall is a simple example. Here the savage performs a process in order to act out a wish and thereby induce its fulfillment.[37] More elaborate illustrations can be given. The Sulka of New Pomerania smokes with an enchanted plant the girl whose love he wishes to compel; he then puts part of the plant into a hill of biting ants and burns the rest in a fire, the biting ants and the heat of the fire being "true material metaphors of the action of love on the feelings." [38] In both practices the structure of a desired process is imitated by actions, as, in verbal metaphor, the sensory or conceptual image of one thing is linguistically substituted for that of another to which, when considered from a particular standpoint, it is sensed to be structurally similar.

Metaphor

Linguistic metaphor itself is an enormously complicated phenomenon which can be considered from many quite different and equally valid points of view—genetic, semantic, structural, material, and other.[39] In the present context, however, it is necessary

---

[37] Heinz Werner, *Die Ursprünge der Metapher* (Leipzig: Wilhelm Englemann, 1919), p. 57.

[38] R[ichard] H. R. Parkinson, *Dreissig Jahre in der Südsee* (Stuttgart: Strecker & Schröder, 1907), p. 190. The quoted phrase is from Werner, who cites the practice in *Ursprünge der Metapher*, p. 58.

[39] For succinct accounts of speculation about metaphor see, e.g., Hermann Pongs, *Das Bild in der Dichtung*, (2 vols.; Marburg: N. G. Elwert'sche Verlagsbuchhandlung, 1927 and 1939), esp. I, 1–24; and Hedwig Konrad, *Étude sur la métaphore* (Paris: Librairie Philosophique J. Vrin, 1939), pp. 27–44. Miss Konrad's work is provided with a full bibliography, and Pongs's is rich in scholarly references.

only so far to consider the subject as to discover whether parallels can be found in primitive speech for the metaphorical expressions which are so striking a characteristic of sophisticated literature. If so, it will appear that still another trait of literary language is present in savage speech; and we may again infer, since metaphors are much less frequent in discursive prose, that during aesthetic creation the psyche falls back into archaic perceptual habits.

A good deal has already been implied about metaphor in the discussion of literary animism, since the sun's hiding of its face or the crying of the wind to the sea imputes "transferred" sensibility to something actually insensible and therefore falls within the limits of the trope called metaphor. Further, we must note again that even abstract terms prove upon examination to have developed from forgotten metaphors.

> Above all the fact must be observed that originally no word had any other meaning than a sensory one, that all roots are auditory signs for sensory impressions and all words, even the most abstract, are derived from such roots.[40]

This insight can be traced as far back as John Locke. Victor Cousin's objection that at least two French words, *je* and *être* ("I" and "be"), were exceptions to the rule was contraverted by Max Müller, who traced the former to a Sanskrit root meaning "to breathe, speak" or to the demonstrative pronoun, and the latter also to the Sanskrit root meaning "to speak" or "life-breath." [41] Whether the rule is unexceptionable or not, it is apparent that transference has been a continually active force in language and that many, at least, of the counters used even in nonliterary speech are faded metaphors. Enough has been said about unconscious metaphor, however, and our attention will now be confined to the conscious transference of meanings.

ITS FUNCTION IN PRIMITIVE SPEECH.   First, it is essential to note that such transference often results, in primitive speech, from a linguistic necessity of the simplest kind: an object seen for the

---

[40] Josef Müller, *Das Bild in der Dichtung: Philosophie und Geschichte der Metapher,* Vol. I (Munich: Kaster & Lossen, 1903), p. 1. Curiously, Pongs seems not to have known this study.

[41] Reported *ibid.,* p. 2.

first time is associated with other objects to which it has some resemblance. Von den Steinen reports typical instances among the Bakairí.

> In the highest degree noteworthy was the quickness with which they classified objects unknown to them among objects with which they were acquainted, and also immediately assigned to them, directly and without modification, a name current among themselves. They cut hair with sharp mussels or the teeth of the piranya fish, and my shears, an object of frank delight to them, which cut off hair so smoothly and regularly, was called simply "piranya-tooth." The mirror was "water"; "Show us the water!" they cried, when they wanted to see the mirror. And I made much less of an impression with it than I had expected.[42]

It is doubtful whether such usages should be classed among true metaphors. The mirror *is* water, in so far as it shares the capacity of water to reflect; the shears *are* piranya teeth, in so far as they are used, more efficiently, for the same purpose. The linguistic association of different things has a practical end and aims at no cognitive enrichment.

In a similar way, it is probable that many other linguistic usages which to us would seem metaphorical lack metaphorical quality for savages. For example, the assertion that such-and-such a man is a lion (in courage) or a hare (in timidity) may imply a fuller identity of essence than among contemporary Westerners.

> *We must think away absolutely the boundaries between man and animal.* A favorite animal may be wiser or more stupid, stronger or weaker, than the Indian; it can have quite different habits of life, only it is in his eyes a *person* exactly like the Indian himself . . . One need only be a medicine man, who can do anything, to change himself from one person to another.[43]

Similar reports have come from all over the world and from a wide variety of low cultures. In the primitive mind, the boundaries between concepts are less firmly drawn than in the scientifically

---

[42] Karl von den Steinen, *Unter den Naturvölkern Zentral-Brasiliens* (2d ed.; Berlin: Dietrich Reimer, 1897), p. 78.

[43] *Ibid.,* p. 306.

or philosophically oriented mind; edges are more fluid, and horizontal or vertical changes in category are easier. Attention seems to be attracted readily to similarities, whereas differences are less likely to arouse and detain notice.

Precisely this point, which has far-reaching significance, has been made by Josef Müller in *Das Bild in der Dichtung*.

> We must propose still another general psychological law for the investigation of metaphor: the *preponderance of considerations of resemblance over the investigation of differences* in ordinary thought, especially for the primitive. . . . Metaphors are not sought, but offer themselves unforced—only to a rich and imaginative intelligence, to be sure; distinctions belong to the penetrating mind and to unflagging industry and are therefore main preoccupations of the learned, whereas the former symbolizing thought is the chief work of the artist.[44]

Thus we return to the observation of Werner that "the isolated phenomena seized by the primitive are unitary complexes not further analyzable by him." [45] When a new complex presents itself, it tends to be identified *as a whole,* and not, as by the scientifically oriented man, in one or more carefully defined aspects, with a previously assimilated complex. When a child (says Müller) who has already seen a bird in flight perceives a butterfly, he may at once cry out "That is a bird too!" [46] The expression is not consciously metaphorical, since it focuses on a resemblance and implies no necessary awareness of difference. And so with the primitive assimilation of new percepts generally: "The new impression is measured by and compared with the earlier as soon as the two are associated; similar ideas acquired earlier press forward at once, as if drawn by a magnet, are recalled and exercise the most powerful influence in the choice of a name." This activity, moreover, is "quite involuntary and can proceed without being noticed." [47] Such associations have great cognitive importance; but the linguistic process differs radically from that in which an object

---

[44] Müller, *Das Bild in der Dichtung,* p. 5.
[45] Werner, *Ursprünge der Metapher,* p. 6.
[46] Müller, *Das Bild in der Dichtung,* p. 3.
[47] *Ibid.*

is deliberately called by a name belonging to something else rather than by its own name.

ITS ORIGIN IN TABOO. Intentional metaphorical *substitutions* (or, if one prefers, "true" metaphors) play a large role in the speech of some primitive societies but not in that of all. According to Werner, whose *Die Ursprünge der Metapher* studies exhaustively the primitive origins of metaphor in this limited sense, among nomadic tribes the deliberate transference of terms is virtually unknown.[48] The reason is unexpected: true metaphor is a product of taboo, and nomadic tribes, which can move away easily from objects that excite apprehension, rarely develop systems of taboos. More sedentary peoples, who cannot so easily avoid fearful objects —for example, the corpses of their dead—develop institutions intended to offer protection from the encompassing dangers. But taboos tend to proliferate, so that after a time an almost unbelievable number of objects can no longer be frankly named.[49] In this situation the only possible recourse is to invent a new terminology. The new names are, of course, not constructed *ex nihilo,* but are based on the existent word hoard. Thus the tabooed objects may easily come to be designated by names properly attaching to other objects, and "true" metaphor, or the identification of one thing by a term known already to belong to a different one, springs into being.

MULTIPLE AND AMBIGUOUS SIGNIFICATIONS. This discovery has great interest, since none of the classical discussions of metaphor offered any hint that the trope had a compulsive origin. So far as the present study is concerned, however, the significance of Werner's book lies chiefly in the light it throws upon the origin of multiple meanings (ambivalence, "ambiguity"). There is no ambivalence in the child's identification of the butterfly as a bird or the Bakairí's identification of the mirror as water, any more than there is ambivalence, or any other approach to consciously poetic quality, in a reference by a modern American to the leg of a chair or the falling of night. In the metaphors arising from

---

[48] Werner, *Ursprünge der Metapher,* p. 139.

[49] In some societies, the proliferation is so extreme that it threatens to prevent all speech. Cf. *ibid.,* p. 77.

taboo, on the contrary, it is deliberately intended that a verbal formula shall be understood to express something other than what is literally signified. An approach is made to conscious artistry, since here speech is deliberately manipulated, and especially happy turns of phrase can evoke admiration or amusement.

Only comparatively simple illustrations can be offered, for explication of complex examples would be wasteful of space. As the first of two instances, I cite a Solomon Island song in which an unfaithful wife repulses her suing husband.

> Kuita   guanai   iru   ciridai   panage
> *Pocket small my-husband the-colored-one into-pillar-house*
> iraguai.
> *inquisitive.*

Here "pocket" is equivalent to "vagina"; but *kuitau,* which sounds like it, means "ladder to the sleeping-house." The sense of the first phrase is accordingly double: "My pocket is too small for you" and "The ladder to the sleeping-house is too short." Since the two meanings coincide, the singer has the satisfaction of making her point twice in a single utterance.[50]

The second example is somewhat more complex, but less so than other examples which I avoid. The source is again the Solomon Islands, where taboos are highly developed.

> Rekuáge   makacíru   kumi-mo
> *In-hill-of-flying-ants   in-stoneheaps   mud-earth*
>
> berebéremom
> *in-which-I-entangle-myself*
>
> tokinominoi   cimukaro   tabe.
> *when-I-once-passed-there   in-Cimukaro   revenge-dance.*

Freely interpreted, the meaning runs something like this: "In the ant-hill of the stone-heap, the vagina is marshy earth in which I entangle myself on my journey to Cimukaro for the dance of vengeance." The first part of the comparison, having to do with entanglement in marshy earth, symbolizes sexual intercourse. More

---

[50] For the song and its interpretation, see *ibid.,* p. 187.

important, however, is a metaphor concealed in the notion of "revenge-dance." At funeral ceremonies it is customary in this area for the male mourners to dance about in a circle and throw their spears into the center; the warrior whose spear falls over and breaks must undertake the duty of avenging the dead man. The throwing of the spears is also a sexual symbol; accordingly, "As the throwing of spears, in certain circumstances, can involve mortal danger because it may entail the obligation to undertake an expedition of revenge, so also is sexual commerce with the derided woman dangerous." [51] Here, obviously, is complexity of the kind prized by critics who derive their poetic standards from John Donne and T. S. Eliot. There is metaphor not only of words but also of ideas. To the astonishment, perhaps, of persons who regard the primitive mind as always simple, it becomes clear that even comparatively recent literary techniques have primitive analogues.

Lability of primitive speech

It is unnecessary to carry the discussion further, since additional illustrations would only reinforce the conclusions already stated. Instead, we may turn our attention briefly to the *lability* of primitive speech implicit in the foregoing examples. In Chapter 3 it was pointed out that in certain ways, having to do chiefly with the delineation of sensory images, primitive languages are more precise than civilized speech. They do not, however, give equal emphasis to the distinguishing of rational concepts, which tend to lack materiality and therefore to escape accurate formulation in tongues oriented toward sensory description. Languages in which sexual enjoyment is designated as "biting" or "eating" are not likely to separate adjacent cognitive areas scrupulously.[52] Not only are ideas associated on the basis of similar affective tonality; they may be positively identified because of an accidental contiguity. Among the Huichol Indians of Mexico, deer, wheat, feathers, and a plant called *hikuli* are so little distinguished that venison broth is thought to be exactly equivalent to *hikuli,* and a ritual arrow may be

---

[51] For the song and its interpretation, see *ibid.,* pp. 183–84.
[52] Cf. Werner, *Comparative Psychology,* p. 85.

fitted out with hairs from a deer's tail instead of with feathers. "Mr. Lumholtz is very insistent on this point; according to the Huichols, a deer *is* hikuli, hikuli *is* wheat, wheat *is* deer, deer *is* feathers." [53] But such cognitive habits result inevitably in semantic diffuseness, and this in turn in the possibility of multiple interpretations. The "ambiguity" of poems, plays, and novels, which occasions both fruitful and fruitless controversy, is thus continuous with a fundamental lability in much primitive speech.[54] In proportion as such speech becomes less practical, it pays for specificity of denotation by indeterminacy of import.

The ambiguity of nonconceptual statement is especially evident in mythology—for example, in that of the Greeks. Whether, as Jung believes, myths are projections of the collective unconscious, or, as others have argued, they are nondiscursive symbols of historical events, they permit a wide latitude of interpretation. On the latter view, what is the significance of the chimera? It was long ago suggested by Pierre François Lafitau that this fabulous creature, part lion, part goat, and part serpent, represented a league of three totem clans, as the Iroquois League, in America, was represented by a wolf, a bear, and a turtle.[55] The suggestion is plausible; but one cannot on that account reject Robert Graves's proposal that the chimera was a calendar symbol in which each part represented a season of the sacred year.[56] Nonconceptual statement is more labile than conceptual, and, after the lapse of time, if not immediately, will carry a range of possible significance. The same thing is true on the Jungian hypothesis. For Jung, Daphne was a symbol of a young girl's frightened recoil from the sexual act; but if the reader is aware that—in Graves's words—she "was anything but a frightened virgin," since her name means "the bloody one" and her priestesses indulged in orgiastic excesses,[57]

---

[53] L[ucien] Lévy-Bruhl, *Les Fonctions mentales dans les sociétés inférieures* (Paris: Librairie Félix Alcan, 1922), pp. 131–37, esp. p. 135.

[54] Werner, *Comparative Psychology*, pp. 152–53, compares savage images with the images seen by modern Westerners in dreams.

[55] Cf. Lang, *Myth, Ritual and Religion*, I, 74–75.

[56] Robert Graves, *The Greek Myths* (Baltimore: Penguin Books, Inc., 1955), I, 9.

[57] *Ibid.*, p. 18.

she must be assigned a different symbolical value.

Beyond this, it is noteworthy that meanings are often deliberately hidden by savages. Werner was so impressed by the role of intentional ambiguity in primitive speech that he declared roundly, "Nearly everywhere that metaphor is used, it tends characteristically not to make objects clearer, to explain and clarify them conceptually, but, on the contrary, to darken and conceal them."[58] For example, the magician must often mutter his incantations in so vague or deceptive a form that they will not be understood if overheard, lest countermagic be used by the expected victim. Threats give special satisfaction if spoken in the enemy's presence in such terms that he will not recognize their tenor. Ridicule is often expressed metaphorically: if the object of scorn penetrates to the speaker's meaning, the mental effort required may prevent him from making an immediate motor response. Bad news might bring retaliation upon the bearer if not sufficiently veiled to occasion a delay between hearing and reaction.[59] For these and other reasons, the purposive lability of much literary statement is not foreign to primitive speech. Further, although the motives for evasion may differ among savages, their techniques bear a striking resemblance to those used by creative writers: ellipsis, nondeclarative statement (the use of optatives, other subjunctives, interrogatives, and the like), and, not least important, metaphor and the direct sensory presentation of objects which have multiple or ambiguous significations.

Magical potencies in words

Since there is no wish in these chapters to draw all the possible parallels between literary and primitive languages, two additional series of comments will suffice. The first will have to do with verbal potencies verging on magic, the second with incantatory rhythms.

"For the poet," say René Wellek and Austin Warren in a well-known book entitled *Theory of Literature,* "the word is not primarily a 'sign,' a transparent counter, but a 'symbol,' valuable for

---

[58] Werner, *Ursprünge der Metapher,* p. 7.
[59] Cf. *ibid.,* pp. 97–98.

itself as well as in its capacity of representative." [60] That this is so hardly needs to be argued. Even unskillful writers feel that word choice is tremendously important—that the "right" word often eludes them and must be struggled for until it is caught. Neither is the matter always one of precise denotation merely; for the poet, especially, words have auras which are not quite the same things as connotations but which may make or mar the aesthetic whole. In extreme cases, the word may be sensed as having an almost mystical identity with its referent. This word only, and no other, will do; the suggestion of a change produces explosive fury, and all paraphrases are rejected as inadequate. The word does not indicate, but is, the thing itself.

This only half-rational attitude of the creative writer strongly resembles an aboriginal persuasion that the name in literal truth *is* the object it designates or, at least, is so intimately unified with the object that possession of the object's name is equivalent to possession of its power. There are ample suggestions of such feeling even in the Hebrew Bible. Adam's naming of the animals apparently made him their master, and the reluctance of the Jews to pronounce the Tetragrammaton, "the ineffable name" of the One God, originated in an impulse toward concealment.[61] But, indeed, it was once apparently common to conceal the names of tribal or family gods, lest power should be acquired over them by enemies; and in many savage communities the "real" names even of private individuals are not divulged until after death. These are familiar examples and need no elaboration. The failure of most primitive men to distinguish between a verbal icon and its referent manifests itself also, however, in less obvious ways, of which two or three may be noticed.

A passage of Von den Steinen's report on the Bakairí shows the cognitive confusion about names in a form so uncomplicated by theory that at first little significance may be seen in it.

---

[60] René Wellek and Austin Warren, *Theory of Literature* (New York: Harcourt, Brace and Company, Inc., 1949), p. 83.

[61] The diabolical power of the reversed Tetragrammaton or of the Lord's Prayer recited backward might also be cited. Here the holy "working" of words becomes malignant when the pronunciation runs in the opposite direction, though the sounds then make no "sense."

Their drive to comprehend the nature of new objects exhausted itself in the questions whether I had made them and what their names were. "Eséti? Eséti? What is it called?" cried the whole company *unisono,* and all plagued themselves orally in an effort to repeat the Portuguese words. . . . When one or another was successful in imitating the appropriate word, the joy was great, and I had the impression that the object itself seemed more familiar to them.[62]

The adjustment is easily appreciated. Even modern Westerners, when they learn the name of an unfamiliar object, feel that they have made progress toward learning its nature and function. In fact, however, the ability to call a certain part of a radio set a "condenser" may imply little real knowledge, and a woman who tells her husband that the car broke down because of carburetor trouble often parrots a mechanic's speech without having acquired any understanding of what has happened. At most, acquisition of a new word makes possible consultation of a dictionary (which may not be intended) or the awakening of understanding in someone who possesses fuller information. Yet the feeling persists that knowledge of an object's name makes the object more familiar.

The naïve recognition of potency in names appears still more clearly in children, who do not ordinarily realize that words are arbitrary symbols. When children five or six years old were asked how people could know that the sun had to be called "sun," they replied, "Because it is hot," "Because it shines," and so on. Upon being asked whether the sun could be called "moon," they said, "No, because it can't be made any smaller." [63] "For the child," says Piaget similarly, "the name is still closely bound up with the thing. . . . As Sully and Compayré have said, children believe that every object has received a primordial and absolute name, which is somehow part of its being." [64] Here we come nearer to the primitive belief reported, among many others, by A. B. Ellis: "The Ewe-speaking natives believe that there is a real and material

---

[62] Von den Steinen, *Unter den Naturvölkern,* pp. 79–80.

[63] Heinz Werner, *Einführung in die Entwicklungspsychologie,* (3d ed.; Munich: Johann Ambrosius Barth, 1953), p. 199.

[64] Jean Piaget, *The Language and Thought of the Child,* trans. Marjorie Gabain (New York: Meridian Books, Inc., 1955), pp. 199 and 220.

connection between a man and his name, and that by means of the name injury may be done to the man." [65] Remnants of the belief remain in much literature—for example, in *Rumpelstilzchen,* in which discovery of the manikin's name infuriates him because he will now be subject to control, and in the Biblical phrase, "In the beginning was the Word," from which was to proceed a power sufficient to create the entire physical universe.[66] "The word and the name," says Cassirer, "possess no mere function of presenting; rather, the object itself and its material powers are held within both. Also, the word and the name do not signify and mean, but *are* and *work*." [67] People who think that puberty initiations so change the character of the initiates that new names must be given them [68] respond to an impulse deeply ingrained in the human psyche.

The creative writer, who recognizes power in words simply as words, is less isolated from this aboriginal tendency than the writer of scientific or philosophical prose. The following dialogue occurs in Shakespeare's *Twelfth Night:*

VIOLA. . . . They that dally nicely with words may quickly make them wanton.
CLOWN. I would therefore my sister had had no name, sir.
VIOLA. Why, man?
CLOWN. Why, sir, her name's a word, and to dally with that word might make my sister wanton.

(Act III, sc. i.)

Though the Clown speaks in jest, the poet's invention of the jest

---

[65] A. B. Ellis, *The Ewe-Speaking Peoples of the Slave Coast of West Africa* (London: Chapman & Hall, Ltd., 1890), p. 98.

[66] Cf. Ernst Cassirer, *Language and Myth,* trans. Susanne K. Langer (New York: Harper & Brothers, Publishers, 1946), p. 45: "In all mythical cosmogonies, as far back as they can be traced, this supreme position of the Word is found." Cassirer cites an Uitoto Indian text which parallels the opening verse of St. John ("In the beginning was the Word").

[67] Cassirer, *Philosophie der Symbolischen Formen,* II, 54 (my italics).

[68] Cf. *ibid.,* p. 55. In many primitive cultures, names are changed as the result of the acquisition of new honors, privileges, etc.; among the Kayans of Borneo a new name is adopted "after any severe illness or serious accident."—Charles Hose and William McDougall, *The Pagan Tribes of Borneo* (London: Macmillan & Co., Ltd., 1912), I, 79.

marks a movement in the direction of an aboriginal assumption about language.

IN RHYTHMS. The relationship between literary rhythms, especially poetic rhythms, and the rhythm of primitive song and incantation is more complicated, although perhaps the assertion of a connection will be less controversial. That in valuing songlike quality poetry has maintained a continuity with the racial past can hardly be questioned. I wish, therefore, in the remarks which follow, to consider especially the affective origin and function of poetic rhythms.

According to Vico, whose speculations are always interesting, the earliest speech was not spoken but sung.

> Since men are shown to have been originally mute, they must have uttered vowel sounds by singing, as mutes do; and later, like stammerers, they must have uttered articulate consonantal sounds still by singing. . . . The first dull-witted men were moved to utterance only by very violent passions, which are naturally expressed in a very loud voice.[69]

Prior to Gorgias and Cicero, Vico continues,

> the Greek and Latin prose writers used certain almost poetic rhythms, as in the returned barbarian times the Fathers of the Roman Church did (and, it will be found, those of the Greek Church did too), so that their prose seems made for chanting.[70]

The theory, although attractive, is pure hypothesis and cannot be built upon. In its ceremonial uses, however, primitive language is very often rhythmic, and in general a tendency toward singsong appears whenever language is intended not merely to express but also to *work:* in incantations, in formalized taunts, in the speech of heralds.

It is probable that the rhythms themselves, quite apart from their verbal content, are felt to have magical potency. The world over, charms of all kinds tend to be rather chanted than spoken.[71]

---

[69] Vico, *New Science*, p. 139 (par. 461).

[70] *Ibid.*, pp. 139–40 (par. 462).

[71] Ralph Linton notes what seems to be an exception among the Tanala of Madagascar, where charms are not recited in set formulas. See Kardiner, *The Individual and His Society*, p. 274.

According to Lang:

> We find among savages the belief in the power of songs of *incan-
> tation.* This is a feature of magic which specially deserves our at-
> tention. In myths, and still more in *märchen* or household tales, we
> shall constantly find that the most miraculous effects are caused
> when the hero pronounces a few lines of rhyme. In Rome, as we
> have all read in the Latin Delectus, it was thought that incantation
> could draw down the moon. In the *Odyssey* the kinsfolk of Odys-
> seus sing "a song of healing" over the wound which was dealt him
> by the boar's tusk. Jeanne d'Arc, wounded at Orleans, refused a
> similar remedy. Sophocles speaks of the folly of muttering incan-
> tations over wounds that need the surgeon's knife. The song that
> salved wounds occurs in the *Kalewala,* the epic poem of the Finns.
> In many of Grimm's *märchen,* miracles are wrought by the repeti-
> tion of snatches of rhyme.[72]

It will be noted that, in Lang's opinion, rhyme has a power of
"working" similar to that of rhythm. Although it is difficult to be
certain that rhyme and rhythm have intrinsic power, the regularity
with which magical words are given rhythmical form may be taken
to imply that verbal form contributes to the charms' effectiveness.

A psychoanalytic view of rhythm and rhyme

The affective basis of rhythm has recently been studied psychoanalytically by Max Rieser in *Analyse des Poetischen Denkens,*
a work which arrives by different avenues of approach at many
of the conclusions already stated here: that poetic thought is
"Regressionserscheinung," that metaphor is based on an "archa-
isches Bild," that symbolism is an "archaische Erscheinung," and,
more generally still, that poetic speech is suffused with "Animismus,
Infantilität und Naivität." [73] The present study, which took shape
before Rieser's book came to my attention, is less uncomplimentary
to literature—indeed, it will be argued in due time that the contact
of literature with an immemorial racial past is a chief source of

---

[72] Lang, *Myth, Ritual and Religion,* I, 102.
[73] The phrases are taken from the *Inhaltsverzeichnis* of Rieser, *Analyse des
Poetischen Denkens.*

its power and value—but a good deal of Rieser's discussion of poetic rhythms compels assent.[74]

The gist of Rieser's argument is that both rhythm and rhyme, by imposing controls on linguistic expression, help the consciousness to achieve a state of relaxed wakefulness in which attention-provoking materials can be contemplated without turbulent feeling. The effect of a stream of new impressions upon the psyche is disturbing, unsettling; the soul desires peace and therefore wishes to escape from the torment which is produced by the effort to assimilate fresh data. Rhythmic alternation of stressed and unstressed syllables, or of long and short, rocks and lulls attention like the beating of a silver hammer on metal: "The regular return of the silvery beat has, besides a wakening effect, the sleep-inducing effect of monotony; rhythm arises like a stream from the poet's excitement." [75] Before composing, the poet finds himself "in the psychic condition of the primitive who breaks out into words to discharge his feeling, the torment of his soul"; [76] but after poetic ordering has reduced affective pressure, the consciousness regains tranquillity and the disturbance ceases. The mind has put itself to sleep by the swing of its rhythmic expression—a desired end, since "the sleep-wish, the wish for the cessation of psychic wakefulness, of psychological tension, is man's basic wish." [77] In the meantime, however, the excitement-producing impressions have been assimilated in such a way as no longer to unsettle the emotions. They have been held before the mind while being ordered and controlled, hence have been transformed from a threat to a possession. And what happens for the poet, when his self-expression has achieved aesthetic status, happens also for his reader or hearer. The wakeful attention which has been given the poem occurs during a trancelike state which inhibits disruptive emotions. Excitement, while remaining excitement, is "distanced," so that stimulus and release achieve an equilibrium. Rhyme, too—though our interest is primarily in rhythm—is an element in the mechanics

---

[74] See *ibid.*, pp. 8–20.
[75] *Ibid.*, p. 17.
[76] *Ibid.*, p. 16.
[77] *Ibid.*, p. 17.

of control and also helps toward the maintenance of psychic balance.

The foregoing description is not, clearly, one which will recommend itself immediately to the more extreme proponents of aesthetic cognition, who will not like to be told that poetic rhythms subserve the death wish. Yet if anyone analyzes introspectively the effect of poetic rhythms he will conclude, I think, in the end, that Rieser's analysis is very plausible. The clearest illustrations are from descriptions of violent or disgusting actions. In Shakespeare's *Titus Andronicus,* for instance, Titus discloses in the following speech the revenge he has taken on two sons of the Empress, who have cruelly ravished his daughter; he has killed them and served their flesh to their mother at a banquet:

> Why, there they are both, baked in that pie,
> Whereof their mother daintily hath fed,
> Eating the flesh that she herself hath bred.
>
> (Act V, sc. iii)

Even with rhythm and rhyme, the speech is revolting enough; without them, we would have no protection at all against our sense impressions, as in reading Mickey Spillane. It is noteworthy that the middle line, in which the matter is most repugnant, has the most singsong rhythm of the three: in the first, excitement tends to break the rhythmic norm, which is then strongly reasserted in the second and modified only by the inversion of one foot in the third. It is as though the dramatist felt subconsciously the need of rocking his spectators soothingly while delivering an especially savage thrust to their viscera. But *all* disruption of psychic stasis, on Rieser's hypothesis, is in some degree unsettling. In poetry and other strongly rhythmic speech, we are at once vitalized by the bombardment of ideas or images and lulled by a persistent beat. The tendency to sleep qualifies, softens, the tendency to strained attention, so that we are assaulted from a tolerable distance or through a protective screen.[78]

---

[78] In the interest of economy I have omitted mention of rhythms other than those of measured language—e.g., of incidents and themes. For these, see, e.g., A[rnold] van Gennep, *La Formation des légendes* (Paris: Ernest Flammarion, 1912), p. 203 f.; and Theodor H. Gaster, *The Oldest Stories in the World* (New York: The Viking Press, Inc., 1952), pp. 12–13.

It will be noticed that Rieser assumes the origin of poetic utterance in excitement, *Erregtheit*. I should myself prefer a milder term, *feelings;* but here is another indication that the cognitive function of literature is often associated with affective dispositions. Whatever may be thought of this general thesis, it is patent that rhythm works upon the mind indirectly, through something other than discursive intelligence. An argument is not made more reasonable by being given rhythmic expression. The poet's commitment to rhythm, like the orator's commitment to rhetoric, implies an interest in something besides pure reason.

Summary

Although the remarks made in the preceding chapters far from exhaust their subject, it must by now be clear that the language of literature, in precisely those ways in which it differs from non-literary language, tends strikingly to resemble the languages spoken by many savages. It is concrete, specific, sensory, and it prefers the delineation of particular instances to the statement of abstract truths. It often registers percepts in clusters and does not, like the more consistently rational languages of philosophy and science, separate out for attention whatever strands of adjacent objects are conceptually related. On the contrary, it regards contiguity as proof of mutual involvement—"uncritically," it would appear to the logical thinker. The readiness to regard as connected whatever objects or ideas lie side by side is reflected also in a tendency toward paratactical syntax. Again, the part is often treated as though the whole were implicit within it: the principle of *pars pro toto,* which we are told is operative in primitive thought, is paralleled in literature by synecdoche, one of the traditional figures of rhetoric. Motor impulses, which tend to be devalued in conceptual thinking, are sensitively registered in literature; fluidity of contour is not cognitively reduced. The animism of primitive thought is reflected in literature by personification and other energizing tropes. A dominant sense impression often replaces a less prominent one which, for discursive thought, has greater semantic import. In description, feelings are allowed to color perceptions, and objects are not rendered with objective truthfulness. Process images frequently act as surrogates for concepts. In metaphor, the affective connotations of one object are often associated with another; more important, the literary consciousness is more sensitive to resemblance than to difference, as is the consciousness of primitives. The language both of savages and of writers has a special lability, so that alternative or even multiple interpretations are not blocked off. Words are not mere signs or symbols of their referents but have intrinsic potencies. Finally, rhythm and rhyme perform nonrational functions, so that in poetry, especially, auditory pattern has nondesignative meaning. The similarities are remarkable—so remarkable, indeed, that the inquiring mind is driven to seek for an explanation.

The explanation (I think) is the one already repeatedly given: during literary composition the writer's mind is often stirred out of the restrictive habits imposed by modern education. As a result, psychic patterns long discredited by the reason, perhaps on inadequate grounds, but still implicit in man's biological nature and deeply embedded in his racial history, reassert themselves powerfully. In proportion as the reader himself has the creative temperament—that is to say, is not cut off from the racial past but is potentially a *whole* man, capable both of discursive thought and of affective response to his perceptions—he too is stirred and reintegrated. A study of literary language thus supports the hypothesis that the cognitive function of literature, whatever it may be, is not identical with the cognitive function of such intellectual disciplines as science and philosophy. The range of literature is wider and its function either different or more complex.

5

Fictive Plot: Its Genesis
and Some Recurrent Motifs

The language of literature, as partly described
in the preceding chapters, is not itself literature, any more than warehouses full of building materials and shops containing carpenters'
and masons' tools are a house. In the present
chapter, we shall consider briefly how the
writer's materials (language and the objects
and psychic states denoted by language) are
shaped by his tools (manipulative processes
determined by patterns of consciousness) into
literary works in which happenings and incidents play a large role; for it is only such
works which may be said to have plots.

Tell-me-why stories

One of the bases of plot is certainly the tendency, already commented on in another connection, for one type of consciousness to use *story* as a means of cognitive adjustment to the environment. The explanation of a pile of jagged rocks, among the Australian Arunta, as caused by the destruction of devil-devil men is typical of the way in which questions about *what* formerly substituted for questions about *how*. Since the primitive has little notion of physical or biological necessity but, instead, imagines every natural object to be possessed of some degree of will, the concept of *working* plays a larger part in his reflections than in ours. But working implies actions, and actions, when skillfully aligned, become story. Thus the end product of reflection is very often not the postulation of a general principle but a series of imaginative incidents possessing the same explanatory function.

The nature of aboriginal consciousness

It is possible, however, if we are willing to speculate, to go beyond tell-me-why stories in a search for the origins of plot. We may begin at the very beginning, when human consciousness was still very like animal consciousness. For the animal, the world must consist chiefly of jumbled and not always discriminable sense impressions colored now and then with affective tonality—as when the environment is sensed to contain a vague threat. From time to time, however, some object or situation leaps momentarily into sharper focus as a result of the stirring into activity of impulse. When the impulse is satisfied or fatigued, attention again becomes diffuse.

In the earliest stages of human consciousness, attention appears to remain diffuse except when drawn momentarily to a point by interest. The tendency, noted in Chapter 2, for savages to be either bored or excited is perhaps vestigial from this aboriginal rhythm. It must not be supposed, however, that the sensory images of primordial men were identical with our own. The lack of cognitive disinterestedness in the quasi-animal mind must almost necessarily have caused a disproportionate magnifying of particular stimuli and the minimizing of the remainder. That this was so is strongly indicated both by primitive languages and by primitive art— for example, the relatively advanced art of the West Coast Indians, which distorts objects in ways that surprise us.[1] In general, as Wilhelm Worringer long ago observed, the tendency in early art is to reproduce not total *Gestalten* but "certain visual peculiarities . . . the relationship of the eyes to the nose or beak, or the relationship of the head to the trunk or the wings to the body." [2] Certain aspects of the sensory field become vivid foreground, while the others remain dull and scarcely distinguished background.

Gods—the sensing and objectifying of mana

At some point in the process of development, if not from the very outset, both background and foreground tend often to be sensed as containing an almost wholly uncomprehended *power*. This power is the *mana* of the Melanesians, the *manitu* of the Algonquins, the *wakanda* of the Sioux, the *orenda* of the Iroquois, the *mulungu* of the Bantus.[3] Its working forces itself most irresistibly upon the attention at precisely those moments when, under the influence of the strong feelings which accompany instinctive drives, a portion of the environment rises into sensory vividness. For example, if a savage protects himself from the assault of a wild beast by entering a stream, the water may not only heighten itself in his consciousness but, by virtue of the protective power which appears to invest it, acquire a kind of sanctity.[4] When the spot is visited again, the almost bestial savage—whom we will

---

[1] See, e.g., Franz Boas, *Primitive Art* (New York: Dover Publications, 1955), esp. chap. vi.

[2] Wilhelm Worringer, *Abstraktion und Einfühlung: Ein Beitrag zur Stilpsychologie* (3d ed.; Munich: R. Piper & Co. Verlag, 1911), p. 67.

[3] Cf. Ernst Cassirer, *Language and Myth*, trans. Susanne K. Langer (New York: Harper & Brothers, Publishers, 1946), pp. 63–64 and 69–70. Cassirer's work is of first importance for the present phase of the study.

[4] The example is from J. Spieth, *Die Religion der Eweer in Süd-Togo* (Göttingen: Vandenhoeck & Ruprecht, 1911), p. 8.

imagine as too "low" to have as yet any language but affective cries—may feel an obscure awe tinged with gratitude. At this stage, his memories are mainly sensory or affective, and it is unlikely that the adventure will long be remembered. After the invention of denotative language, however, the *naming* of such a protective force may confer upon it greater cognitive durability. The reinvocation of the name can initiate a reliving of the experience, and a social dissemination of the name can resist the disintegration of the memory. What at first was mere feeling has attained a quasi-objective status, and a felt power is well on the way to crystallization in the form of a god.

If this guesswork has been even approximately accurate—and it is supported by much anthropological evidence, of which a good deal is summarized in Cassirer's *Language and Myth*—we should not be surprised that the earliest recorded gods are attached to specific localities or functions. This specificity continues well into civilized times; for example, among the Romans.

> The primitive god, like primitive action, is limited to a very restricted sphere. Not only does every occupation have its particular god, but each phase of the total action becomes the domain of an independent god or daemon who governs this precise sphere of action. The Roman *Fratres Arvales,* when making atonement for the removal of trees from the sacred grove of the goddess Dia, divided the deed into a number of separate acts, for each of which a special deity was invoked.[5]

It was the same in Roman agriculture. The three ploughings, the sowing, the weeding, and the harrowing had each its own god, whom it was necessary to invoke by his own name and in the right order. And so, perhaps, typically: "Every different concrete activity first becomes truly conscious . . . by viewing itself objectively in the image of the appropriate special god." [6] We need not wonder, accordingly, that monotheism is rare and late and polytheism normal. Among the Greeks also there was a god for every noteworthy place and for every important activity. How numerous these

---

[5] Cassirer, *Language and Myth,* p. 41.

[6] Ernst Cassirer, *Philosophie der Symbolischen Formen,* Vol. II (Berlin: Bruno Cassirer, 1925), p. 251.

had become by classical times, one can remind oneself by glancing through the pages of Robert Graves's *The Greek Myths* or Hermann Usener's *Götternamen*.[7]

What happened among the prehistoric Greeks and Romans happens still among primitive men. The Ewe of Africa bring offerings to their chopping knives, their axes, their planes, their saws, and other tools, and recognize spirits called *trō* in hollow trees, in springs, in nests of termites. "The moment," says J. Spieth in *Die Religion der Eweer in Süd-Togo*, "in which an object or its striking characteristics enters into any remarkable relationship with human spirit and life, whether this is agreeable or repellent, is the birth-hour of a *trō* for the consciousness of the Ewe." [8] The *trō* is perhaps rather daemon than god; it "denotes a being which brings man into bewilderment"; [9] but, if not a god, it is capable of developing into one. The world is still alive for the Ewe, and its energies manifest themselves spontaneously.

The beginnings of myth: the influence of language

If the world is thus *peopled* for the primitive consciousness, or is filled with vitalities which can become hypostatized as personalities, it is not surprising that the interrelations of phenomena are often given *narrative* formulation. The imputation of spontaneous activity even to inanimate objects leads to the pre-eminence already noted of "working" over "being"; and working implies the activity of processes. In Cassirer's words, "the world of mythical *objects* reveals itself almost everywhere as a mere objective projection of human *actions*." [10] The opportunities for such projection are, however, so deeply embedded in the languages which grow out of primitive mind states that the development of myths seems to be contemporaneous with that of language. If Max Müller was wrong

---

[7] Hermann Usener, *Götternamen: Versuch einer Lehre von der religiösen Begriffsbildung* (Bonn: Friedrich Cohen, 1896); Robert Graves, *The Greek Myths* (Baltimore: Penguin Books, Inc., 1955).
[8] Spieth, *Religion der Eweer*, pp. 7–8.
[9] *Ibid.*, p. 37.
[10] Cassirer, *Philosophie der Symbolischen Formen*, II, 228.

in believing that myths were generated by a disease of language—
that mythology is in fact "the dark shadow which language throws
upon thought, and which can never disappear till language becomes
entirely commensurate with thought" [11]—he was right in doubting
that language merely records verbally series of images that have
already been finally articulated by the imagination. Myth *is* language, together with the images evoked by words and rituals, and
language develops concurrently with the myths produced by the
interaction of images and words. With art, myth and language "begin
as a concrete, undivided unity, which is only gradually resolved
into a triad of independent modes of spiritual creativity." [12]

An example will show how even the basic linguistic category of
gender, where it exists, might provoke the invention of a mythical
plot. Let us suppose (what is perhaps improbable) that before the
invention of any myths about the sun or moon the words for the
two luminaries have fallen, because of obscurely felt sexual tonalities, into the classes, respectively, of masculine and feminine nouns.
The sun and moon dominate the sky at different times, and both
proceed across the heavens in the same direction. It might thus be
easily supposed that the moon, which takes care to avoid proximity
to the sun, flees from it; and flight might imply a wish to preserve
chastity. The sun, in consequence, becomes a lustful god with a
history of rapes and attempts at rape, and the moon a symbol of
purity. The sun, moreover, is observed to stimulate the growth of
plants and, in time, is imagined to impregnate the earth goddess.
Rituals will be invented to invite or induce the union. In contrast,
the moon, which will become the patroness of certain priestesses and
young girls who have no inclination to marry, will be regarded as
inimical to fertility, and the dark of the moon will be thought an
especially propitious time for planting. The development can proceed to almost any length; and if, while it is continuing, hitherto-
unnamed objects are absorbed into the mythical plot, they will acquire suitable genders. The influence of the myth on gender, and
of the genders on myth, would therefore be reciprocal. Each would
grow to the enrichment of the other. The images, too, which are

---

[11] Quoted in Cassirer, *Language and Myth*, p. 5.
[12] *Ibid.*, p. 98.

generated by narrative exigencies, may be hypostatized and given names of appropriate gender. As a result, the patterns of human consciousness are linguistically fixed at the same time that a mythological narrative widens the cognitive range.

MYTHS AS EXPLANATORY OF PERCEPTS. Where there is no grammatical gender, other psychic forces work toward the development of story. Frank H. Cushing relates the perceptual qualities of Indian corn to a creation myth which invests them with historical meaning.

> The Zuñi has observed that the [Indian] corn plant is jointed; that its leaves spring from these joints not regularly but spirally; . . . that the matured plant is characterized, as no other plant is, by two sets of seeds, the ears of corn springing out from it two-thirds down and the tassels of seeds, sometimes earlets, at the top; also that these tassels resemble the seed-spikes of the spring-grass or pigeon-grass; that the leaves themselves . . . are fluted like plumes, and that amongst the ears of corn ever and anon are found bunches of soot; and, finally, that the colors of the corn are as the colors of the world—seven in number.[13]

Here are the perceptual data. They are accounted for not in terms of botanical principle (what primitive group has evolved a science of biological law?) but by a genetic myth, a story of what happened "in the beginning," *in illo tempore*. A youth and maiden danced round the sprouting corn,

> and they grasped, one on either side, the first plants, dancing around them, gently drawing them upward as they went . . . until all had grown to the tallness of themselves and were jointed where they had grasped them; yea, and leaved as with waving plumes of the macaw. . . . As the dawn approached, the youth and first maiden were led apart as before by the Mother-making matron, and together embraced the first of the full grown plants, and so, in turn, the youth and each of the other maidens embraced the other plants. . . . Lo! where the mid-persons of the youth and

---

13 Frank H. Cushing, "Outlines of Zuñi Creation-Myths," in J. W. Powell, *Thirteenth Annual Report of the Bureau of Ethnology to the Secretary of the Smithsonian Institution, 1891–92,* (Washington, D.C.: Government Printing Office, 1896), p. 376.

the maidens had touched most unitedly and warmly the plants, new parts appeared to the beholders, showing, through their coverings, many colors, soft hair shrouding them [an equivalent of the pubic hair of the dancers], as if to make precious their beauty.[14]

After this, Kwélele (identity uncertain) touched the plants "with his flame-potent fire-wand," whereby "the new parts were hardened, some to fruitfulness; others, being too closely touched, burned to the very heat of generative warmth" (hence the soot).

The pressure for cognitive assimilation, felt by the primitive as well as the modern Westerner, has thus been relieved by the invention of a fiction. This is to say that the sorting out of a group of sensory qualities has led to their alignment in a sequential order. That the relations are ordered sequentially must be due, in large part, to the poverty of primitive languages in forms expressive of causal nexus. Indeed, the tendency, commented on earlier, of primitive speech toward parataxis suggests that another very deep source of mythological plots can be located here. What substitute is there for causal analysis besides story? The Bushman, it will be remembered, could not express the attitude of white men toward his tribe abstractly, but was forced instead to draw a series of progressive verbal pictures descriptive of motor activities. The genetic myth about the corn plant is only one example of thousands which indicate that cultures not provided with linguistic forms capable of expressing relationships abstractly can formulate their solutions of intellectual problems satisfactorily as stories. Reciprocally, of course, the readiness of the primitive mind to accept narrative explanations inhibits the development of abstract linguistic patterns. The development is circular and self-perpetuating.

STRUCTURAL AND TONAL ANALOGIES IN MYTH AND LITERATURE. In the growth of specific narratives, much will depend on an intuition of fitness—that is to say, on structural or tonal analogies which are felt but not rationally analyzed. Wundt said, perhaps too emphatically, that "not intelligence, not reflection over the ways in which phenomena arise and cohere, but affect is the creator of

---

[14] *Ibid.,* pp. 394–95.

mythological thought." [15] It might be more accurate to observe that, at this stage, reflection is imperfectly conceptualized and that, in consequence, sensory configurations which in a different intellectual milieu might be recognized to symbolize the structures of feelings or to have describable affective tonalities are absorbed into myths on the basis of a felt congruity.

Such congruities often arise so oddly that a rationally oriented mind is amused by them. The extent to which, for example, motor images furnish a part of the savage's intellectual capital is implied by an adoption ritual current among the Klemantans of Borneo—a ritual which is not itself mythological but which illustrates the sub-rational association that is frequently active in story making.

> Some of the Klemantans (Barawans and Lelaks in the Baram) practise a curious symbolic ceremony on the adoption of a child. When a couple has arranged to adopt a child, both man and wife observe for some weeks before the ceremony all the prohibitions usually observed during the later months of pregnancy. Many of these prohibitions may be described in general terms by saying that they imply abstention from every action that may suggest difficulty or delay in delivery; *e.g.* the hand must not be thrust into any narrow hole to pull anything out of it; no fixing of things with wooden pegs must be done; there must be no lingering on the threshold on entering or leaving a room. When the appointed day arrives, the woman sits in her room propped up and with a cloth round her, in the attitude commonly adopted during delivery. The child is pushed forward from behind between the woman's legs, and, if it is a young child, it is put to the breast and encouraged to suck. Later it receives a new name.[16]

In birth, a large object must go through a narrow opening; hence it is felt that the processes of sticking or delay must not (as it were) be suggested to the embryo by actions of the parents. The Klemantan imagination is not so limited to verbally formulated ideas that

---

[15] Wilhelm Wundt, *Elemente der Völkerpsychologie* (Leipzig: Alfred Kröner Verlag, 1913), p. 92.

[16] Charles Hose and William McDougall, *The Pagan Tribes of Borneo* (London: Macmillan & Co., Ltd., 1912), I, 78.

the similarities of motor patterns have ceased to be directly apprehended.

Comparable forces are active both in myth making and in modern storytelling. Associations may rest on motor resemblances, as in the adoption ritual, or an object's visual traits may generate motor activity. Movement in the latter direction occurs at the beginning of a Hupa legend called "Dug-from-the-Ground," which begins as follows:

> An old woman was living with her granddaughter, a virgin, at Kintcuwhwikut. The girl used to go to dig roots and her grandmother used to say to her "You must not dig those with two stalks." The girl wondered why she was always told that. One morning she thought, "I am going to dig one," so she went across the river to Tceindiqotdin and began digging. She thought, "I am going to take out one with a double stalk." When she had dug it out she heard a baby cry. She ran back to the river, and when she got there she heard someone crying "mother" after her. She jumped into the boat and pushed it across. When she got across, the baby had tumbled down to the other shore. She ran up to the house and there she heard it crying on that side. She ran into the house, then she heard it crying back of the house.[17]

The two-forked root suggests human legs, and human legs evoke the image of motion; so the process of digging up becomes equivalent to childbirth, and the child, once born, immediately makes use of his legs to scamper about vigorously. In this story the visual element is important; but it at once generates a motor suggestion. Motor analogies appear to be important also, though in a more obscure way, in certain ritualistic practices, such as the custom, in New Guinea, of swinging on vines, sawing with strings, and playing tops with acorns in order to induce newly planted yams to grow.[18]

---

[17] Pliny Earle Goddard, *Hupa Texts,* University of California Publications in American Archaeology and Ethnology, Vol. I, No. 2 (Berkeley, Calif.: University of California Press, 1904), p. 146. I have altered "stock" to the more conventional "stalk."

[18] See L[ucien] Lévy-Bruhl, *La Mentalité primitive* (Paris: Librairie Félix Alcan, 1922), pp. 355–56; also Sir James George Frazer, *The Golden Bough: A Study in Magic and Religion,* Vol. VII (*Spirits of the Corn and of the Wild,* Vol. I) (3d ed.; New York: The Macmillan Company, 1935), pp. 92–112.

Primitive narrative, then, reflects an unanalytic sensitivity of the savage mind to structural likenesses—visual, motor, and other. The use of similar analogies in sophisticated literature reveals that the creative mind has preserved the sensitivity, though the connections apparent to it have little importance for discursive thought. This is not, of course, to say that only the artist's mind is capable of perceiving such analogies. The secretary of an academic department housed in a building adjoining that in which I work told me recently that when workmen were making holes in the walls with pneumatic drills for the installation of ventilating pipes, more than one professor shouted to her over the din, "Remind me to see my dentist." A perception which flashes across the nonaesthetic mind and disappears may, however, be fitted by the novelist or dramatist into a *structure* which the perception itself helps determine.

The importance to literature of such motor analogies, quickly apprehended by the primitive and often taken quite seriously by him, is enormous. The seriousness of the primitive apprehension can be inferred from the readiness of uneducated people even today to read meanings into sensory processes which to the discursive mind appear inconsequential and therefore trivial. In 1066, according to a legend, the stumbling of William the Conqueror on the English beach might have so lowered the morale of the Norman army as to change history had the King not quick-wittedly cried, raising his soiled hands aloft, "Thus do I take possession of England!" Other structural similarities also—for example, of shape—exert a powerful influence on literature. In a recent poem by a member of the "beat" generation, we read:

> I remember when I first got laid, H. P. graciously took my cherry, I sat on the docks of Provincetown, age 23, joyful, elevated in hope with the Father, the door to the womb was open to admit me if I wished to enter.
> There are unused electricity plugs all over my house.[19]

---

[19] From Allen Ginsberg, "Transcription of Organ Music," in *Howl and Other Poems* (San Francisco: City Lights Books, 1956), pp. 26–27. The perception was no doubt assisted by the fact that such outlets are called "female"; but this designation, in turn, rests on analogies of shape.

The analogy here is crude, though not without humor. Often the association is so subtle that it is appreciated only subconsciously, if at all. In Chaucer's *Summoner's Tale*, the line, "And fro the bench he droof away the cat," (D, 1775) is usually enjoyed for its "realism." Yet the motor image is indicative of the Friar's purpose in entering the goodman's house, since the narrator's intent is to stigmatize the begging orders for their selfish appropriation of property belonging to others.

Dreams as a source of narrative motifs

The foregoing suggestions might easily be elaborated into a volume; we must pass on, however, to a third source of narrative motifs, the irrational conjunctions of objects and actions in dreams. According to J. S. Lincoln, it has been shown that "the essential dream mechanisms of non-Europeans are the same as those of ourselves." [20] The valuation given dreams, however, is different, since, among primitives, dream happenings are often believed to have a reality equal, or even superior, to that of waking events. It has more than once been suggested that the almost universal belief in immortality was stimulated by the vision in sleep of men already dead; and Ellis has urged that the presence in dreams of such objects as weapons, clothing, bushes, rocks, and the like is responsible for the conviction that everything without exception has a soul.[21] It is widely known, however, in these post-Freudian times, that dreams are irrationally structured. If the almost unavoidable tendency for the "telling" of a dream to be a narrative process strengthens the assumption that dreams had an influence on the beginnings of fictive plot, it will appear likely that many of the irrationalities encountered in myths are analogous to those met with in dreams. Freud himself, at the very outset of his psychoanalytic experiments, was struck by

---

[20] Jackson Steward Lincoln, *The Dream in Primitive Cultures* (London: Cresset Press, [1935]), p. 104.

[21] A. B. Ellis, *The Ewe-Speaking Peoples of the Slave Coast of West Africa* (London: Chapman and Hall, Ltd., 1890), pp. 18–19.

the fact that the dreams he had written down sounded like short stories.[22]

The influence of dreams on story is complex but must not detain us for long. It may be remembered, however, that in dreams even cultured Westerners regress in some degree to the primitive perceptual world. One indication of this is the fact that many, perhaps most, dreams are played out wholly in grays. If the cause is regression to superseded modes of perception, such dreams are almost unbelievably archaic, for there do not, so far as I know, now exist in any part of the world savages whose sensoriums are so little developed as to be incapable of color vision. Other characteristics of dreams help us to understand the primitive mentality: the vagueness of outlines, the chaotic shifts and mixtures of settings, the ambiguous identity of human figures, the uncomprehended juxtapositions of incidents, the unfocused dread which may accompany the appearance of objects and persons. If the highly developed modern mind behaves in such ways when rational control is suspended, it is probable that in the very remote past much or most experience was equally puzzling.

At such an almost inconceivably remote period, myth must have had its origin. "Many mythical concepts are dreamed, and it has been amply demonstrated that the psychological pattern of the myth is identical with that of the dream." [23] Moreover, "many motives of legends and fairy tales have justly been traced to dreams; many mythical concepts and motives of art and even works of art have been inspired by them." [24] Behind the tales and legends, as behind the postulating of gods, must have lain strong psychic pressures—an uneasy desire to assimilate, to adjust, to *know*. We must not, however, expect dream knowledge to be formulated in the same way as discursive knowledge. In so far as dreams formed the model for myths, the articulation of experience in myths was rather affective than rational. As the numinous situations from which gods

---

[22] Sigmund Freud, *The Standard Edition of the Complete Works,* ed. James Strachey (London: Hogarth Press, Ltd., 1955), II, 160.
[23] Lincoln, *The Dream in Primitive Cultures,* p. 87. (Quoted from B. Laufer.)
[24] *Ibid.,* p. 50.

arose were charged with emotion, so too were many dreams; but in dreams there was even less opportunity for rational monitoring.

In such ways as these, the origin of story, if not fully explained, can be made credible. Matters so large and remote can never be adequately investigated, and theories about them cannot be experimentally verified; consequently, we must either renounce curiosity or be satisfied with an account which is plausible because it is not contradicted by large bodies of available information. Curiosity, however, is necessitated by the plan of the present study.

Lévi-Strauss's method of analyzing myths

The next step must be to inquire whether savage myths of the kind we have been examining are continuous with sophisticated modern fiction. A convenient point of departure can be found in a recent suggestion of Claude Lévi-Strauss, a distinguished French anthropologist, about a technique for the analysis of myths. If modern fiction is illuminated by an analytic process developed for application to myths, some basic continuity will be apparent.

Fundamentally, Lévi-Strauss argues, the significance of a myth lies in the story it tells. Myth is "the part of language where the formula *traduttore, traditore* reaches its lowest truth-value. . . . Poetry is a kind of speech which cannot be translated except at the cost of serious distortions; whereas the mythical value of the myth remains preserved, even through the worst translation." In myth, indeed, "meaning succeeds practically at 'taking off' from the linguistic grounds on which it keeps on rolling." [25] The first step in the analytic process, therefore, consists of "breaking down [the] story into the shortest possible sentences, and writing each such sentence on an index card bearing a number corresponding to the unfolding of the story." [26]

When this has been done, the cards are arranged in such a way as to permit both diachronic and synchronic reading. We must treat

[25] Claude Lévi-Strauss, "The Structural Study of Myth," in Thomas A. Sebeok (ed.), *Myth: A Symposium* (Bloomington, Ind.: Indiana University Press, 1958), pp. 52–53.

[26] *Ibid.*, p. 53.

the myth like "an orchestra score perversely presented as a unilinear series and where our task is to re-establish the correct disposition." [27] Thus the series of symbolic figures 1, 2, 4, 7, 8, 2, 3, 4, 6, 8, 1, 4, 5, 7, 8 would be rearranged as follows:

$$
\begin{array}{ccccc}
1\ 2 & 4 & & 7\ 8 \\
 2\ 3 & 4 & 6 & 8 \\
1 & 4\ 5 & 7\ 8 \\
\end{array}
$$

Interpretation requires a recognition both of the order of succession (the numbers read from left to right and from top to bottom) and of the synchronous arrangements of elements (the columns read vertically). The "gross constituent units" which constitute the vertical columns are synchronous in the sense that they are qualitatively similar and therefore should be considered simultaneously, although they are separated in actual narration.

When this scheme is applied to a simplified version of the Oedipus legend,[28] four columns are produced, the second and fourth of which reverse and contradict the first and third. All the incidents in the first column (Cadmus seeks his sister, Europa, who has been carried off by Zeus; Oedipus marries his mother; Antigone, despite Creon's prohibition, buries her brother Polyneices) suggest an "overrating" of blood relationships. The incidents in the second column (the Spartoi kill each other; Oedipus kills his father, Laius; Eteocles kills his brother, Polyneices) imply, by way of contrast, the "underrating" of blood relationships. The two incidents in the third column, the killing of the dragon by Cadmus and the destruction of the Sphinx by Oedipus, are said, for reasons which we have not leisure to examine, to constitute a *"denial of the autochthonous origin of man"* (that is, his origin from the earth). The fourth column consists of names—Labdacus, Laius, Oedipus—which are interpreted to indicate difficulties in walking ("lame," "left-sided," "swollen-foot"). Since it is a "universal character of men born from the earth that at the moment they emerge from the depth, they either cannot walk or do it clumsily," the column reasserts the autochthonous origin of man. As a whole, the myth "has to do with the

---

27 *Ibid.,* p. 54.
28 For the following interpretation, see *ibid.,* pp. 54–57.

inability, for a culture which holds the belief that mankind is autochthonous . . . , to find a satisfactory transition between this theory and the knowledge that human beings are actually born from the union of man and woman." The four columns, read from left to right, state a relational equation: "The overrating of blood relations is to the underrating of blood relations as the attempt to escape autochthony is to the impossibility to succeed in it. Although experience contradicts theory, social life verifies the cosmology by its similarity of structure. Hence cosmology is true."

Much is puzzling here: the reasons why these elements of the myth are chosen for inclusion (is the story of Cadmus properly a part of the Oedipus legend? why is the plague omitted?), some details of the interpretation (is it an overrating of relationship for a brother to seek a lost sister?), and, not least important, the total reading. Yet the interpretative method, which is later illustrated more fully by application to all the known versions of a Zuñi origin myth, is worth adapting to literary fiction. The experiment is attractive because the discovery that an approach to myth can yield hints for the understanding of fiction would suggest a basic kinship. The chief difference will be that because we work in our own language some attention can be paid to metaphor of word as well as of idea.

THE METHOD APPLIED TO *Great Expectations.* For the example of fiction we shall go to a novel, since prose fiction is the lineal descendant of oral narrative; to a work old enough to be unaffected by the current interest in myths (post-Frazer novelists would be suspect), yet recent enough to be indisputably modern; to the product of a richly creative mind not likely to have been biased by an aesthetic theory: in short, to Dickens' *Great Expectations.* Since the modern novelist is to some extent, at least, a conscious artist and would be offended by the suggestion that details of treatment have no importance, we shall choose a climactic passage and not attempt to reduce the whole novel to a texture of gross incidents. I begin with a condensed paraphrase of some two pages of Chapter XXXIX.

Pip was twenty-three years old. He had moved to rooms in the Temple, by the river. He felt restless and unsettled, but had formed a habit of regular reading. Herbert had gone to Marseilles; hence

Pip was alone. He felt dispirited, anxious, disappointed, solitary. The weather was wretched—stormy, wet, gloomy. The wind had stripped the lead off roofs, torn up trees, and carried off the sails of windmills; there had been reports of shipwrecks. The day just ended had been worst of all. The Temple was then more lonely and exposed than it is now. The wind shook Pip's rooms like surf or the blast of cannons, so that he could have fancied himself in a storm-beaten lighthouse. The smoke, instead of going up the chimney, sometimes rolled down it. The staircase lamps had been blown out, as had the lamps in the court; the lamps elsewhere were shuddering, and the fires on barges were being carried away before the wind like red-hot splashes in the rain. Pip read with his watch before him, intending to stop at eleven o'clock. When eleven came and he shut his book, the many church clocks in the City, striking the hour, sounded curiously flawed by the wind. Just then a footstep became audible on the stair. Pip started nervously, thinking of the footstep of his dead sister. The step stumbled as it came on. Pip took his reading lamp to the head of the stairs. He saw and heard nothing; he called, and was answered. A man came momentarily within the circle of light thrown by the lamp and then passed into darkness again. The strange face Pip had seen appeared touched and pleased. Moving the lamp, Pip observed that the stranger was dressed roughly but substantially; that he was old; and that he was strong but weather-beaten. The man held out his hands.

When the elements of the story are sorted out under headings that suggest themselves irresistibly, interesting relationships appear.

One set of details has to do with physical situation. At the age of twenty-three, Pip is situated in "rooms in the Temple, by the river"; he is "alone," the Temple then having been "more lonely and exposed than it is now." The stress here is on isolation, physical solitude. The solitude is further emphasized by the presence in the near vicinity of the river, normally a bustling avenue of the workaday commerce with which Pip is unconnected, and even now, we are to learn, occupied by moving barges in spite of the inclement weather.

A second global cluster has to do with Pip's mood, which is in keeping with his situation. He feels "restless and unsettled," "dispirited, anxious, disappointed, solitary"; under the influence of the storm he "could have fancied himself in a storm-beaten light-house." The coal fires on the barges appear to him "like red-hot splashes in the rain": we cannot be mistaken in recognizing a suggestion that natural forces, which can here be equated with "the world," assist in quenching the ardors of young manhood. Later, he thinks of the footstep of his dead sister, with whom his relations had been consistently painful.

The mood engendered by solitude, as well as by other circumstances which have been explained in previous chapters and exert a pressure on the passage, is outwardly symbolized by depressing weather; and this provides the basis for a third cluster of narrative details. The weather is "wretched—stormy, wet, gloomy." The wind has played havoc with physical objects, including a number made by man in a futile effort to protect himself against nature (the world); it has stripped the lead off roofs, torn up trees, carried off the sails of windmills, caused shipwrecks, and at present is shaking Pip's rooms "like surf or the blasts of cannons." Of many bad days, the present one has been "the worst of all." The smoke, which is a by-product of man's effort to obtain warmth and comfort, is driven down the chimney to plague him. The lamps, set up by human beings as a protection against natural darkness, have lost much of their usefulness; those on the staircase and in the courtyard have been blown out, others further away are shuddering, and even those on the barges are threatened with extinction. When the clocks of the many churches in the neighborhood strike eleven, the sound is "curiously flawed by the wind"—another symbol of interference with human purposes. The convict Magwitch, when he appears, is revealed as having been long buffeted by wind and rain: he is "weather-beaten" by exposure to such storms as rage now about Pip.

A fourth cluster has to do with human actions, and this, surprisingly, has more elements than any of the others. As rephrased, the passage seems relatively static, and in the original version the narrative momentum is minimal. Yet this column includes fourteen items, whereas the three former columns contained only four, nine, and five, respectively.

Upon inspection, the items subdivide themselves easily into two groups, one having to do with Pip, the other with Herbert and the stranger, whose lives impinge upon Pip's. "Herbert had gone to Marseilles": clearly, the absence has been contrived to produce a solitude which is further enhanced by depression and the storm. Thereafter, for some time, our attention is focused upon Pip; he "had moved" to the Temple, "had formed a habit of regular reading," "read with his watch before him, intending to stop at eleven o'clock," and when eleven came "shut his book." So far, the image is that of an unsettled man who has established a single consistent habit. When the step is heard, he starts nervously, takes his lamp to the head of the stairs, where he sees and hears nothing but receives a reply to his call, and, finally, moves the lamp and observes a stranger. Everything about the stranger is disturbing—his footstep, which "becomes audible" unexpectedly and stumbles in its progress, the manner in which he enters a circle of light and then immediately passes again into darkness, and, not least startling, his sudden gesture of friendship ("the man held out his hands"). The descriptive details given about the stranger, which constitute a fifth and final cluster of elements, are ambivalent: the unknown face appears "touched and pleased," but the man's dress is rough; although old, he is apparently strong. The facial expression at once reassures and perplexes; the age, which might imply weakness, is balanced by strength and roughness.

If we now attempt to read the global units from left to right, as Lévi-Strauss suggests ("if we want to *understand* the myth, then we will have to disregard one half of the diachronic dimension . . . and read from left to right, column after column, each one being considered as a unit" [29]), we discover some such sequence as the following: physical isolation—spiritual depression—violent weather—completion of unsatisfying routine—disturbing intrusion—benevolent threat. This is reassuring, because application of a method of mythical analysis in no way outrages the critical intelligence. Evidently modern fiction is not so discontinuous with preliterate myth as to become nonsense when treated in the same way. We must attempt, however, to go further. In the illustration from the Oedipus legend, the serpent and the Sphinx were interpreted as chthonic

---

[29] *Ibid.*, p. 55.

creatures which symbolized obstacles to the autochthonous origin of man, and a set of names was asserted to imply that man nonetheless was born from the earth.

At once it becomes evident that, without intending to do so, we have already construed certain symbols—the river, the coal fires on the barges, the smoke, the flawed striking of the clocks, Pip's habit of reading, perhaps also the storm. The storm, we must remember—since the story is fiction—was not actually "there" but was imagined. Pip's psychological state and the results of an anticipated visit have been permitted to generate an objective equivalent, something possessed of sensory qualities which can be elaborated. The description of an affective state is difficult, that of a visual, auditory, tactile object, easy; moreover, literature, which, like the other arts, is an art mainly of presentation, requires maximal concretion. As the wild weather engrosses our attention, we recognize subconsciously the spiritual equivalents of the clouds, the wind, the darkness, the rain. The storm is not only object but metaphor; it grows out of the storyteller's mood and creates an answering mood in the reader. That mythical objects and happenings often had a similar origin cannot be doubted. Indeed, the words and phrases of the fourth paragraph of the original version (omitted from the summary in order to distract attention from language) have affective valences even if syntax is totally disregarded: "heavy veil," "the East," "cloud," "wind," "furious gusts," "torn up," "carried away," "gloomy," "shipwreck," "death," "violent blasts," "rain," "rages of wind." The power of language, which we have tried to separate here from the power of fictive invention but which is really not wholly independent of it, makes itself felt in Dickens' prose through the multiplication of images, so that there is less cold and violence in the summary than in the actual narrative. The cold is in Pip's heart, the violence is preparatory for the psychological blow which is to result from the convict's self-revelation as the benefactor whose money has made Pip a gentleman. But there are other symbols, too, which may or may not be apprehended by the critical intelligence but are solidly embodied in the myth (the shortened version) as well as in the novel.

One of these appears in the "curiously flawed" sound of the

clocks. Magwitch, too, is flawed; he is also, from the point of view of the gentleman Pip has become, odd, curious. There is *transference* here; the qualities of one fictive object are anticipated in the description of another. Then comes the footstep, which induces the memory of Pip's dead sister. It was while Pip lived with his sister that he had met the convict, and it was his sister, also, whom he had feared while stealing the food which the starving man had demanded. Quite irrationally—mythically—the memory of the sister is invoked in preparation for an encounter which is, so to speak, to occur *in illo tempore,* although also, synchronously, in a very different present. The recollection evoked by the footstep is a symbol of the then-within-the-now and reminds one that the rituals from which myth is often said to have descended are thought to occur at the moment of the archetypal act which is being repeated. The footstep, in coming on, *stumbles;* and this again is irrationally anticipatory, since the discovery of his benefactor's identity marks a stumbling and a fall for Pip's presently overinflated ego. The stumbling is realistically motivated by the darkness, but it is mythically functional in predicting an effect of the impending meeting. The stranger steps momentarily within the circle of light thrown by Pip's lamp and then passes again into darkness: so he had appeared twice *in illo tempore,* out of the marshes and back into them, and a third time, to vanish into the looming convict ship.

Still another suggestion arises from a reperusal of our findings to this point: the passage asserts repeatedly, again in nonlogical ways, that nature, "the world," is too powerful for man, who secludes himself in vain against it. Pip's sanctuary, the Temple, is shaken as if by surf (a natural force) or the blasts of cannons (man-made disturbances); the flawing of the clocks' sound, the stripping of roofs, the damaging of windmills, the shipwrecks at sea, the reversal of the smoke, the interference of the weather with the lamps, all imply the inability of men to manage their lives as they wish. Perhaps our vertical columns have resulted from a wrong principle of division; if we had searched from the outset for nonrational meanings, the schema would have taken a different form. However arrived at, the insight blends beautifully with the purport of the whole novel: because man is not his own master, it behooves him to sympathize with the weaknesses of others. Pip's estrangement from Joe Gargery and Biddy as a consequence of a fortunate accident is therefore morally blameworthy. The remainder of the story will subject him to a series of calamities which will destroy his fence against human involvements and revivify his warmheartedness at the expense of his dignity.

Having perceived so much, we observe that many other details have some tincture of symbolical—that is, presented, not explicated —meaning. Pip's residence in the ancient and respectable Temple is a visible embodiment of his admission to the honorable class of gentlemen. (The shaking of the Temple, because the status of its occupant is to be menaced, illustrates the difficulty of keeping metaphor firmly under control.) His giving over of reading at eleven foreshadows the putting aside of selfish pursuits at the end of a late adolescence. Henceforward, Pip is to stop preparing himself for gentility and enter into praiseworthy, if distressing, human relationships of a kind calculated to produce the self-forgetful warmheartedness that Dickens admires. The convict's slow ascent of the stairs is, from one point of view, the rise to equality and even dominance of someone very "low," who is at first "looked down upon" as inferior; his substantial but rough clothing is the outward manifestation of a heart which is morally sound but not equipped with superficial graces. Everywhere significance is carried down into the minutiae. In life, it is not consistently true that appearance is a metaphor of character, that living quarters are ideally appropriate to their inhabitants, that people who come upstairs increase their importance as they ascend, that dreadful happenings occur on nights when the weather is dreadful. In Dickens' myth, however, there is fitness in every detail.

How does this come about? Not, certainly, because Dickens created his symbols by a process identical with that by which we have interpreted them, though working in an opposite direction. He was not so conscious an artist. We approach nearer to an answer if we say that the suggestions thrown up by his creative imagination impinged, as it were, on inclined surfaces which determined the direction of their import; each had to adapt itself to a bias set partly by the logical intelligence but also partly by the psychic tilt which we call a mood. As in the origin of primitive myths, affect played a considerable role. The congruence of the narrative elements comes about almost necessarily, provided the slopes are firmly established; the idea, for example, of congenial company, absorbing occupation, pleasant sunshine, or a cheerfully glowing fire would have been deflected into an area outside the mythic frame. The overt actions, falling into such a context, are also tonally appropriate. This is in no way surprising, since the nature of the projected actions has been responsible for the creation of this context rather than another. Given the isolation, the mood, and the weather, the convict's step cannot be imagined as springy; it must "sound" ominously, then stumble. When Pip comes to the head of the stairs, his lamp cannot be permitted totally to dissipate the thick gloom; the convict will at first be outside the circle of light, come into it, and at once pass again into darkness. Playing the scene out in his visual imagination, the author is satisfied, for it resonates a pattern solidly established by earlier appearances and disappearances. The source of the metaphorical relevancies is thus to be found less in rational processes than in a creative mental activity marked by the nonrational sensitivities in which all symbols have their ultimate origin. But these sensitivities are "primitive"; hardheaded men ignore them on principle, scientists take pains to eliminate them from cognition; besides artists, only women and children take them seriously. In making his fictions powerful, the modern novelist falls back toward the psychic patterns which governed the projection of myths.

A general conclusion drawn by Lévi-Strauss from his analysis of myths is that "two opposite terms with no intermediary always tend to be replaced by two equivalent terms which allow a third one as a mediator." Thus the polar opposites "life" and "death" are irreconcilable; but if "agriculture" (which produces growing things) is substituted for "life," and "war" (which causes destruction) replaces "death," the middle term "hunt" (the provision of food by means of killing) is engendered.[30] The application of this formula to *Great Expectations* as a whole will be a further test of the continuity of myth and modern fiction.

---

[30] *Ibid.*, p. 62.

No difficulty is encountered in the attempt. In Dickens' mind, both social respectability and warmheartedness were "good"; but all too frequently, experience revealed, the aloof and self-valuing gentleman was not warmhearted. Let "gentility" be replaced by "Pip," a man conceived as ascending to social respectability from a situation which had opened his eyes to human suffering, and "warmheartedness" be replaced by "Joe Gargery"; the ultimate result is the middle term "refined compassion." Myths, however, we are further told by Lévi-Strauss, are "much addicted to duplication, triplication or quadruplication of the same sequence"; their structure is "slated." [31] Beside Pip, accordingly, we have Estella and Miss Havisham, beside Joe we have Biddy; and Herbert Pocket is from the beginning—although for a while affected by Pip's uncertainty and irresponsibility—the warmhearted gentleman that Pip is to become. The duplications are of course not mere repetitions: "A theoretically infinite number of slates will be generated, each one slightly different from the others." [32] Thus Estella, because she has escaped youthful hardships, has a more difficult time than Pip in achieving the admired virtue; Miss Havisham dies almost at the moment she discovers her error; and Biddy, although she achieves a satisfactory education in some mysterious way, remains permanently in a low social status. The structure of the novel, like that of myth, "closely corresponds, in the realm of the . . . word, to the kind of being a crystal is in the realm of physical matter." [33] The patterns repeat themselves, but always with slight differences.

Protagonist and antagonist

Backing away from Dickens and Lévi-Strauss to obtain another kind of synoptic view, we observe the tendency in all fiction, mythical or consciously feigned, for the protagonist to have an antagonist, the good force to be resisted by an evil force to which it will succumb or over which it will rise. The cause appears to be, at least in part, an instinctive Manichaeism encouraged by, if not originating

31 *Ibid.*, p. 65.
32 *Ibid.*
33 *Ibid.*

in, such natural opposites as day and night, summer and winter, life and death, pleasure and pain. Lang says of the good and evil powers of the Hottentots, "We have here an example of the constant mythical dualism which gives the comparatively good being his perpetual antagonist—the Loki to his Odin, the crow to his eagle-hawk." [34] And again, of America: "From north to south the more general beliefs are marked with an early dualism." [35]

THE ANTAGONIST AS A PROJECTION OF FELT RESISTANCES. In struggling to achieve his objectives, man meets resistances, over which he is helped, sometimes, by forces apparently originating outside himself. Both the resistances and the help are hypostatized, the former as bad or unfriendly powers, the latter as good or friendly. The movements toward a goal are dynamic in nature, hence tend by an internal momentum toward plot; but the hypostatization leads to the creation of dramatic or narrative personae, which then develop an intrinsic life. *Process* becomes *incident,* and critical moments become *crises.* The inception of the purpose becomes Aristotle's "beginning," the movement toward it the "middle," the final achievement or frustration the "end." Psychic states, as well as physical and social obstacles, are made *objects* or *happenings,* and the concatenated series becomes *story.*

How this works out in the oldest literary document in the chief Western tradition can be seen from a typical excerpt. Menelaos (Atreides) is fighting with Paris (Alexandros):

> Then Atreides drew his silver-studded sword, and lifted up his hand and smote the helmet-ridge; but the sword shattered upon it into three, yea four, and fell from his hand. Thereat Atreides looked up to the wide heaven and cried: "Father Zeus, surely none of the gods is crueller than you. Verily I thought to have gotten vengeance on Alexandros for his wickedness, but now my sword breaketh in my hand, and my spear sped from my grasp in vain, and I have not smitten him."
>
> So saying, he leapt upon him and caught him by his horse-hair crest, and swinging him round dragged him towards the well-

---

[34] Andrew Lang, *Myth, Ritual and Religion* (London: Longmans, Green & Co., Ltd., 1913), II, 46.
[35] *Ibid.,* II, 71.

greaved Achaians; and he was strangled by the embroidered strap beneath his soft throat, drawn tight below his chin to hold his helm. Now would Menelaos have dragged him away and won glory unspeakable, but that Zeus' daughter Aphrodite was swift to mark, and tore asunder for him the strap of slaughtered ox's hide; so the helmet came away empty in his stalwart hand. Thereat Menelaos cast it with a swing toward the well-greaved Achaians, and his trusty comrades took it up; and himself sprang back again eager to slay him with spear of bronze. But Aphrodite snatched up Paris, very easily as a goddess may, and hid him in thick darkness, and set him down in his fragrant perfumed chamber; and herself went to summon Helen.[36]

The basic matter here is the failure of Menelaos to defeat Paris in single combat. In a modern story, the actions imputed to gods would be ascribed to chance or "natural" causes. For Homer, the splintering of the sword was the fault of Zeus, the breaking of the chin strap the work of Aphrodite, and the escape of Paris a supernatural abduction. There is no chance (*il n'y a pas de rapports fortuits*); every happening is traced to an intelligent source, which then becomes an actor in the narrative, although often invisible to human sight. And the gods, in the *Iliad,* are in fact almost as busy as the human beings. Poseidon rallies the Greeks on the beach; Ares enters the battle directly; a river god, enraged by the choking of his bed with corpses, pursues Achilles with his waves across the plain; Apollo shakes the aegis; spears are turned aside from their targets, heroes are warned against encounters, wounded favorites are instantaneously healed of mortal injuries. The network of hypostatized causes leads, however, clear out of the epic itself. The elopement of Paris with Helen was an outgrowth of the beauty contest among Hera, Athena, and Aphrodite. Troy was doomed because the gods had been cheated in its first building. In the whole Olympian mythology, indeed, there is a coherence depending chiefly on the interplay of wills and almost nowhere on the passive resistance of of mindless objects.

This is not the place to study the gradual transformation of the

---

[36] *Iliad* iii. 361–83. The translation is by Andrew Lang, Walter Leaf, and Ernest Myers and is now published by Random House, Inc.

personified *mana* which we call gods and goddesses to insentient forces oblivious of man and his projects. My own guess would be that the process coincided approximately with the inductive revolution; but I should add immediately that it is not yet complete and may never become so. In Sir Thomas Malory, at any rate, as in other authors of his period, the old tendency is still strong. If gods no longer deflect spears and dash reins out of warriors' hands, their purposes still rule the future and can be interpreted by a seer. Actions are determined by something besides physical and psychological law. By Jane Austen's time, however, the occult is on its way out—it is parodied in *Northanger Abbey*—and chance is recognized to be operative in human affairs. The ill feeling between Darcy and Wickham, thinks Jane in *Pride and Prejudice,* must be based partly on misunderstanding: "Nothing therefore remained to be done, but to think well of them both, to defend the conduct of each, and throw into the account of accident or mistake whatever could not be otherwise explained." [37] Yet, in general, the role of chance in literature is still much smaller than in life, and resistance still tends to be personified as villain. In experience, the enemy is often shadowy and pervasive, not concrete and localized—lack of capacity, self-division, uncertainty, awkwardness, group expectations, society as a whole, and the like. In a novel, the awkwardness of a suitor may generate, by a kind of creative animism, an embodied Suavity who stands in graceful and mocking proximity to the loved one, apparently deflecting to itself the sorely wanted affection. The need of art for an objective correlative is perennial.

THE PROTAGONIST IN *Märchen*. The protagonist himself —the hero, as he becomes in many narratives—is usually at the center of the fictive actions. (Sometimes, of course, there are several protagonists.) In one archaic literary type, the *Märchen*, he is,

> as a rule, a boy who goes into the world and has adventures. Many kinds of magic come to his help in them; and he either wields it himself, or it is imparted to him by kindly sorcerers. Thereupon ill-disposed demonic creatures, who would destroy him, come

---

[37] Jane Austen, *Pride and Prejudice,* I, chap. xvii.

against him; and the action consists mostly in his overcoming of these. Thus his good fortune comes, for the most part, from without.[38]

"A peasant had a son who was the size of a thumb." "A poor woodcutter lived by a great wood with his wife and two children. The boy was named Hänsel and the girl Gretel." "A poor man had four sons. When they were grown, he said to them, 'Dear children, you must go out into the world.' "[39] The age of such a story, in a given version, may perhaps be computed very roughly by the amount of magic in it. In its essence, the subject is the contact with a hostile or indifferent world of a young man unprovided with such adventitious help as may be furnished by wealth and friends. In the end, he ordinarily, although not unexceptionally, acquires wealth, or a princess, or both. The hearer is accordingly cheered. Misfortunes of birth can be compensated, bad luck overcome, wit and courage rewarded. A modern parallel is the Horatio Alger story, or any story of a youth's upward progress against odds. The doggerel charms given the boy by friendly powers are gone, the inexhaustible purses and the axes that chop by themselves, superseded. Yet the basic pattern, which corresponds to that of relief from common environmental stresses, remains.

IN MYTH—THE "MONOMYTH." On a higher level, the hero is more imposing; story becomes *myth*. The incidents acquire cultural meaning because they have left visible traces in social institutions or the cosmos. In recent years, it has become increasingly clear that behind an astonishing number of myths lies a common pattern. The pattern eludes perception until the attention is directed to it because it is the condition of mythical thought; it is not so much *what* we see when our minds work mythically as *how*. In Joseph Campbell's formulation, which is as concrete as the materials permit, the monomyth runs as follows:

> The mythological hero, setting forth from his commonday hut or castle, is lured, carried away, or else voluntarily proceeds, to the

---

[38] Wundt, *Völkerpsychologie*, pp. 372–73.
[39] The stories are from Grimm: "Der kleine Däumling," "Hänsel und Gretel," and "Die vier kunstreichen Brüder."

threshold of adventure. There he encounters a shadow presence
that guards the passage. The hero may defeat or conciliate this
power and go alive into the kingdom of the dark (brother-battle,
dragon-battle; offering, charm), or be slain by the opponent and
descend in death (dismemberment, crucifixion). Beyond the threshold, then, the hero journeys through a world of unfamiliar yet
strangely intimate forces, some of which severely threaten him
(tests), some of which give magical aid (helpers). When he arrives at the nadir of the mythological round, he undergoes a supreme ordeal and gains his reward. The triumph may be represented
as the hero's sexual union with the goddess-mother of the world
(sacred marriage), his recognition by the father-creator (father-
atonement), his own divinization (apotheosis), or again—if the
powers have remained unfriendly to him—his theft of the boon he
came to gain (bride-theft, fire-theft); intrinsically it is an expansion of consciousness and therewith of being (illumination, trans-
figuration, freedom). The final work is that of the return. If the
powers have blessed the hero, he now sets forth under their protection (emissary); if not, he flees and is pursued (transformation
flight, obstacle flight). At the return threshold the transcendental
powers must remain behind; the hero re-emerges from the kingdom
of dread (return, resurrection). The boon that he brings restores
the world (elixir).[40]

It is true, as Campbell remarks, that "The changes rung on the
simple scale of the monomyth defy description." Archaic traits
are excised or rationalized; imported elements are adapted to local
settings and customs; many dislocations occur. [41] Yet, on the whole,
the fixity of the outline is remarkable. One recognizes immediately
the plot not only of many classic legends but also—when mundane
equivalents are substituted for cosmological—of many contemporary novels. The father-creator becomes the parent, the head-
master, the boss, the general, or anybody else who is endowed
with authority and power. The descent into hell becomes the
stresses and terrors of any fictive adventure, or, more generally still,
merely the fictive "middle." The return is the end of struggle, the

---

[40] Joseph Campbell, *The Hero with a Thousand Faces* (Bollingen Series XVII,
Bollingen Foundation, Inc., 1949), pp. 245–46.
[41] *Ibid.*, p. 246.

stasis in which the plot eventuates. No doubt, if the pattern is to be useful, one must adopt a policy of broad constructionism. But the monomyth exists, and recognition of it simplifies the analysis of story.

Lord Raglan has argued for a different analytic scheme, which is not, however, incompatible. In a standard pattern of heroic action the semidivine nature of the premodern hero—the Achilles, the Beowulf, the Siegfried, the Roland, the King Arthur—appears plainly.

(1) The hero's mother is a royal virgin;

(2) His father is a king, and

(3) Often a near relative of his mother, but

(4) The circumstances of his conception are unusual, and

(5) He is also reputed to be the son of a god.

(6) At birth an attempt is made, usually by his father or his maternal grandfather, to kill him, but

(7) He is spirited away, and

(8) Reared by foster-parents in a far country.

(9) We are told nothing of his childhood, but

(10) On reaching manhood he returns or goes to his future kingdom.

(11) After a victory over the king and/or a giant, dragon, or wild beast,

(12) He marries a princess, often the daughter of his predecessor, and

(13) Becomes king.

(14) For a time he reigns uneventfully, and

(15) Prescribes laws, but

(16) Later he loses favour with the gods and/or his subjects, and

(17) Is driven from the throne and city, after which

(18) He meets with a mysterious death,

(19) Often at the top of a hill.

(20) His children, if any, do not succeed him.

(21) His body is not buried, but nevertheless

(22) He has one or more holy sepulchres.[42]

---

[42] Lord Raglan, *The Hero: A Study in Tradition, Myth, and Drama* (London: Methuen & Co., Ltd., 1936), pp. 179–80.

According to Lord Raglan, on a scale of these twenty-two points Oedipus scores twenty-one; Theseus, twenty; Romulus, eighteen; Hercules, seventeen; Perseus, eighteen; Jason, fifteen; Bellerophon, sixteen; Pelops, thirteen; Siegfried, eleven; King Arthur, nineteen; and Robin Hood, thirteen; and Jewish, Javanese, African, and Celtic heroes make scores ranging from nine to eighteen points.[43] We have here, accordingly, not merely a catalogue of heroic traits but an archetypal plot, a motif of circumstances so frequently encountered that it becomes almost coextensive with heroic story and drama.

THE WEAKENING OF THE HEROIC MOTIF. It will be observed that none of the Western heroes mentioned is contemporary or even recent. The heroic motif, which seems to have had an almost compulsive strength in the age of myth, has no authority in the age of reason.

The reason for this is easily found. How near the older heroes were to gods is implied by Wundt's belief that the gods were formed after their image, not they after the image of the gods: "Gods do not precede heroes, but, contrariwise, heroes the gods. . . . The hero first prepared the way for the god, not the other way round." [44] In contrast, the tendency nowadays is for the chief character to be especially bumbling and ineffectual and for the apparent superman to be set against him as opponent. If in the end the feeble protagonist triumphs, it is because there is a kind of evil in strength, a *hybris*, once again, of the body and will which nature or humankind cannot tolerate. How far the distrust of strength goes can be seen in a currently popular theme of science fiction. The protagonist, although intimately at home with space suits, disintegrator guns, and air locks, spends his time resisting the efforts of a much more knowledgeable genius to control the universe. In the older dictionary sense, as "a warrior chieftain of special strength" or "an immortal being intermediate in nature between gods and men," the hero has thus gone over to the enemy. He does not, like King Arthur, at one rush slay single-handed

---

[43] See *ibid.*, pp. 180–89. Lord Raglan's scoring is perhaps liberal; I am myself unable, for instance, to give either Oedipus or Arthur so high a rating.

[44] Wundt, *Völkerpsychologie*, p. 372.

960 men.[45] He is closer to the child hero of the fairy tales in his essential weakness. This, however, is in the main a development of the last two or three centuries. Dryden's Almanzor and Milton's Samson are still larger than life; and the line stretches back to Achilles and Hercules.

"Reality" of fictive personages

It will be seen that fictive character varies from age to age; that, more or less directly, it typifies a cultural attitude. If we inquire more narrowly, however, into the relationship between fictive personages and flesh-and-blood human beings, very complex problems arise. In what way, especially, are the characters of a play or novel "real" to a reader or spectator? We shall leave to one side every aspect of the problem but this; for the mental habits of primitives throw some light on what is called "reader identification." Despite the protests of aestheticians, it is certain that many persons find pleasure in throwing themselves imaginatively into the situations of one or more fictive characters, and pre-eminently into those of the protagonist.

The traditional explanation is that literary personae are representative. In a phrase of Aristotle (*Poetics* 15), they are "true to life," although, of course, they do not live in the same way as ordinary people. The soldier is soldierly, the king kingly, the slave humble, and so on. In the view of many literary critics, the creator of fiction works largely with archetypes—for the philosophical idealism of Aristotle dominated not only ancient criticism but also the criticism of the Renaissance and the Enlightenment, and it lingers still in the academies. The presumption is that the writer eliminates what is factitious and narrowly particularizing in his personages in order not to distract attention from their fitness to "stand for" permanent tendencies in human nature.

Among savages, the relationship presumed to obtain between

---

[45] Cf. the following in the *Historia Britonum,* by Nennius: "Duodecimum fuit bellum in monte Badonis, in quo corruerunt in uno die nongenti sexaginta viri de uno impetu Arthur; et nemo prostravit eos nisi ipse solus, et in omnibus bellis victor exstitit." Quoted by John Rhys in the Preface to Sir Thomas Malory, *Le Morte d'Arthur* (London: J. M. Dent & Sons, Ltd., 1953), I, ix.

an individual and its species is quite different. We can approach
this more mystical view by observing a primitive attitude toward
animal sacrifices. Among certain California Indians, it was formerly
the custom to hold a yearly festival at which a buzzard was killed.
The details of the ceremony need not be described; the point is
that "as often as the bird was killed, it became multiplied; because
every year all the different Capitanes celebrated the same feast of
Panes, and were firm in the opinion that the birds sacrificed were
but one and the same female." [46] Sir James Frazer, who reports
the ceremony from Spanish sources, comments on this remarkable
belief as follows:

> The unity in multiplicity thus postulated by the Californians is very
> noticeable and helps to explain their motive for killing the divine
> bird. The notion of the life of a species as distinct from that of an
> individual, easy and obvious as it seems to us, appears to be one
> which the Californian savage cannot grasp. He is unable to con-
> ceive the life of the species otherwise than as an individual life,
> and therefore as exposed to the same dangers and calamities which
> menace and finally destroy the life of the individual. Apparently
> he imagines that a species left to itself will grow old and die like
> an individual, and that therefore some step must be taken to save
> from extinction the particular species which he regards as divine.[47]

Because the species is a single object, the different birds sacrificed
in different localities at the same time can be considered one bird.
The relationship between the part and the whole is that of equality,
even of identity. Every part *is* the whole; hence each part is
identical with every other. There is no thought of representation
at all. In a much-criticized word of Lévy-Bruhl's, the "participation" of the species in the individual is complete.

An idea as strange as this is difficult to assimilate. Must not
even the dullest savages have perceived that during the sacrifice
of the sacred buzzard (or ram, in ancient Egypt, or serpent, in
West Africa [48]) other members of the same species went on quite

[46] Frazer, *The Golden Bough,* VIII (*Spirits of the Corn and of the Wild,* Vol.
II), 170–71.
[47] *Ibid.,* VIII, 171–72.
[48] Cf. *ibid.,* VIII, 172–75.

unconcernedly about their ordinary business? Yes, but the relationship of percepts to convictions is not everywhere and always what it has become among educated Caucasians since the seventeenth century. In the main, the human mind has spun its most fundamental truths quite as much from its inner resources as from external sensory impulses. When convictions and percepts differ, the historical tendency has been either to subtilize the belief without abandoning it or to deny the percept, not to begin afresh in an attempt to conceptualize the empirical evidence.

I propose that in the beginning the relationship between the fictive protagonist and the tale's auditor depended on a somewhat similar participation. We forget too easily that the separation of subject and object is not a psychological *given*. What is apprehended through the senses or through the imagination may be so thoroughly internalized that it tends, in the untutored mind, to become part of the content of personality.[49] The aboriginal relationship between mythical personages and the hearers of tales or observers of dramas could hardly have been that of reflecting subject and typical or archetypal object. The literary transaction was neither so cool nor so highly conceptualized. Instead, the observer or hearer *participated* psychologically. He was *rapt into* the presented or reported events. In the proportion in which the experience was absorbing, the auditors lost self-consciousness and lived wholly within the myth, identifying themselves principally, no doubt, with the protagonist, if there was one, but not inhibiting their soul stuff from flowing into the situations in whatever other ways the narrative or dramatic structure permitted.[50]

---

[49] Cf. Cassirer, *Philosophie der Symbolischen Formen,* II, 216.

[50] The plausibility of this view is not compromised by the fact that not all existing primitive cultures make much either of storytelling or of ritual dramas. For example, the adult Manus, of the Admiralty Islands, do not tell legends to their children (see Margaret Mead, *Growing up in New Guinea* [New York: William Morrow & Company, Inc., 1930], p. 126) and seem not to take much interest in stories themselves. Among such people, absorption strong enough to produce identification of the kind just described may not occur. For two reasons, however, the exception is not significant. First, in these pages we are concerned with those tendencies of primitive men which throw light upon literature as we know it, not with all tendencies of all primitive men. The tendencies must be widely enough diffused to allow assurance that they represent permanent human possibilities, but they need not be universal. Secondly, the Manus are not, any

If the foregoing speculations have been sound, the Aristotelian view of the separateness of spectator and fictive object, and of the archetypal nature of fictive personages and situations, was much too highly conceptualized to describe accurately the psychological realities of ordinary aesthetic contemplation in ancient Greece. The high-ranking tiers of Athenian spectators who watched a tragedy of Aeschylus or Sophocles in the amphitheater, or the groups who heard Homer declaimed, must have done little more than empathize—as Aristotle himself suggested indirectly in his discussion of pity and fear. Moreover, what was "imitated" in the fictive actions themselves was not so much human character and recurrent human situations as the curves of emotional processes. For example, the curve of a tragedy, from initial relaxation through growing tension to release and restored tranquillity, seemed "right" because it was the familiar curve of a certain type of emerging and subsiding interest, only more vividly and memorably drawn; moreover, the feelings could be observed in others as well as experienced in oneself and were increased by social contagion.

Character motifs as transactional

The meaning of this discovery for the present chapter is that important character motifs may be *transactional* in nature (and therefore, perhaps, not really character motifs at all). From this point of view, some such division as that used by Georges Polti in his once-famous *Les Trente-six situations dramatiques* would appear to have potential value. Three of Polti's thirty-six "situations" are the following: "Supplication—a persecutor, a suppliant, and an undecided power"; "Rescuer—unfortunate person, threatener, rescuer"; "Vengeance in pursuit of crime—the avenger, the guilty." Here the quality of a central emotion, rather than the personality of the fictive actors, receives emphasis, and critical

---

more than any other surviving savages, really "primitive." They are not "first men," but merely men relatively far back on the evolutionary scale. At some point, the Manus may have taken—like other people—a turn away from communal feeling toward jealousy, mutual suspicion, dourness, preoccupation with private affairs, self-centeredness. The possibility of such a cultural choice is always open; but more often the trend toward gregariousness predominates, at least within the limits of village or clan.

attention is shifted from archetypal character to archetypal situation. It is not my purpose to argue that the traditional analytical methods are "wrong." It would appear, however, that if reader empathy has always been more important in aesthetic experience than in aesthetic theory, attention can sometimes profitably be turned to the affective motifs which are objectified by more than their own number of plot types.[51]

Fictive time

Still another archaic element in plot appears in the peculiarities of fictive time. It has often been observed that in literature time does not flow evenly, as in philosophical theory, but is *dinghaft* (material) and accelerates or decelerates in proportion to the density of incident. The same thing is true of the primitive time sense. Literature perpetuates a consciousness of time which before the dissemination of scientific thought patterns obtained in all experience.

The most convenient description of primitive time is given by Werner in *Comparative Psychology of Mental Development*. Such time "is not so much an abstract measure of order as a moment embedded in the whole concrete activity and social life of the tribe." The words used to express time concepts "represent really no more than certain salient events within a continuum of action." Thus cattle-raising Uganda tribesmen speak of "milking-time," "watering-time," "home-coming time for the cattle," and so on. The Eskimos of Greenland have a system of fish-catching times. The Trobriand Islanders have a system of gardening times. Again, differentiation may be based, usually in a subsidiary system which crosses the basic one, on affective qualities: there are lucky and unlucky times, holy and unholy times. The various units are not always so arranged as to be successive and continuous. They may overlap, or there may be gaps between them: "The Tumerehá Indians say that the year has ten months and two more during

---

[51] Polti thought that his thirty-six situations could be related to thirty-six emotions: "In life there are no more than thirty-six emotions." See Georges Polti, *Les Trente-six situations dramatiques* (Paris: Mercure de France, 1912), pp. 12–13. I need hardly say that the theory is suspiciously simple.

which the year is dead. . . . The Malecites Indians have a concrete qualitative sequence of lunar periods marked by frequent gaps." Balancing the moments when there is no time, however, are other moments when there is more than one time.

> Present and future may become congruous, for example, since the simultaneity of events is defined not so much by their objective synchronism as by their coincidence in effect. . . . Omens, dreams, and magic ritual are to a certain degree simultaneous with the event that occasions them, or which they occasion. Mythical happenings long past can be vital and effective in the present.

In a word, time does not exist independently of events and qualities, or it exists as something so vaguely sensed as not to demand conceptualization.[52] It is no accident that savages rarely know their ages. Moreover, for early men the cyclic element in time, the tendency for seasons and rituals to recur at more or less regular intervals, seems to have been more important than the succession of moments along a horizontal line—as in Malory's *Morte d'Arthur* Whitsuntide and Candlemas are thought more deserving of mention than the years of the Christian era or of Arthur's reign.

In early stages of development, the modern child recapitulates some of these notions. "Each day, for example, is divided off into breakfast, midday nap, supper, and so on; each year into birthday, Easter, Christmas." [53] A child may believe that a calendar creates time and may tear off calendar sheets in order to hasten an eagerly awaited event.[54] Researches have shown that a sense of impersonal or "universal" time is acquired very gradually.[55] At the beginning, the child, like the primitive, bases his concept of time on "an egocentric and concrete mode of experience." [56] Finally, the same peculiarities reappear in certain neurotic disturbances.[57] There is every reason to believe that the understanding of time common

---

[52] Heinz Werner, *Comparative Psychology of Mental Development*, (rev. ed.; Chicago: Follett Publishing Co., 1948), pp. 182–85.

[53] *Ibid.*, p. 187.

[54] *Ibid.*, p. 186.

[55] See Werner's report of findings by David and Rosa Katz, E. C. Oakden, and M. Sturt, *ibid.*, p. 187.

[56] *Ibid.*, p. 188.

[57] See *ibid.*, pp. 188–90.

among Western adults, although "natural" enough in corforming to the realities of physical nature, is historically eccentric.

The treatment of time in literature conforms rather to historical mind than to sidereal law. Rarely, as in Honoré de Balzac's *Eugénie Grandet,* is the lapse of time made to seem important—and real—despite the lack of dramatic incident. As Percy Lubbock has explained, Balzac's tremendous picture of the daily routine at Eugénie's has informed the bare statement that "five years passed" with deep and poignant meaning.[58] One stretches out the dismal existence in imagination and is appalled. In somewhat the same way, the tragedy of *Ethan Frome,* by Edith Wharton, lies not so much in the smashing of two bodies against the elm tree as in the years of dumb and hopeless suffering which followed. In even these two works, however, the empty years are filled with known routines; and, in general, time is present in literature in the proportion in which it is occupied. The moving-picture technique of causing a clock to tick or water to drip from a faucet during periods of tense waiting shows an instinctive realization that fictive time must be fleshed out with processes. Psychological incident, too, is procedural and will serve, especially, when the mental states include material images or attention is frequently diverted to an object in the setting: rain on the windowpane, a torn lampshade, a paperweight. When nothing at all happens, however, fictive time does not exist. The steady movements of the heavenly bodies by reference to which philosophical time is measured cease. Within the fictive universe, the past contains only those moments which are recalled in the present; the present consists of internal and external incident; and, after action stops, the personages remain forever in the postures in which they were left by the denouement. Moreover, the story as a whole floats in a time world of its own, which is fixed in historical time only to the extent that the manners and furnishings are peculiar to a specific period. For the most part, fictive time is free, like primitive time, and renews itself in a fresh *now* at cach reading. Not only is Malory's Whitsuntide

---

58 Percy Lubbock, *The Craft of Fiction* (London: Jonathan Cape, Ltd., 1931), chap. xv, esp. pp. 225–30.

mere Whitsuntide and not the Whitsuntide of a particular year; it can be drawn into the reader's present at will. The universality of literature, about which Aristotle remarked, depends on the quality of fictive times as well as on the typicality of happenings and character.

Against this background, but without any effort to make constant reference to it, we shall examine, finally, some of the minor motifs of fiction—patterns which have not been used a few times only, but are solidly in the literary tradition either because they have long been known or because they correspond to some basic complex of psychic elements and tend to be often reinvented. There will be no occasion for surprise if the human mind repeats itself unconsciously from generation to generation in response to fundamental biological tendencies.

Dreams, omens, presages

We begin by considering dreams, omens, and presages. The predictive value of certain passages in *Great Expectations* has been noticed; and similar foreshadowings occur in most fiction. Calpurnia's dream in Shakespeare's *Julius Caesar* is an example. Often, however, the presages are more subtle. Kenneth Burke, in a brilliant essay, has pointed out that before Caesar's death the audience's minds were poisoned against him by his partial deafness, his susceptibility to the falling sickness, his inferiority to Cassius in swimming, the barrenness of his wife, and his crying out like a sick girl during an illness in Spain.[59] Considered from another angle of vision, these details are portents. The deafness portends an unwillingness to listen to sound advice; the weakness in swimming foreshadows destruction by a political torrent in which Cassius will be his enemy; Calpurnia's barrenness, besides implying a lack of masculine force in her husband, presages the total cessation of his power; Caesar's susceptibility to illness and pain foretell an affliction from which he will not recover. Analogous

---

[59] See Kenneth Burke, "Antony in Behalf of the Play," in *The Philosophy of Literary Form: Studies of Symbolic Action* (Baton Rouge, La.: Louisiana State University Press, 1951), esp. p. 332.

predictions can be found everywhere in a variety of forms—in the
Iliad, where divine decrees are announced unambiguously; in
Richard Wright's *Native Son,* where the cornering of the Negro
murderer at the end is symbolized at the beginning by the cornering
of a rat; in Eve's premonitory dream of sin in *Paradise Lost.* The
influence of formal considerations also comes to bear, since the
dropping of hints which are not to be followed up would leave
structural joints loose. Yet the continuity between such literary
techniques and a savage assumption about experience is striking.
Reports on primitive peoples in every part of the world have
insisted that for the primitive chance does not exist. Every happening is significant, exactly as in literature.

The tendency of primitives to give credence to dreams has already been mentioned and is too well known to require discussion.
From Biblical times to the present, dreams have been anxiously
"interpreted" for their relation to the future; and in many cultures
dream events are thought to be quite especially "real." [60] Other
happenings which would seem to us accidental—that is, not connected with intelligent purpose—are thought to have occult causes
and hence to be premonitory. The Kaffirs of Africa run from a
man who falls into unexpected distress; in Fiji the crew of a
capsized canoe can lawfully be eaten; among the Eskimos a man
whose kayak overturned was allowed to drown, although his father
could easily have reached him an oar.[61] Such misfortunes express
the disfavor of spirits or powers and therefore presage a bad end.
For the savage, the network of causality is unbroken, and significance looms in every element of experience. Similarly, Jean Piaget
found that "the idea of chance is absent from the mentality of the
child," [62] who must grow out of psychic habits comparable to those
of savages. The primitive recognition of absolute meaningfulness
is thus institutionally perpetuated in literature. Whenever, in a
modern play or novel, an omen is fulfilled or an irrational hint is

---

[60] See Lévy-Bruhl, *La Mentalité primitive,* chap. iii, "Les Rêves," for a collection of typical examples.

[61] For these and other examples, see *ibid.,* pp. 317–31, esp. pp. 320–21.

[62] Jean Piaget, *The Language and Thought of the Child,* trans. Marjorie Gabain
(New York: Meridian Books, Inc., 1955), p. 156.

picked up, a savage assumption about reality is made operative in the fictive present. The pulling of a narrative together by non-rational means, perhaps in the interest of aesthetic form, makes the fiction more convincing for the part of the reader's mind which has resisted a discursive education.

The marvelous

From dreams, omens, and presages it is an easy transition to the marvelous, of which also literature is full. Vico long ago observed that "The poets nowhere exert themselves more actively than in singing the marvels performed by magicians through works of incantation." [63] The Gothic novel of the eighteenth century was a reaction against increasingly rationalistic thought modes and readily became popular. In our own time, space fiction provides an escape from humdrum perceptions while at the same time capitalizing on the prestige of science. In the main, there has recently been a movement away from wonders; but the affinity between literature and a magical world view remained strong at least through the Renaissance. Aesthetic creativity feels a drive not only to reproduce common experience (as in representational painting), but also to widen experience (as in fantastic, allegorical, and abstract painting). In doing so, it often breaks through the limits of the rationally comprehensible.

Animals in fiction

An illustration of a more concrete sort of continuity is provided by the treatment of animals in literature. Foxes, birds, horses, and the like have been in fiction from the beginning, although more functional in the *Odyssey* (Circe's swine) than in Conrad's *Heart of Darkness* (which is about the jungle) and in Lucius Apuleius' *Golden Ass* than in Tobias Smollett's *Roderick Random*. From time to time they usurp centrality: in *Aesop's Fables,* in fairy tales, in nursery rhymes, in moving-picture cartoons, in stories like *Black Beauty* and *Shaggycoat the Beaver,* in the fourth book of

---

[63] Giambattista Vico, *La Scienza nuova, e Opere scelte,* ed. Nicola Abbagnano (Torino: Unione Tipografico-Editrice Torinese, 1952), p. 321.

Gulliver's Travels, in George Orwell's *Animal Farm,* in Chaucer's *Nun's Priest's Tale,* in a recent series of films about Francis, the Talking Mule. Whenever this happens, they possess strikingly human traits—not only human feelings and some power of reason but often the capability of human speech. When they remain outwardly animal, they nonetheless retain vestigial human characteristics. A dog in a realistic novel may look bored, sniff critically at his food, show anxiety, resist an unwise purpose of his master. To nongenetic theory, it may seem that animals are used as deliberate surrogates for people, as "symbols." The roots of the practice, however, lie deeper, for in savage thought there is no dichotomy between brutes and men. Commerce between them is easy, and transformations from one form to the other are common.

The most familiar proof that the animal and human realms overlap is furnished by the widespread practice of totemism, which everywhere rests on a supposed blood relationship of the clan to its totem animal. In more advanced cultures—for example, the ancient Egyptian—the gods were represented in the forms of animals and birds. Anthropomorphic deities (Zeus, Odin) often turned themselves into animals. Again, primitive hunting rituals assume what has been called "the solidarity of life" among all animate species. The co-operation of the prey may be implored; the speaking of its name may be tabooed lest it should take alarm; if the hunt is successful, thanks may be offered to the victim for submitting itself to death, and its pardon implored for the further violence of cooking and eating it.[64] Beneath all these strange customs is the belief that animals have an intelligence similar to man's and magical power possibly greater.[65] The basis of the practices appears to be a tendency of primitive man to read his own nature into objects other than himself, as a child projects its mentality into dolls and toys. The fact that animals were never heard actually to talk or seen to behave rationally had not the slightest effect on

---

[64] See Heinz Werner, *Die Ursprünge der Metapher* (Leipzig: Wilhelm Engelmann, 1919), p. 85; and Frazer, *The Golden Bough,* VIII, 169–273.

[65] For examples see Lang, *Myth, Ritual and Religion,* I, 81, and Raglan, *The Hero,* p. 261. Raglan has a chapter on "Shape-Shifting and Talking Animals."

the belief. The mind has ways of getting round such difficulties: rationalization in the adult Westerner, something less complicated but harder to analyze in the child and in primitive men.

In the face of this evidence, there is not (I think) much doubt that an archaic mental attitude toward animals has been established as a convention in literature. When vitalistic assumptions began to decay, the old plots continued to be imitated. In consequence, the modern author who writes an animal fable can feel confident that his fiction will not arouse dismay. A receptive attitude toward such fictions exists alongside an expectation that extra-literary reflection will be discursive.

Primitive initiations as ancestral to fictive conversions

A long list of other continuities could be added, having to do, for example, with the literary uses of ghosts, of the savage impulse to revenge, of sworn brotherhood, and of the pursuit motif, which recapitulates the emotional experience of the primitive hunt and just now is very popular. I conclude this section of the chapter, however, with comments about savage initiation ceremonies, which appear to be ancestral to fictive conversions. The relationship is so close that Joseph Campbell based his description of the mono-myth largely on Arnold van Gennep's *Rites de passage*.[66] We shall have no space, however, for more than a hurried recapitulation of a few especially noteworthy convergences.

A frequent theme, in both novels and drama, is the attaining of a new consciousness within which experience acquires deeper meanings. *Wilhelm Meisters Lehrjahre*, by Goethe, provides an especially clear illustration. In Book VII, after the title character has been led through various adventures, he is taken into a converted chapel and made to undergo a curious ritual. Various persons whom he had met casually step within a picture frame and utter oracular statements; an "indenture" is handed him; he dis-

---

[66] Arnold van Gennep, *Les Rites de passage* (Paris: Librairie Critique, Émile Nourry, 1909).

covers that a charming but mysterious boy about whom he has wondered is his son. "Hail to thee, young man," says an officiating *abbé,* "Thy Apprenticeship is done; Nature has pronounced thee free." [67] Although much of this may appear ridiculous to the contemporary American reader, the intention is unmistakable. Wilhelm's adolescence is over. He has become a member of an inner circle, with a man's understanding of the hidden relationships in experience.

The sense that at certain stages human life turns a corner, that happenings or calamities frequently produce new personalities, appears not only in the *Erziehungsroman* but everywhere in fiction. Dante's *Vita Nuova,* Samuel Butler's *The Way of All Flesh,* and Conrad's *Victory,* like hundreds of similar works, lead their protagonists to new characters marked by profounder awarenesses. Conversions are, in fact, common in literature because they occur often in life. Anthony Trollope, in his *Autobiography,* began a new life at the moment of his arrival in Ireland; [68] Edmund Gosse's *Father and Son* described his emancipation from an early "dedication," by public immersion, to Christianity.[69] All such metamorphoses may be viewed as initiations into fresh attitudes; and among savages the importance of initiations is institutionally recognized.

The most important of such initiations occurs at puberty. The male candidates are often secluded from women and younger children, submitted to special taboos, treated brutally, made to undergo painful trials, and at last reunited with the tribe on a new footing. The rites may require weeks or even months, and are often accompanied by mutilations which make the new status visible at a glance. In addition, the initiate may cut his hair in a new style, acquire the right to carry a spear or other weapon, and perhaps dress or ornament himself differently. The acquisition of the higher status involves, however, the loss of the former one; and this loss

---

[67] I quote Thomas Carlyle's translation, entitled *Wilhelm Meister's Apprenticeship and Travels* (Boston: Houghton Mifflin Company, n.d.), Book VII, chap. ix.

[68] Anthony Trollope, *An Autobiography* (London: Oxford University Press, 1936), p. 54.

[69] Edmund Gosse, *Father and Son* (New York: Oxford University Press, 1934), esp. pp. 174–80 and 303–308.

is sometimes dramatized as actual physical death, as in some versions of Campbell's monomyth. On Melville Island, the candidate is supposed to be killed in a structure made of bark; [70] in New South Wales, he is met by a being who "takes the youth to a distance, kills him, and in some instances cuts him up, after which he restores him to life and knocks out a tooth"; [71] in New Guinea, he is swallowed and disgorged by a mythical monster; [72] in Liberia, he is killed by a forest spirit and given a new soul.[73] The initiates' bodies are often whitened to suggest a return from the grave, and the widespread practice of requiring them to sit with downcast eyes in the presence of women and children implies the breaking of former ties.

The stages of the initiation, which have been described by Van Gennep as separation, isolation, and aggregation,[74] have a parallel in many fictive plots—obviously, in the older literature, faintly, but still significantly, in the later. The boy or girl who is to be initiated in a recent novel is gradually separated from childhood, undergoes a series of painful trials, and is at last aggregated to an adult community of the approved kind, at which point the work usually ends. This is to say that the literary pattern has very deep roots in the racial past. It communicates, by literary structures analogous to the ritual patterns of the primitive initiation, a sense of transition formerly objectified in elaborate communal ceremonies and still sought by boys who form secret societies and invent initiatory rites.[75]

---

[70] Baldwin Spencer, *Native Tribes of the Northern Territory of Australia* (London: Macmillan & Co., Ltd., 1914), p. 107.

[71] Quoted from A. L. P. Cameron, "Notes on Some Tribes of New South Wales," in Frazer, *The Golden Bough*, XI (*Balder the Beautiful*, Vol. II), 227.

[72] *Ibid.*, p. 240.

[73] Cassirer, *Philosophie der Symbolischen Formen*, II, 203.

[74] For Van Gennep's book, see Note 66, above. This simple schematization, although not proposed by Van Gennep in precisely these terms, is clearly indicated by him. It is assumed by Henri A. Junod, on Van Gennep's authority, in *The Life of a South African Tribe* (Neuchâtel: Imprimerie Attinger Frères, 1913), I, 73–92, except that I have substituted "isolation" for Junod's "margin."

[75] In an interesting essay called "The Night Journey in *The Ambassadors*" (*Philological Quarterly*, XXXV [1956], 24–38), by Robert A. Durr, a well-known novel by Henry James is analyzed as a *rite de passage*.

Summary

The gist of the foregoing discussion, in all its parts, has been that both the materials and the forms of fiction owe much to primitive origins. The thesis, indeed, is not basically different from that of Andrew Lang's early *Myth, Ritual and Religion,* which undertook to show that all cultures have passed through a savage state and that the irrationalities even in Greek and Roman religion were residual from the primitive state. My purpose has been to argue a similar hypothesis with regard to literature; but two cautionary remarks are appropriate.

First, we must not be disconcerted if we find large differences between the primitive origin and the modern analogue. The slight bulge beneath the windows of recent automobiles barely suggests the fenders and running boards from which it has evolved within recent memory; and the difference between the same automobile and a horse-drawn carriage is so great that the continuity of design is not generally recognized. Yet the temporal distance of the two is hardly greater than a half century. The transformations with which we have been concerned extended over countless ages. It should not be surprising that the continuities can be established only by anthropological research, and then sometimes only tentatively.

Secondly, too much weight should not be given to rationalized explanations of behavior patterns. When a death occurs, it is now customary, or was customary when I was a child, to leave a window in the death chamber slightly open "so that the air can circulate." The practice is certainly harmless and may be wise, but it is undoubtedly continuous with a nineteenth-century European folk practice of opening a window or door to let the soul escape, and that, in turn, with the making of a hole in the burial house, the coffin, or the roof among the Iroquois, the Malagasy, and the Chinese.[76] The behavior pattern persists, the explanation of it has changed. The rationalization of irrational habits is of course absurdly easy; accordingly, it is safest, in a study of literature, as

---

[76] Edward B. Tylor, *Primitive Culture* (London: John Murray, 1920), I, 453–54.

of folk customs, to focus attention on the practices and not on the explanations. The matter and forms of literature can readily preserve a continuity with primitive thought ways which is lacking from creative purposes. The conclusions offered in the present chapter would not be affected, for instance, by an incontrovertible discovery that Homer did not really believe rivers to be inhabited by intelligent spirits. He writes *as if* he believed in the spirits; and his literary practice, which is all that concerns us here, is consonant with a primitive belief. The modern reader, in turn, gives easier credence to the flight of Achilles from the river than he would give to a fiction which had no basis in the innate tendencies of the savage and childish mind. No matter how cultured, he is not *all* discursive intelligence.

Fictions as projected states of mind

If our speculations have not been wild, the role of feeling in literature is much greater than some recent critics have been willing to admit. Both myths and art works are at least partly projective; they embody states of mind which seek objectified expression because they are affectively charged. What exists within the creative psyche partly, no doubt, as discursive thought, but also partly as feeling or attitude, wins expression as a concrete aesthetic object capable of being set adrift from its creator. The materials within the object are those which, by their modes of activity, their sensory qualities, their symbolic values, the sequence of their affective implications, or in some other way, either separately or as a group resonate the state of mind which demanded externalization. The object's form sets the limits within which the psychic processes indicated by the materials have been allowed to develop. Observers of the same biological nature as the creator, and with much the same racial—at best, also much the same cultural—history, can then, by allowing the art work to *initiate* psychic processes in them, relive the creative experience at a somewhat greater psychological distance. Their senses run over the work's contours and report the qualities of its materials. What was chosen by the creator as an objective correlative of pain means pain to them also; what was chosen as an embodiment of joy means joy. They are vitalized as the artist was vitalized. The modern dissociation of sensibility is resolved as whatever notions the work may contain develop in a richly affective context; and finally, the process having run its course, the readers are content, as the artist before them had been content, to separate themselves from the work and leave it suspended in aesthetic space.

At best, the experience can be profoundly satisfying. In literature, the medium of aesthetic projection is language, which, as we saw in previous chapters, still retains many primitive traits. The materials which are projected, however, are often fictions. That these too recapitulate immemorial patterns, under the influence of aroused affections, it has been the purpose of the present chapter to show.

6

The Major Literary Types:
Tragedy and Comedy

Up to the present point, the discussion has been broadly of "literature"—poems, folk tales, novels, plays, and whatever else has traditionally been considered verbal art. The question now arises whether the general conclusions will be borne out by a more detailed investigation of individual literary types. We turn first to an examination of tragedy, about which there has been an especially long-lived and influential theory; a theory, moreover, which asserts very persuasively a mimetic theory of art more directly than any other in contradiction with the findings of the preceding chapters. The challenge must be met head-on;

and this can best be done by genetic study. We shall no longer merely observe parallels but instead will watch an aesthetic evolution in process.

Origin of tragedy in Greece

The project would be impossible, or nearly so, were it not that tragedy came rather suddenly into existence at a known spot in the last half of the sixth century B.C. It did not, of course, originate in a final and unalterable form, and its roots were in other more archaic activities which will claim attention as we proceed; but within three lifetimes it had reached and passed its crest, and in less than another century Aristotle was able to reflect on it as something relatively fixed and analyzable. For several hundred years thereafter, it lingered among the Greeks and their successors to Mediterranean dominion, the Romans; then it sank out of sight for a millenium, to re-emerge, with differences, in the Renaissance. Outside the Graeco-Roman tradition, according to Gilbert Murray, there is little or nothing comparable.[1] Although we shall see later that the assertion is too sweeping, it has some basis of truth. For the present purpose, accordingly, tragedy provides the best possible starting point. It is a "great" art form whose origins, if not immediately open to view, are at least less impenetrably hidden than most.

Gaps in our knowledge of backgrounds

This is by no means to say that all the necessary evidence is immediately at hand. The researches of many scholars in Greek and Near Eastern prehistory have unearthed vast stores of information about ancient religion and mythology, out of which tragedy evidently grew. Yet there is no consensus: the inferential findings far outrun the substantive, so that in adopting any detailed theory one must run counter to others equally plausible. As Martin P. Nilsson remarked, at a time when less bewildering quantities of

---

[1] Gilbert Murray, *Aeschylus, The Creator of Tragedy* (Oxford: Clarendon Press, 1940), p. 5.

information were available than now, the search for a single source of tragedy leads into uncharted wilderness.[2] We may take courage, however, from the realization that for our purposes no single origin need finally be preferred to alternative ones which have similar aesthetic implications. Though the method to be pursued is historical, the aim is the testing of a relationship already tentatively established between literature and nonrational states of the psyche.

Anthropological views of Greek tragedy

The reinterpretation of Greek tragedy in the light of anthropological findings was begun more than half a century ago by scholars who were no longer satisfied with the cryptic statements made about tragic origins in Aristotle's *Poetics*. A convenient summary of new ideas accessible as early as 1911 can be found in an article published in that year by the Swedish scholar Martin P. Nilsson.[3]

TWO EARLY THEORIES: W. SCHMID AND ALBRECHT DIETERICH. Only two early theories can be mentioned here, and those only briefly. W. Schmid, in 1901, inquired why the all-important dithyramb, which apparently should have had only Dionysian content, handled heroic materials belonging properly to the hero cults and replied that, as a result of deliberate machinations by seventh- and sixth-century tyrants, the festival days of the heroes and that of the lower-class Dionysian cult were made to coincide.[4] Albrecht Dieterich, in 1908, suggested a more complex origin. The masked figures he explained as derivative from mummings and animal dances like those still observable among savages in many parts of the world; the dancers themselves he identified with the souls of the dead, and Dionysus, their leader, with the god of the dead. The occasion of the ritual was the Anthesteria, the Greek All Souls' Day; the *thrênos* in tragedy derived from lamentations

---

2 Martin P. Nilsson, "Der Ursprung der Tragödie," in *Neue Jahrbücher für das klassische Altertum,* Vol. XXVII (Liepzig: B. G. Teubner, 1911), p. 609.

3 See *ibid.* For the whole essay, see pp. 609–42.

4 For a summary, see *ibid.,* pp. 614–15; for the theory itself, see W. Schmid, *Zur Geschichte des griechischen Dithyrambos* (Tübingen: Programm, 1901).

sung earlier at the graves of heroes, and the dramatic dialogue from the Eleusinian liturgy.[5]

MARTIN P. NILSSON. Both these views, for reasons which need not be gone into here, and the view also of Ridgeway, to which we shall turn in a moment, seemed unsatisfactory to Nilsson. His own theory laid special stress on the importance of death laments as a tragic source. These were at first sung by relatives of the dead person, later by professional mourners; and they persisted in the final choruses of many tragedies, which are in the Doric idiom instead of the Ionian idiom—derived from the epic—of the dramatic dialogue.[6] An advantage of this view is that the sad earnestness of tragedy, unaccountable on the hypothesis of an origin in the satyr play, is made to appear natural. A serious disadvantage, admitted by Nilsson himself, is that the origin of the mimetic element remains problematic and must be sought elsewhere.[7]

WILLIAM RIDGEWAY. In the meantime, William Ridgeway, a member of the Cambridge school of classical anthropologists, had proposed that tragedy developed from mimetic dances performed at the graves of heroes on memorial days. The dances had as their purpose the invocation both of the heroes' protection and of their interposition for the obtaining of good harvests. On top of the ancestor worship, however, orgiastic fertility rituals came in from Thrace; and these were engrafted on the old ceremonies, so that the tombs of the heroes became altars of Dionysus. The only truly Dionysian element in the developed drama was the dithyramb, from which satiric plays evolved. The decisive contribution of Thespis was to elevate the mimetic dance into true drama.[8] This view, first presented in 1910, was expanded on a broader basis five years later in *The Dramas and Dramatic Dances of Non-European Races, in Special Reference to the Origin of Greek*

---

[5] For a summary, see Nilsson, *op. cit.*, pp. 616–17; for the theory itself, see Albrecht Dieterich, "Die Entstehung der Tragödie," *Archiv für Religionswissenschaft*, XI (1908), 163–96.

[6] Nilsson, *op. cit.*, pp. 624–25.

[7] *Ibid.*, p. 642.

[8] See William Ridgeway, *The Origin of Tragedy* (Cambridge: University Press, 1910), p. 108, for his own summary.

Tragedy. The first chapter of the later work was given over to a refutation of competing theories, including those of L. R. Farnell (tragedy arose from "a European winter mummery") and Gilbert Murray (it originated in rituals celebrating the death and rebirth of the Year-Spirit). Here are several indications of many that attempts were being made to elucidate Greek art and religion by means of comparative anthropology.

JANE ELLEN HARRISON.   Still another hypothesis was put forward by Jane Ellen Harrison, also a member of the Cambridge school, in the interval between Ridgeway's two books. Tragedy may be traced to its roots in a Dionysian rite modeled on the initiation rites for young men, Dionysus being a *projected* god of rebirth who sprang from the hypostatization of a group emotion. The emphasis of Miss Harrison's first important book, *Ancient Art and Ritual* (1913), is vigorously anti-Aristotelian.

> At the bottom of art, as its motive power and its mainspring, lies, not the wish to copy Nature or even improve on her . . . but rather an impulse shared by art with ritual, the desire, that is, to utter, to give out a strongly felt emotion or desire by representing, by making or doing or enriching the object or act desired.[9]

Of Aristotle's definition of art as the imitation of natural objects, she says flatly, "Never did a statement so false, so wrong-headed, contain so much suggestion of truth." [10] The ritual out of which tragedy developed was not a representation but a presentation of something desired. The bas-reliefs which accompany the Osiris inscription at Denderah show the god rising gradually from his bier; and this example Miss Harrison thinks typical. "In ritual, the thing desired, *i.e.* the resurrection, is acted, in art it is represented. . . . Countless bas-reliefs that decorate Egyptian tombs and temples are but ritual practices translated into stone." [11] The savage is a man of action; "Instead of asking a god to do what he wants done, he does it or tries to do it himself." [12] The peasants

---

[9] Jane Ellen Harrison, *Ancient Art and Ritual* (New York: Henry Holt and Company, Inc., 1913), p. 26.
[10] *Ibid.,* p. 22.
[11] *Ibid.,* pp. 17–18.
[12] *Ibid.,* p. 30.

in Swabia and Transylvania leap high into the air to make the hemp grow tall.[13] Hence the appropriateness of the Greek word for drama, *drómenon,* "a thing done." [14] The rebirth of Dionysus, being wanted, was acted out; and the ultimate result was Greek tragedy as we know it. In a later book, *Themis: A Study of the Social Origins of Greek Religion* (1927), she developed her point of view further, beginning with an analysis of a *Hymn of the Kouretes,* recently discovered at Palaikastro, in Crete.

GEORGE THOMSON.   This part of our survey, which is meant only to be suggestive, will be concluded by a consideration of "George Thomson's very learned attempt to bring Greek tragedy into concrete relations with cult and rituals and with a definite democratic social revolution at the time of Aeschylus" [15]—an attempt which draws from a wide range of sources and synthesizes views that it would be uneconomical to consider separately. Final acceptance of any theory must be the responsibility of specialists; but the *direction* taken by classical anthropology in its effort to throw light on the origins of tragedy has significance for the present study quite apart from the accuracy of the detailed findings.

Aristotle, it will be remembered, had said in the *Poetics* that tragedy "originated with the leaders of the dithyramb." What exactly was the dithyramb? Thomson believes it to have belonged originally to a Dionysian *thíasos,* or band—actually, a secret society which had grown out of a totemic clan and preserved something of the clan's structure and functions. In the beginning, except for a male priest, the society was composed of women only. Its principal rite, derived from initiation ceremonies, comprised three parts: an orgiastic sortie into the fields, a sacrament which consisted in dismembering a victim and eating it raw, and a triumphant return. The ritual was projected (note the Freudian term) as a myth of Dionysus' passion, but its function was to make the soil fertile. Celebration of the rite tended, therefore, to be limited to the peasantry, and as time went on became identified with a

---

[13] *Ibid.,* p. 31.

[14] *Ibid.,* p. 35.

[15] René Wellek and Austin Warren, *Theory of Literature* (New York: Harcourt, Brace and Company, Inc., 1949), p. 105.

popular movement against the landed nobility. The declining social status of women caused the rite to pass into the hands of men and to undergo further modification. From this point we may follow Thomson's own words:

> It ceased to be secret, and began to disintegrate. The orgiastic procession became a hymn, which was developed most rapidly in the Peloponnese; the sacrament became a passion-play, developed principally in Attica, where the popular movement, after beginning later, progressed further. From the first arose the dithyramb, from the second tragedy. Both were urbanised and consciously directed by the tyrants, the former maturing under the influence of aristocratic lyric. Thus, looking back over our argument, we may say definitely that the art of tragedy was descended, remotely but directly, and with each stage in its evolution conditioned by the evolution of society itself, from the mimetic rite of the primitive totemic clan.[16]

The roots of the developed art form go deeper than Aristotle suspected, though he was right in asserting a relationship with the dithyramb.

The analysis can be pushed further. It has been said that, as the social status of women declined, the *thíasos* declined also. In time the dithyramb, or what was to become the dithyramb, ceased to be sung as a processional hymn and, the chorus being brought to a stand at an altar, became a *stásimon,* or "standing song." Its theme was in all probability the myth which corresponded to the rite about to be celebrated—the passion or suffering of Dionysus. The choir had a leader, who no doubt impersonated the god, or came to impersonate him, as in many cultures.

> It is plain that we have here the germ of a ritual drama. When the leader of the dithyramb begins to speak in character to his chorus, the dithyramb is becoming a passion-play. As Aristotle said, the art of tragedy was evolved "from the leaders of the dithyramb." [17]

---

16 George Thomson, *Aeschylus and Athens: A Study in the Social Origins of Drama* (London: Lawrence & Wishart Ltd., 1941), pp. 195–96.
17 *Ibid.,* p. 172.

At this point, the dithyramb segmented, one part allowing the music to dominate the words; in the other part, the music dropped away, and "the leader became an actor, then two actors, and finally three. . . . The performance which began and ended in this way was, in origin and essence, an *agón*—an ordeal or contest, a purge or purification which renewed life." [18] Hence came the basic substance of tragedy—struggle or pain leading to a defeat in which there was also victory.

The date at which the ceremony began to resemble the mature Greek tragedy can be roughly fixed by the association of Thespis with the tradition. According to Horace, a late and consequently dubious authority, Thespis and his troupe toured the Attic countryside in a wagon.[19] If the report is trustworthy, as Thomson believes, the actors would have been members of religious guilds derived from the Dionysian *thíasos,* and their performances would have had a religious significance associated with the fertility of the fields. It is likely that "those qualities of boisterousness and crudity which Aristotle noted as characteristic of early tragic diction" developed then. The period during which the Dionysian ritual, having ceased to be the property of a secret society, was performed by religious guilds perhaps ended about 534 B.C., when Thespis won the tragic prize, a goat. Only a few years later Aeschylus was born; and in his lifetime the history of tragedy proper begins. The elevation of tragedy to a city festival at Athens resulted from the encouragement of Peisistratus,[20] who is believed to have desired public support from the peasants against powerful nobles.

If this hypothetical reconstruction is even approximately accurate, why did the subject matter of tragedy not continue to be simply the birth and resurrection of Dionysus? I offer a simple explanation which, although adequate, is purely supposititious: that the institutionalizing of tragic contests under Peisistratus forced the dramatists to seek fresh materials suitable for absorption into the established form. It is easy to imagine an official proclamation

---

[18] *Ibid.,* p. 173.
[19] *Ibid.,* p. 192.
[20] *Ibid.,* pp. 192–93.

to the effect that *"Drómena* in Thespian form, but dealing with any sacred or heroic subject, are solicited for performance at the next City Dionysia, the prize to be a goat." The tragic competition must have had a beginning—that is, a year when it was not held must have been followed by a year when it was held—and the transition must have been bridged by some action of Peisistratus, if it was indeed he who instituted the festival.

However that may be, it is worth noting that a search of the kind just undertaken for the origins of tragedy in ritual is justified by a rather vigorously supported hypothesis that ritual precedes not only art but also mythology. The thread that unites the confusing and contradictory Greek myths, says Thomson, "is ritual, which is older than the gods." [21] The insight has been shared by many other anthropologists and mythologists: by Miss Harrison, by Gilbert Murray, by Lord Raglan, by Robert Graves, by Ernst Cassirer ("It has been rightly emphasized that in the relationship of myth and rite the rite is earlier, the myth later" [22]). The very low savage acts out his fears and hopes before he fictionalizes or mythologizes them; and conceptualization comes last of all. At the beginning, accordingly, myth is closely bound up with ritual and cannot profitably be considered apart from it. In detail, Thomson's conclusions may be wrong; but his search has been made in the right quarters.

Ritual and drama outside Greece

Other scholars have conducted similar researches into the dramatic rituals of the Near East, thus implicitly denying Murray's dictum that tragedy can be found only within the Greek tradition. (The truth of Murray's assertion depends on the definition of tragedy, a matter into which it would be digressive to enter here.) In *Thespis: Ritual, Myth and Drama in the Ancient Near East,*

---

21 *Ibid.,* p. 130.
22 Ernst Cassirer, *Philosophie der Symbolischen Formen,* Vol. II (Berlin: Bruno Cassirer Verlag, 1925), p. 52.

Theodor Gaster finds ample evidence that seasonal rituals tending toward drama existed elsewhere.

> Recent studies have shown that the Pattern may be recognized behind the conventional structure of Greek comedy and tragedy and behind the European Mummers' Play. Using the same line of argument, it is here shown that several of the longer mythological texts recently recovered from the Ancient Near East are likewise but literary adaptations of the Seasonal Pattern, and therefore essentially dramatic, each incident of the plot being projected from an element of the original ritual. It is therefore possible to claim these texts as ancient dramas and as the prototypes of Greek comedy and tragedy and indeed, of modern theatrical forms.[23]

The function of the mythological plot is "to bring out in articulate fashion the inherent durative significance of the ritual program" [24]: that is, to furnish a narrative equivalent for the ceremonies which will provide a preconceptual explanation for the continuing importance of the ritual. The effect of the plot, once invented, is "to turn presentation into *re*presentation, to introduce the element of mimesis and to confer upon the participants the added and parallel rôle of actors." [25] In this way, myth and ritual are correlative, and drama is a result of their organic combination. The form of the plot is similar to that of the seasonal ritual and consists ordinarily either of a combat (an *agón*) or of a death-and-resurrection, the "god" who takes the central role being "nothing but a durative projection of the king" [26] on whose health and vigor the success of agriculture is thought to depend. From this beginning, drama can develop in various ways; yet it can never "wholly forget the rock whence it was hewn," for the ritual pattern remains, and the central theme is always that of "Conflict, Discomfiture and Restoration." [27]

---

[23] Theodor H. Gaster, *Thespis: Ritual, Myth and Drama in the Ancient Near East.* Reprinted by permission of the publisher, Abelard Schuman, Limited. © 1950 by Henry Schuman (New York). P. 49.

[24] *Ibid.*

[25] *Ibid.*

[26] *Ibid.*, p. 50.

[27] *Ibid.*, p. 55. The whole of Gaster's book deserves study.

Dramatic ritual and the primitive time sense

The relation of dramatic ritual to the primitive time sense, touched on by Gaster, is developed on a still broader geographical basis by a Rumanian scholar, Mircea Éliade, in *The Myth of the Eternal Return*. People living in traditional (that is, nonprogressive) cultures are everywhere ahistorical; by their rituals they undertake to annihilate time, to return, when life and energy appear to be exhausted, to the mythical beginnings. Only what occurred at the beginning, *in illo tempore,* has firm reality; hence ritual actions are paradigms of eternal archetypes.

> A sacrifice . . . not only exactly reproduces the initial sacrifice revealed by a god *ab origine,* at the beginning of time, it also takes place at the same primordial mythical moment. . . . Through the paradox of rite, profane time and duration are suspended.[28]

For example, when the Fijians feel that the vitality of the cosmos is running out they return ritually *in principium.*[29] On a smaller scale, such a return can be accomplished by an individual who is engaged in some quite ordinary pursuit: "The Melanesian fisherman, when he goes to sea, becomes the hero Aori and is projected into mythical time, into the moment when the paradigmatic voyage took place." [30] All ritual is imitative of archetypes and has as its effect the restoration of an aboriginal moment. It does not follow that because all traditional societies have rituals all must develop drama. We are helped by Éliade's discussion, however, to an understanding that drama as near to religious ritual as the Greek derives much of its power from the ability of ritual to obliterate the psychic distance between a mythical age and the present. The impressionable spectators so empathize the enacted events that separate times coalesce and become indistinguishable.

---

[28] Mircea Éliade, *The Myth of the Eternal Return,* trans. Willard Trask (Bollingen Series XLVI, Bollingen Foundation, Inc., 1954), p. 35.
[29] *Ibid.,* p. 81.
[30] *Ibid.,* p. 36.

The form of Greek tragedy

Let us see whether some such analysis as Thomson's helps us to account for the form of extant Greek tragedies. Although by far the greater number of tragedies actually produced is gone irrecoverably, the few that remain are well known, and Aristotle's analysis has helped disseminate a certain understanding of their formal peculiarities; an understanding, however, which will perhaps not survive the present examination unchanged.

According to Thomson, the outline of a pre-Aeschylean tragedy is not difficult to imagine.

> The chorus entered with a song or recitative, and after taking up their positions round the altar they sang a *stásimon*. Then the hero appeared, explained his identity and expounded the situation in a dialogue with the chorus. Then he disappeared, and, after another *stásimon* from the chorus, a messenger entered to announce the hero's death. There followed a lament, the messenger retired, and the chorus left the orchestra in the same manner as they had entered.[31]

Simple as the pattern was, it had emerged from something more elaborate, if less neatly formed, and was rapidly to undergo elaboration in a direction suggested by its source.

That source, as has already been seen, was very likely the initiation ceremonies once, perhaps, familiar to all Greek youths and still existing, no doubt with modifications, in various mysteries. As was seen in the last chapter, the basic pattern of initiation ceremonies is fairly constant the world over: the candidates leave their homes with adult guides, undergo trials, suffer a pretended death, are shown sacred objects and taught esoteric lore, and at length return to their homes as adults—quite different persons, whose discontinuity with the uninitiated youth is dramatized in curious ways. The Greek form of the initiation has been speculatively reconstructed by Thomson as follows: it consisted, in order, of a *pompé* (an escorted procession), an *agón* (contest, trial), a *sparagmós* (rending, tearing, as in the Dionysian celebrations),

---

[31] Thomson, *Aeschylus and Athens*, p. 179.

an *anakálypsis* (unveiling of the reborn god), an *ainígmata* (teaching by means of dark sayings or riddles), a *dokimasía* (examining, catechizing), and, finally, a *kômos* (festal procession back to the village). All these parts of the total ritual have left an impression upon mature Greek tragedy.

The tragic equivalent of the *pompé* is the *párodos,* or entrance of the chorus. The protagonist's *agón* is initiated by the *peripéteia,* or reversal of fortune, which in turn is followed by a *kommós,* or ritual lament, comparable to that which accompanied the rending (*sparagmós*) of the sacrificial victim at the Dionysian ceremonies. The tragic *anagnórisis,* or recognition, is co-ordinate with the *anakálypsis,* or unveiling of the reborn god. The catechizing of initiates, or *dokimasía,* has left a vestige in the *stichomýthia* of tragedy, which often has a riddling character, "as though the speakers were more concerned to veil their meaning than to elucidate it." Finally, the *éxodos* of the chorus is parallel to the *kômos* in which the just-made adults are led back triumphantly to the village.[32]

The correspondences are striking. That both initiation ceremony and tragedy should begin and end in a procession is not in itself very meaningful, since the Greek theater provided no other means of introducing and dismissing the chorus; and the equating of the tragic recognition with the unveiling of a disguised god is perhaps somewhat forced. Nevertheless, a rather surprising similarity remains. When we remember that the tragic competitions were held at the greater, or City, Dionysia, a festival named from the Dionysian mystery, the hypothesis that there was a direct development from the initiation ceremonies for youths through the mysteries to tragedy becomes very persuasive.

CONFORMITY WITH A RECURRENT PATTERN OF CONSCIOUSNESS. Dionysus, who is now often thought to have been originally a vegetation deity, became in the course of time a seasonal god who was regenerated yearly. Such gods are met everywhere in primitive religion, and the seasonal festival has been relied on by innumerable peoples to restore the dead year and reinvigorate an

---

[32] See *ibid.,* p. 192, for a tabular statement of the above correspondences. The remark about *stichomýthia* has been taken from *ibid.,* p. 189.

exhausted earth. A family resemblance in all such rituals permits us to connect Greek tragedy with a pattern of consciousness apparently always accessible to the human mind and therefore very elemental. The ease with which modern minds resonate to Greek tragedy is thus partly a consequence of the primitive residue in Greek thought of the classical period.

Theodor Gaster, in *Thespis,* studies the seasonal ritual in the ancient Near East and finds a roughly anologous pattern. "Drama," he says in his first chapter, "is everywhere more than mere mimesis. In whatever form and at whatever level we encounter it, it consists essentially not in a single mimetic act but in a series of acts, arranged in a specific pattern and manifesting a specific 'plot.' " [33] The plot is a mythologized version of "the mechanism whereby, at a primitive level, Society seeks periodically to renew its vitality and thus ensure its continuance" [34]; it is ritual become story. Since the rituals are everywhere similar ("seasonal rituals follow a uniform pattern" [35]), the myths also have a family resemblance. In dramatized form the plot works out something as follows: energy is paralyzed, and the normal activities of society are suspended; there is howling and wailing; an attempt is made to get rid of evil influences in order to prepare for reinvigoration; a ritual combat of some kind is held, and evil is expelled from the topocosm; finally, there is jubilation, accompanied on the social level by such orgiastic practices as communal meals and mass mating.[36] The last step is missing from individual Greek tragedies, although it may originally have appeared in the satyr play which followed each trilogy and has left traces in Aristophanic comedy. The remaining four steps are easily traceable in many plays—for example, in Sophocles' *Oedipus.* At the beginning, Theban life is at a standstill because of the plague; an *agón* follows, resulting in the discovery that the King's murder of his father and incestuous union with his mother have been responsible for the civic calamity; and, finally, the exile of the guilty sovereign prepares for a resumption

---

[33] Gaster, *Thespis,* p. 3.
[34] *Ibid.*
[35] *Ibid.,* p. 6.
[36] For details, see *ibid.,* pp. 6–33.

of normal life. The wailing and lamentation, which in the more primitive rituals end with the successful issue of the *agón,* because of the poet's sympathy with the protagonist, here extend beyond the *anagnórisis;* but the essential conformity of the plot to the usual schema is clear. In Gaster's words, "even after it had emerged from the embryonic stage and long outgrown its primitive functional purpose, Greek drama nevertheless retained the basic form and structure of its rude prototype." [37]

It would be possible, if there were space and necessity, to trace other variations of the pattern over much of the earth's surface. For example, the mummer's play, which in England sometimes took the form of an *agón* between St. George and the Dragon or, later, a Turk, was found by Karl Young to have originated in a seasonal ritual intended "to secure the fertility of the earth, of animals, and of human beings." [38] Karl Theodor Preuss discovered similarities between Greek tragedy and the old magico-religious drama of Mexico; [39] and Alfred Winterstein, in a monograph to which we shall recur later, came to the same conclusion about a wide variety of carnival mummings still performed in remote districts of Europe. [40] It is unnecessary and inaccurate to assert that Greek tragedy in its developed form was "nothing but" a fertility ritual. The resistance of classicists to the ruthless reductionism of much anthropological scholarship is thoroughly justified. Yet the continuity of Greek tragedy with something much older may well account for some of its power even over sophisticated modern readers. Like the poet described by T. S. Eliot, the good reader is at once more civilized and more primitive than the average man; and we need not wonder if he feels the pull of psychological patterns so "natural" that they have been institutionalized by the majority of historical cultures.

ADDITIONAL FORMAL DETAILS. An examination of the tragic

---

[37] *Ibid.,* p. 55.

[38] See Herbert Weisinger, *Tragedy and the Paradox of the Fortunate Fall* (London: Routledge and Kegan Paul, Inc., 1953), p. 212.

[39] See A[rnold] van Gennep, *La Formation des légendes* (Paris: Ernest Flammarion, 1912), pp. 112–13, for comments.

[40] Alfred Winterstein, *Der Ursprung der Tragödie* (Leipzig: Internationaler Psychoanalytischer Verlag, 1925), pp. 10–96.

pattern in terms of isolated aspects supports the conclusions suggested by the total configuration. The lamentation, for instance, is immemorially old; if the artfully composed *thrênos* or *kommós* differs enormously in complexity from the howls and shrieks of mourning savages, it is nonetheless clearly derived from ululation and occupies with respect to the whole tragedy a place analogous to that occupied by wordless keening at an Irish funeral or the yells and self-lacerations of an Australian tribeswoman at the death of a relative. The suffusing of the *kommós* with thought—sometimes very profound and subtle thought—is a result of the same conceptualization which has complicated the remainder of the tragic pattern. Grief now activates the cortex as well as triggers physical reflexes—if it did not, it would be less meaningful to sophisticated readers—but the basic emotion remains.

One reason why the *kommós* was free to become partly intellectualized can be found in the opportunity for nonrational expression provided by the choral dance. Dancing, however, is also very old; no communal activity is more archaic. "It is astonishing," says E. J. Eyre of the very "low" Australians, "to see how perfectly the time is maintained, and how admirably exact is the coincidence of the motions of the dancers with the intonations of the music." [41] The effect of shared action, as of shared speech, which in Greek tragedy accompanied it, is an enhanced feeling of group solidarity; and the disappearance of dancing from modern tragedy is a serious loss. The modern protagonist, who must express his grief by staring numbly out of a living-room window or, at most, by letting his head sink upon his arms while his wife or sweetheart strokes his hair pityingly, lacks the expressive resources—very ancient resources indeed—of his Greek prototype.

For some time, in the typical tragedy, he has lacked also the resources of verbal and musical rhythm. Although comparatively little is known about Greek music, its contribution to the affective pull of classical tragedy must have been very great. The respect shown for music in Plato's *Republic* suggests that it was already a highly developed art. Tragic speech, too, was rhythmic when

---

[41] Quoted by Ernest Grosse, *The Beginnings of Art* (New York: D. Appleton & Company, Inc., 1928), p. 222.

not accompanied by music, and in its systole and diastole resembled one of the two oldest known musical patterns, that of regular movement between two pitch norms at more or less regular time intervals. Charles Darwin believed that animals enjoyed rhythm; and it is virtually certain that they can perceive it.[42] By using measured instead of unmeasured speech, Greek tragedy preserved contact with the racial habit of fitting ritual speech to a rhythmic accompaniment.

Archaic tendencies in later tragedy

Although the discussion might be prolonged indefinitely, we have perhaps dwelt long enough on the origins of Greek tragedy to show that it contained many primitive elements and maintained continuity with patterns of consciousness deeply rooted in the racial past and still observable in undeveloped areas of the world. It next becomes appropriate to inquire whether all tragedy, Renaissance and modern as well as ancient, is also in some degree archaic. Have the writers of tragedy always reverted for important effects to prerational psychic habits? And are the spectators or readers of tragedy still driven to a sympathetic relaxation of normal cognitive controls?

The question cannot be addressed until a preliminary objection has been met fairly. The origins of Renaissance and post-Renaissance tragedy cannot be traced here in the same way as the origins of Greek tragedy; will there not, therefore, be danger lest generalizations so formulated as to capitalize on findings made up to this point apply only loosely, or not at all, to tragedies of other times and places? Very likely, and the reader of these pages is invited to test whatever conclusions may be arrived at against all his own reading. Yet there seems still, as during the centuries when Aristotle's *Poetics* was authoritative, to be an assumption that despite local and temporal differences tragedy is always fundamentally the same thing. The *Prometheus Bound* of Aeschylus, the *Phèdre* of Racine, and the *Lear* of Shakespeare belong to the same "type" or "genre"; there is potentially (it seems to be thought)

---

[42] Cf. *ibid.*, p. 222 n.

an adequate "idea" or "view" of tragedy which will be relevant to all works admitted to be tragic. If it were not so, the tragic theories of Georg Wilhelm Hegel, A. C. Bradley, Joseph Wood Krutch, Maxwell Anderson, and many other recent and less recent men of letters would be predestined to fatuity. The assumption may of course be wrong or, if not wrong, frivolous. W. M. Ivins, Jr., has argued that art works are interesting not because of qualities which they have in common with other art works but because of their uniqueness.[43] If this is so—and certainly it is so for many people— the best tragic theory could do no more than specify invariables which are aesthetically unimportant. Nevertheless, let us see what can be done. Every class concept must, or should, contain some constant; and our effort to isolate one or more constants in all tragedy by searching for irrational and regressive psychic patterns, if it does not lead to a total tragic theory, may at least open our eyes to aesthetic data not regularly noticed.

Three modern theories

I propose to summarize three theories advanced by others and then to consider whether some fairly trustworthy inferences cannot be drawn from all three.

LEO KAPLAN.   The first theory was proposed by Leo Kaplan some forty years ago in a stimulating article entitled "Der tragische Held und der Verbrecher." [44] The gist of the theory runs as follows:

> The tragic hero is the criminal in us; he takes upon himself both our fault and the punishment appointed for us. In a word, the idea of the scapegoat is realized in tragedy. . . . By the punishing of the actor the crime is atoned for, the desire for a clear conscience gratified, the damaged norm reëstablished, the evil deed compensated. *The dramatic-tragic action is a materialization of our own criminality.*[45]

---

[43] W. M. Ivins, Jr., "A Note on Ipseity," *Journal of Aesthetics and Art Criticism,* VII (1948), 38–41.

[44] Leo Kaplan, "Der tragische Held und der Verbrecher," *Imago,* IV (1915), 96–124.

[45] *Ibid.,* p. 119.

This view brings us at once very near to the whole complex of motives and psychic responses in ritual sacrifice, from which, as we have seen, the descent of Greek tragedy can be established; yet it is not on that account irrelevant—for instance—to *Macbeth,* or to any other tragedy in which the protagonist has dared greatly.

Kaplan develops his thesis persuasively. The suppressing of basic drives not countenanced by communal morality is not easy. Among primitives, especially, "every new breach of the moral order threatens to awaken the 'criminal complex' and to lend it new force; every crime offers the instincts a welcome example for imitation." [46] In proportion as the forbidden urge grows stronger, more energy is required to resist it, so that the thought of breaching the social norm gradually becomes very attractive; and the spectacle of dramatic transgression provides an opportunity for psychic release. By identifying with the protagonist, the observer obtains vicarious satisfaction. At the same time, the socialized part of the individual consciousness is scandalized, for "the tragic hero violates the norm suggested to the individual psyche by the communal will." [47] Hence there must be punishment: the norm must be reasserted, the social standards vindicated. When this has been done, gratification is complete. Because the spectator has sinned and been purified, he can leave the theater "calm of mind, all passion spent."

The desire for punishment, for atonement, Kaplan believes to have been established during childhood—a Freudian view, consonant with the assumption that no part of the cultural heritage is transmitted biologically.

> The need for atonement has its basis in childhood. If the child is punished by his parents, it feels the punishment as an alienation of the parents' love and solicits this so much the more. The parents too, on their side, strive to repay their harshness to the punished child by subsequent tenderness. *The child accordingly accustoms itself to regard punishment as a reprisal through which it obtains the right to make new demands for testimonies of love.*[48]

---

[46] *Ibid.,* p. 120.
[47] *Ibid.,* p. 96.
[48] *Ibid.,* p. 105.

In the child's life, the highest authority is exercised by the parents; in religious thought, it is exercised by God; in civil life, it is exercised by the judge. In tragedy, however, we ourselves take over the responsibility of judging: we allow the hero to come to grief in spite of the fact that he embodies our own wishes.[49] The function of tragedy is therefore to "thrust latent criminality back within bounds by the help of a projection mechanism." [50]

The theory is illustrated by references to Dostoevski's fiction—an interesting method, which suggests that in modern times a psychic function once performed by drama has been taken over by prose fiction. The crime of Raskolnikov, in *Crime and Punishment,* is an obvious example: it embodies in an extreme form the juvenile tendency, usually repressed, to wildness, to the violation of prohibitions, to the taking of a dare. Once the deed is committed, however, the moral censor begins to exert pressure. Raskolnikov feels an almost irresistible impulse to confess.

> The urge of the guilty man to concealment demands for its continued functioning a "psychic expenditure" (Freud)—that is, a consumption of energy. If secrecy is abandoned, however, and the fault acknowledged, the "psychic expenditure" ceases, and this is always sensed as a relief.[51]

The sympathetic Sonya, whose own conscience is not without a weight of guilt, advises Raskolnikov to go to a crossroads, kiss the ground, bow in all four directions, and then say aloud, "I have murdered!" whereupon *God will grant him life.* Even this, however, is not enough. As the desire to assert his superiority to social convention by the taking of life could be satisfied only by a criminal act, so now a moral conscience created in the same mind by social forces requires that he expose himself to retributive punishment.

The possibility of obtaining vicarious satisfaction—a possibility exploited by the tragic spectator, as also in the ritual sacrifice of a scapegoat in primitive religious ceremonies—is presented scenically within the same novel. When the murder is already on

---

[49] *Ibid.,* p. 101.
[50] *Ibid.,* p. 120.
[51] *Ibid.,* p. 115.

Raskolnikov's conscience, he happens to be present at the suicide of a worthless creature named Marmeladov. Later, as he walks from the dead man's home, he feels a lightening of his psychic burden.

> He went slowly, without haste—feverish, but unaware of the fact, merely filled with a singular, new, boundless feeling of full and powerful lust for life. *This feeling was comparable to that of a man condemned to death who learns suddenly and against hope that he has been pardoned.* . . . What had worked this transformation in him? He himself did not know; but it was clear to him, as to a drowning man clutching at a straw, that he might still live, that there was still life for him, and that his own life was not extinguished with that of the old man.[52]

The sensation of reprieve is experienced also by the roomers among whom Marmeladov had lived. Kaplan comments as follows:

> The roomers of the big house in which Marmeladov lived all appeared, gaping, about the unfortunate man as he was brought home. They "pressed first into the doorway, then came in bright throngs into the room itself." Katherina Ivanovna drove them all away. "The roomers, one after another, pressed out through the door *with that curious inner gratification which one always observes even among those nearest to the victim when misfortune comes unexpectedly to someone else,* and from which absolutely no man is free, notwithstanding his sympathy and compassion." This "curious inner gratification" of which Dostoevsky speaks here is like the "pleasure in tragedy": we feed on others' sorrows.[53]

The roomers, with their shamelessly laughing faces, accept Marmeladov as their "hero," who must come to grief that they may be satisfied: "The 'sinner' is punished, and the public can return to its daily routine." [54]

The theory is persuasive. There cannot, I think, be much doubt that through empathetic self-identification with literary personages the reader can, and does, enjoy fruitions which are denied him

---

[52] *Ibid.*, p. 113.
[53] *Ibid.*, pp. 106–107.
[54] *Ibid.*, p. 107.

in everyday life. The principle applies to comedy as well as to tragedy: a whole theaterful of spectators who are not themselves given to rowdy actions cannot only approve but heartily relish undergraduate rowdiness in a moving picture about college life. Impulses ordinarily inhibited are harmlessly indulged in an aesthetically ordered daydream. In tragedy the impulses given free rein are not harmless; injury results to an imaged social body. Because the spectator's will has assented to the protagonist's rashness, his conscience becomes uneasy. The breach of the moral law demands expiation; hence a scapegoat is offered to the parent-judge-God. When all is finished, the spectator can rise from his seat psychically healthy, "purged" by the discharge of criminal tendencies, reassured that his habitual observance of moral law is the best policy, and once more resigned to unadventurous living. An inference from the theory explains the low state of modern tragedy. The modern protagonist dares too little, stays too timidly within the mores; he is not so much executed as exterminated. His fate is therefore painful, not satisfying. The usual housewife's objection to tragedy, that she "has enough trouble without going to sad movies," thus has a certain cogency after all.

ALFRED WINTERSTEIN.   The second of the three theories, advanced by Alfred Winterstein in *Der Ursprung der Tragödie* (1925), is more elaborately Freudian and, because of its length and complexity, can be summarized here only cursorily. Winterstein begins with a detailed examination of carnival rites still celebrated in various remote areas of Europe and reduces them all to a generally similar pattern, which he then interprets psychoanalytically. The blackened faces of the mummers indicate that daemonic forces in nature are represented. A murderer, who sometimes wears a mask (ultimately derived from the animal and other masks worn by primitive dancers, often in combination with animal skins), is, however, like the bogy man invoked to frighten children, a representative of the ancestors or, more properly, of the terrifying side of the individual father, which arouses death anxiety in the son. In the end, the whole schema is seen to be the familiar one of the father-mother-son. The carnival mummings derive from the aboriginal family group and objectify the son's psychic predicament.[55]

Next follows an analysis of primitive initiation ceremonies, in which there is also regularly death and rebirth; but here the presentation is mainly from the father's point of view. The candidate is brought by the ceremonies into relationship with the tribal spirit by dying and being reborn with a new soul.[]The death ritual, Winterstein thinks, is correctly interpreted by Theodor Reik as an expression of the suppressed hatred of the older men toward their sons, and the rebirth ritual is an outgrowth of the love which accompanies and balances the hatred. The ground of the hatred is fear of incest, which motivates also a retaliatory attack on the sexual organs of the young men (circumcision). [56]

The beginnings of Greek tragedy derive from a celebration in which initiated young men, and perhaps also young men not yet initiated, took leading roles. Such a group would have a strong feeling of group solidarity, increased to magical potency by such rhythmic activities as singing and dancing. The masculine libido would be aroused, and a feeling of identification with the fathers, sought by the wearing of masks and other disguises, would be attained—a process which would involve the obscuring of individual personality.

> The dancers relive in their memory the vicissitudes of death and rebirth, and old feeling-complexes are stirred again. . . . As a result of a psychic distancing which takes place at the same time, the secret process of suffering and regeneration is viewed as something lying outside the individual personality and by a kind of abstraction is connected with the leading dancer, the representative of the youthful group.[57]

The gulf between leader and group may gradually have widened until the leader appeared to the *thíasos* as something mysterious and strange—a god, a supernatural visitant from a different world. When this occurred, a ceremony which once had embodied group

---

[55] Winterstein, *Ursprung der Tragödie*, pp. 46–47.
[56] *Ibid.*, pp. 77–78.
[57] *Ibid.*, p. 181.

wishes and fears would have been sensed as the reflection of an independent external reality. Projection would have given way to "imitation," and the development of tragedy would have begun.[58]

The further tracing of psychological origins must be brief and can be given most economically in quotation.

> In tragedy, which presents the fate of heroes and only exception-ally that of gods, the hero, the successor of the god Dionysus, as a human being, is pulled back nearer to the "ideal observer" (A. W. Schlegel) and to the chorus. . . . The separation of con-scious and unconscious, of moral Censor and forbidden wishes, is carried through more strongly than before. This explains the split in the consciousness of the chorus, which on one side sympathizes with the bold revolt of the hero against the human or divine au-thority, but on the other side is awed by it and warns the hero to tame his pride and to bend himself humbly to the law. The hero is simply a projection of primitive drives, forbidden but none the less felt by the chorus, and not only by it—drives in which the titanic aboriginal wishes of childhood play so meaningful a rôle.[59]

In its role as judge, the chorus assents to the hero's destruction. It is a double of the observer and voices the moral ideas and inhibitions produced by culture but often violated by impulsive desires.

> When the spectator in the Athenian theater not only saw repre-sented on the stage what he unconsciously wished and feared, what caused related, never completely silenced strings to resonate deep within him, but also heard his moral conscience speak through the mouth of the chorus, the double distancing signified a real sav-ing of psychic expenditure, since the feeling of distance did not allow the repugnant identification with the sufferings of the hero to develop, but heightened the illusive character of the drama and —so to speak—by means of a short circuit produced a catharsis of pity and fear.[60]

Here again the analysis eventuates in a conclusion not entirely disharmonious with the traditional Aristotelian doctrine of ca-

---

[58] *Ibid.,* p. 182.
[59] *Ibid.*
[60] *Ibid.,* p. 184.

tharsis, though arrived at by a different route and by no means identical in psychological emphasis.

Winterstein's theory is not applied to modern tragedy, though he comments on the recurrence of a death-and-rebirth pattern in the medieval trope which is supposed to have been the point of departure for modern drama.

> Quem quaeritis in sepulchro, Christicolae?
> Jesum Nazarenum crucifixum, o caelicola.
> Non est hic, surrexit sicut praedixerat.

There is thus a connection of sorts between carnival rites, primitive initiation ceremonies, Greek tragedy, and modern drama. The strongest hint of a general theory of tragedy occurs, however, in a statement which I have purposely omitted from the foregoing summary: "The tragic hero is Dionysus, who took the guilt of his brothers upon himself and absolved them by his own painful death-sacrifice. *Every tragic hero is a scapegoat.*" [61]

With this laconic assertion we prepare to make a transition to the third and final theory to be summarized here. I wish, first, however, to interpose a few remarks in defense of Winterstein's psychoanalytical approach, which to persons unfamiliar with depth psychology—and there are many such even now—may seem strange to the point of absurdity.

The point to be made is the elementary but important one that the unconscious levels of psychic activity, precisely because they are unconscious, tend automatically to be denied by the reason. How, then, is it possible to be sure what subrational associations are or are not made in the unconscious? At another point, Winterstein discusses symbolic values in common stage properties. Phallic symbols can be suspected in the pointed hats of actors, in the swords and whips of policemen, and in arrows. By another analyst, the burlesque comedian in the American theater has been identified as a father symbol, deprived of threat and rendered absurd; his limp cane is an impotent phallus, his broad tie a relaxed scrotum.[62]

---

[61] *Ibid.*, p. 185 (my italics).

[62] Martin Grotjahn, in a Jake Gimbel lecture entitled "Psychoanalytic Remarks about the Comedy, Clowns, and the Circus," delivered at the University of California (Berkeley) on March 3, 1955.

Such views, expressed by men whose profession is the exploration of the subconscious, may not all be sound, but it is unlikely that they are all completely without foundation. The human mind, of course, has no difficulty in finding collateral significances which it can then insist are basic. The assurance in Psalm 126, "They that sow in tears shall reap in joy," is easily interpreted as meaning much the same thing as the Beatitude, "Blessed are they that mourn, for they shall be comforted." The verse will bear such a reading; but, according to an expert, the original meaning was: "Ritual weeping, when done properly, by homeopathic or imitative magic will induce rainfall and good harvests." [63] In the same way, the limp cane of the burlesque comedian can readily be invested— perhaps was invested even by its first user—with a significance easily comprehensible by a consciousness working within its normal range: since the function of a cane is to support weight, limpness is a contradiction of its purpose. Yet, deep below the threshold of consciousness, other identifications or substitutions may be made. If the cane were made suddenly to squirt water, a masculine audience would roar with laughter. Who is to say with confidence that the reason would be the sudden making of an identification and not the bringing to consciousness of an identification already prepared in the unconscious? I do not urge the "rightness" of Winterstein's views; but refutation of them is no easy matter.

HELEN ADOLF.   The third and last theory was proposed by Helen Adolf in "The Essence and Origin of Tragedy," an article printed in the *Journal of Aesthetics and Art Criticism* in 1951.[64] After a rapid enumeration of other theories, she offers the following formula: "Tragedy arose out of human sacrifice; it still is a substitute for it." This view, she claims, "has long been an open secret among poets."

> Goethe wrote: "In der Tragödie geschieht [die Katharsis] durch eine Art Menschenopfer, es mag nun wirklich vollbracht oder unter Einwirking einer günstigen Gottheit durch ein Surrogat gelöst werden, wie im Falle Abrahams und Agamemnons." Jean Girau-

---

[63] Cf. Gaster, *Thespis*, pp. 16–17.
[64] Helen Adolf, "The Essence and Origin of Tragedy," *Journal of Aesthetics and Art Criticism*, X (1951), 112–25.

doux, discussing the theatre of Racine, affirms: "Sur cette scène devenue une espèce d'autel, Racine pouvait devenir sans difficulté le poète qui a le plus rapproché la tragédie du sacrifice humain." Finally, Gerhardt Hauptmann not only called human sacrifice "the bloody root of tragedy," but he went down to those very roots by reviving the horror of such rites in his *Atrides* tetralogy.[65]

We cannot, however, accept an argument from authority but must indicate briefly the nature of Miss Adolf's empirical evidence.

That evidence, like the evidence of many of the scholars cited earlier—Winterstein, Thomson, Gaster, Murray, Harrison, Ridgeway—is drawn from non-European sources as well as European. The old Quichés drama, *Rabinal-Achi*, revived in Guatemala in 1856, includes a ritual slaying. Human sacrifice was occasionally practiced (says Miss Adolf, on authority which she indicates in a footnote) by the Greeks until the time of the Emperor Hadrian; but the Greek mind was uneasy about it, and the avoidance of bloodshed on the Greek stage may have resulted from a wish to forget the barbaric beginnings of a favorite art form.[66] The hypothesis enables us to avoid a difficulty implicit in the view that the roots of tragedy lay in a ritual dramatizing the death and resurrection of the Year Daemon. Such an origin would have produced a sequence of emotions different from that actually embodied in existent tragedies—a curve upward from sorrow to joy, not downward from joy to sorrow. It therefore seems advisable, thinks Miss Adolf, "to interpose, between vegetation-ritual and drama as terminal points, the concept of sacrificing a human victim." This view, moreover, enables us rather to capitalize on than to resist "the modern tendency of abandoning the pure cantata or oratorio theory by stressing the tragical rift already present in the earliest lyrical tragedy.[67] What happened was that the old *drómena* were revivified by coalescence with heroic sagas.

It would be an oversimplification, however, to assume that where a sacrifice had been enacted, a play or image was directly sub-

---

[65] *Ibid.*, pp. 112–13.
[66] *Ibid.*, p. 114.
[67] *Ibid.*, p. 115.

stituted for reality, although a very definite relationship exists between games and funeral sacrifices. Substitution of animal victims (a bull, a goat) probably came first, accompanied by songs and mimetic dances (dithyramb), which commemorated the mythical prototype of the immolation. Then the shift of interest set in, and the threnodies and the trappings pertaining to the cult of the dead were added.[68]

Thus tragedy was created by "the conflict between two opposed forces: the (subconscious) craving for sacrifice, and the (conscious) struggle against it." *Phóbos* and *éleos*, "terror" and "pity," are accordingly not only the effects of tragedy but also its source.[69]

The remainder of Miss Adolf's article is given over to an examination of the implications of her theory. Not all her conclusions need concern us; but her answer to the question, "Is tragedy necessary?" bears on the relevance of her historical views to tragedy of all times and places. Since tragedy is a spontaneous growth hardly anywhere outside Greece, it appears to be unnecessary "that human sacrifice be substituted by a presentation, on the aesthetic level, of the conflict between our conscious and subconscious motivations." [70] Among the ancient Jews, a pact between man and God required only ceaseless obedience and periodical ceremonies of atonement from man. In the Middle Ages, Christ Himself was "the sacrifice to end all sacrifices." Tragedy subsisted in the sacrament of the mass itself. In modern times, there has again been tragedy sufficiently like Greek tragedy to bear comparison with it. A distinction must be made, however: in some plays sacrifices are offered, whereas other plays are "postludes to sacrifice." In the latter type, "serenity prevails, since for both the author and his protagonist the real fight is already over and victory has been won." On the whole, it may be said, "that sacrifice does not invariably evolve into tragedy, but that tragedy and even serious drama cannot do without some kind of sacrifice, either past or present." The reason is that sacrifice is part of the life process

[68] *Ibid.,* p. 116.
[69] *Ibid.,* pp. 117–18.
[70] *Ibid.,* p. 120.

itself: "For life is a combustion, feeding higher entities at the expense of lower ones." We sense this truth and recognize that the life of the spirit "cannot be entrusted to institutions but must be fed again and again by an individual's voluntary act of devotion." [71] In the end, we are reminded of the appearance of the ancient tragic mask, which is at once cruel and humane—something to be approached only rarely, and then with a prayer that the sacrifice may not be in vain.[72]

COMMON ELEMENTS IN THE THEORIES. Although the approaches made by Kaplan, Winterstein, and Adolf differ, the findings possess striking points of similarity. "The tragic hero is the criminal in us; he takes upon himself both our fault and the punishment appointed for us"; "Every tragic hero is a scapegoat"; "Tragedy arose out of human sacrifice; it still is a substitute for it." Obviously, the three writers have arrived at a common insight. Though we may yet have reservations, remembering how much of the historical reconstruction is speculative and how dangerous is the interpretation of unconscious drives, especially at a distance of centuries, still the three discussions have some cumulative force. And corroboration is accessible from many other sources. While the Aristotelian theory that poetry derives from an imitative impulse retains its authority in the academies ("The reason why men enjoy seeing a likeness is, that in contemplating it they find themselves learning or inferring, and saying perhaps, 'Ah, that is he' "), perceptive scholars have again and again noted historical and psychological facts which point to a more complex origin.

As Ridgeway remarks, the orchestra of the Greek theater was said by Pollux always to have contained a *thyméle,* "whether it was a *bema* (a step or platform) or a *bomos* (an altar or a tomb)." The *Etymologicum Magnum,* however, says: "The *thymele* of the theatre bears down to the present day a name derived from the circumstance that upon it the sacrifices are cut up, i.e. the sacrificial victims." [73] Assuming the truth of the tradition, can we create in ourselves an appreciation of why the spectacle of a sacrifice, either

---

[71] *Ibid.,* pp. 120–23.
[72] *Ibid.,* p. 125.
[73] Ridgeway, *Origin of Tragedy,* p. 40.

of a living animal or of a hero impersonated by an actor, should have been spiritually satisfying?

The question has been confronted by Edwin O. James in a book called *Origins of Sacrifice*. The fundamental principle of sacrifice, according to this writer, is always the same: "the giving of life to promote or preserve life, death being merely a means of liberating vitality." The basic significance of the ritual lies

> in the setting free of life for one or more of the following reasons: (a) to augment the power of the god or spirit approached to enable him to perform his beneficent functions on earth; (b) to meet the forces of death and destruction by a fresh outpouring of vital potency, and so to strengthen the worshipper against malign influences, and to "cover" or "wipe out" the transgression; (c) to establish or re-establish a bond of union or covenant with the benevolent powers in order to maintain a vital relationship between the worshipper and the object of worship, and so to gain free communication between the natural and supernatural order.[74]

More simply, in Cassirer's words, "Every widening and heightening of the individual's powers is bound up with a compensating contraction." [75]

Further illumination is offered by Sir James Frazer at the beginning of his volume *The Scapegoat*. The notion (says Frazer) that we can shift our guilt and the sufferings due them to another being is familiar to savages.

> It arises from a very obvious confusion between the physical and the mental, between the material and the immaterial. Because it is possible to shift a load of wood, stones, or what not, from our own back to the back of another, the savage fancies that it is equally possible to shift the burden of his pains and sorrows to another, who will suffer them in his stead.[76]

Hence the endless multiplicity of "unamiable devices" for palming off trouble on someone else described in the four hundred pages

---

[74] Edwin O. James, *Origins of Sacrifice* (London: John Murray, 1933), pp. 256–57.

[75] Cassirer, *Philosophie der Symbolischen Formen*, II, 274.

[76] Sir James George Frazer, *The Golden Bough: A Study in Magic and Religion*, Vol. IX (*The Scapegoat*) (3d ed.; New York: The Macmillan Company, 1935), p. 1.

which follow. Spiritual burdens may be transferred to sticks, stones, or leaves; to images; to animals; or to human beings. The transference may be public or private and may involve all sorts of ludicrous or repulsive techniques—the pegging of sickness into a tree, the burning of a witch on Walpurgis Night, the expelling of a demon in a boat or toy chariot, the sliding of a scapegoat down a long rope in the western Himalayas. In some form, the practice has been traced in virtually every part of the world. The impulse which underlies it is apparently potential in man's biological nature and therefore accessible to everybody by a relaxation of intellectuals controls. We feel we can get out of a hole by *doing something*, by finding a surrogate, by shifting the burden, by making George do it. The mill must be given something to grind, but it will be as well satisfied with barley as with wheat.

The pattern of substitution is very deeply ingrained in human conduct. The infuriated employer can strike a desk instead of the defaulting worker; the homeowner who avoids painting the high eaves may pull a great many weeds in his garden; the teacher who has given bad lectures may make his examination especially difficult. Were it not for such subterfuges, the pressure of responsibilities would often be intolerable. Life cannot always be faced honestly. Our attitudes, moreover, seldom have a purely intellectual basis. Feelings are prior to concepts, and in the best-educated man serenity is as much a matter of balanced drives as of behavior approved by the reason.

Lucretius' view

To all these explanations of the satisfaction derived from tragedy may be added another: a sense of enhanced personal vitality produced by the spectacle of others' suffering. The classical statement of this truth is made at the beginning of the second book of Lucretius' *De rerum natura*. It is sweet, says the poet, when on the great sea the water is buffeted by violent winds, to look from the shore upon the great struggle of another, not because it is a delightful joy that another should be in trouble, but because it is sweet to perceive evils from which you yourself are free.

Suave, mari magno turbantibus aequora ventis,
e terra magnum alterius spectare laborem;
non quia vexari quemquamst iucunda voluptas,
sed quibus ipse malis careas quia cernere suave est.

(II. 1-4.)

In the same way, it is sweet to behold great contests of war set in array on the plains without having any part in the danger. Lucretius was not an unsympathetic man—in some of his verses one feels the pulsation of an almost violent compassion—but he expressed here an enduring psychological truth.

It will be recalled that as Raskolnikov helped carry home the mangled body of Marmeladov, he felt "that he might still live, that there was still life, and that his own life was not extinguished with that of the old man." Similarly, the lodgers who occupied the same house with Marmeladov showed "that curious inner gratification which one always observes even among those nearest to the victim when misfortune comes unexpectedly to someone else." In comparison with Hamlet, whose last breath has promised silence, we feel enormously alive. If we should choose, we could still make considerable noise. The realization is so powerfully borne home, however, that we need do nothing of the sort; in the quiet which follows the cessation of the hero's torments, it would seem brutal to rejoice openly at our own abounding health. Like Nietzsche's tragic spectator, we remain sunk in contemplation, sitting peacefully in a bobbing skiff on an ocean just now swept by a storm.[77] Our reassurance is too deep to need expression.

CORROBORATION FROM THE PRACTICE OF SELF-TORTURE. Only some such view of the relationship of suffering to well-being can account adequately for the widespread practice among primitive races of self-torture, which is by no means limited to experiences of grief. "Orgiastic self-tortures," says Yrjö Hirn, "may be adduced as the most remarkable proofs of this desire for an enhanced sense of life which lies at the bottom of all our appetence";[78] and the remark, although pre-Freudian, has cogency. What more swiftly

---

[77] Friedrich Nietzsche, *Die Geburt der Tragödie aus dem Geiste der Musik* (Leipzig: E. W. Fritzsch, 1872), p. 16.
[78] Yrjö Hirn, *The Origins of Art* (London: Macmillan & Co., Ltd., 1900), p. 64.

than pain can convince us that we exist, that there is blood in our veins and flesh on our bones, that the life which may have begun to seem dull and uninteresting is still precious? One satisfaction produced in spectators by tragedy is thus not wholly different from that obtained by lying in a position which increases the pain from a sore muscle. The effect of both vicarious and physical pain is an enhanced feeling of our own vital reality.

Tragedy and psychic release

A final suggestion may be added: the death of the tragic hero offers the same relief as awakening from a frightening dream. I quote from Otto Rank's *Der Künstler:*

> The desire for the destruction of the hero, for his "death," is comprehensible only through a comparison with the awakening from a heavy dream or with the feeling of joy after recovery from an illness (neurosis). This "death" is sensed by neither the spectator nor the artist as "dying." . . . The hero has died; his "death" is the visibleness of a wish-fulfillment in its highest form.[79]

The nightmare is not sought, and the horrifying events in a good tragedy are "distanced"; but a tragedy which does not evoke feelings of horror cannot produce the satisfaction of relief and therefore lacks the proper tragic effect.

The skein at which we have been pulling is tangled, and I am aware that many knots remain to be untied. The explanations which have been offered are partly contradictory, and if, as I believe likely, there is an element of truth in most, or in several, no doubt their separate roles can never be fully explicated. It is apparent, however, that no aesthetic theory which regards literature as primarily cognitive can account for its psychological function. Tragedy offers not only a clarification of problems (nothing that has been said is meant to imply that tragedy is *merely* affective), but also a psychic release. Like all art forms, it appeals not only to reason but also to something deeper. If it does not—if it leads to a conviction merely that nineteenth-century German weavers

---

[79] Quoted by Winterstein, *Ursprung der Tragödie*, p. 166 n.

were mistreated, or that the shoddy airplane parts manufactured by a wartime profiteer may lead to a death in his own family, or that Americans have had "the wrong dream"—it "proves" points that could be recommended powerfully to the intelligence by reasoned treatises. Of course Gerhart Hauptmann's *Die Weber* and Arthur Miller's *All My Sons* and *Death of a Salesman* do more than recommend these convictions. At present, however, responsible criticism prefers the analysis of cognitive meanings to the exploration of affective significance. By doing so, it emasculates art and reduces it to a single one of its aspects. The damage is not rectified by chanting "Affective fallacy!" to justify the narrowing of critical scope.

If the foregoing account of tragedy has been even approximately accurate, common assumptions about the genre need revision. True, concerning the details of the historical development there is not now, and perhaps never will be, settled agreement. George Thomson's *Aeschylus and Athens* undertook to synthesize a large body of discoveries and interpretative hypotheses accessible to the classicist about 1940; Mario Untersteiner's *Le Origini della tragedia e del tragico,* reprinted in 1955 but first circulated in Italy during the war, offers a less schematic view on the principle that "la spiritualità greca si presenta come una sintesi, instabile e in continuo fermento, di un travaglio svoltosi nel corso di secoli e secoli." [80] I am acquainted, however, with no really scholarly refutation of Aristotle's assertion that tragedy had a religious source. (It "originated with the leaders of the dithyramb.") Even though the specific history proposed above contains errors of detail, I do not think that the general hypothesis is likely to be invalidated by them. In the same way, the claim that tragedy has maintained fairly steadily a vitalizing contact with its past can be made confidently despite the virtual impossibility of analyzing correctly what goes on beneath the threshold of consciousness in writer, actor, or spectator. No purely cognitive account of what happens in *Lear* or *A Streetcar Named Desire* exhausts our response to the play.

---

[80] Mario Untersteiner, *Le Origini della tragedia e del tragico* (Torino: Einaudi Editore, 1955), p. 19.

If we do not, as we watch and listen, feel a satisfaction analogous, if only at a distance, to that felt by the primitive Greek at the consummation of a blood sacrifice, some other deep-lying stratum of the psyche is invaded. At such points as this, the literary theorist can afford to display a generosity denied to the purely historical critic. It is one of his few sustaining comforts on a journey across treacherous ground.

Archaic tendencies in comedy

In the remainder of the present chapter, I intend to suggest, more briefly, that what is true of tragedy is true also of comedy: that here, too, there is continuity with a transcended and forgotten past. The danger of error will be even greater, for, in proportion as the discussion is compact, data are certain to be excluded. Yet I can attempt to indicate, by a series of controlled hints, that an archaizing literary tendency appears also in the second major variety of drama.

Recurrent comic elements: cheerfulness

Comedy includes at least three separable elements, not all of which need appear in any single play. The first is cheerfulness. If based on organic euphoria—a simple consciousness of vitality superior to inconvenience or temporary frustration—cheerfulness tends to express itself in sheer exuberance of language and incident, as in the comedies of Ben Jonson. Here the exposition of every idea or feeling explodes with the energy of fireworks, so that the vitality of language far exceeds that of the concept, and the generation of stratagem by stratagem bespeaks a fecundating principle in life itself. If based on cosmic optimism, the mood reveals itself, more soberly, in the manipulating of the plot toward a final gratification of desires. In either event, the total effect is that of fulfillment, hence cheerfulness. The life principle shows itself stronger than the death principle, and the spectator leaves the theater heartened for the resumption of his daily responsibilities.

Cheerfulness, so defined, is continuous with a drive toward fulfillment institutionalized in the ceremony in which the Old Comedy of the Greeks had its beginnings. According to Aristotle, comedy originated with the leaders of phallic songs, which themselves were clearly parts of a ceremony meant to reinvoke fertility in fields, animals, and men. "Invigoration," says Theodor Gaster of Near Eastern cultures, in *Thespis,* "is also effected by rites involving sexual intercourse"; [81] and the continuity between Greek comedy and rituals in which the phallus was carried about on a long pole is indicated by the artificial phalli worn by comedians represented on Greek vases and friezes.[82] Such celebrations tend to be un-inhibited, even wildly orgiastic; they are accompanied by a relaxa-tion of normal restraints analogous to, but often far exceeding, the license of the modern pre-Lenten carnival. Mating is therefore implicit in the situation from which comedy arose and even today is basic to the typical comic plot. Benjamin Harrison Lehman writes:

> Never in comedy are we without love, and almost never without lovers. . . . The elements, within and around lovers, which stand in the way of their fulfilling themselves and their biological func-tion, are in comedy usually treated with sympathetic derision. It is folly to oppose this compulsion to mate, and what opposes prop-erly falls under a derisive light.[83]

A recent dramatist has expressed the same insight: "When you write for the theatre you must choose between your version of a phallic revel and your vision of what mankind may or should become." Early Greek comedy "was dedicated to the spirits of lust and riot and earth, spirits which are certainly necessary to the health and continuance of the race"; and musical comedy (together, I may add, with old-fashioned American burlesque) is

---

[81] Gaster, *Thespis,* p. 24.

[82] For a rich collection of these and other illustrations, see Margarete Bieber, *The History of the Greek and Roman Theater* (Princeton, N.J.: Princeton Uni-versity Press, 1939).

[83] Benjamin Harrison Lehman, "Comedy and Laughter," in *Five Gayley Lec-tures, 1947–1954* (Berkeley, Calif.: University of California Press, 1954), pp. 82–83.

"simply our approximation of the Bacchic rites of Old Comedy." [84]
Whether or not combined with coruscating energy of language,
which adds to the gratification of vicarious mating the sensation
of vitality in a joyous proliferation of ideas and images, a mood
of cheerfulness thus dominates much comedy. Obstacles are overcome, resistance subjugated or eluded, inhibitions denied, cautions
ignored, and desire triumphantly satisfied. The most direct assertion
of animal high spirits may have appeared in Old Comedy, which
was nearest to the actual phallic ritual; but through the centuries
comedy has glorified the satisfaction of appetite.

SATIRE. A second recurrent element in comedy is satire. This
is so pervasive that at times it has quite usurped critical attention.
According to Aristotle, the "characters of a lower type" imitated
in comedy suffer from "some defect or ugliness which is not painful
or destructive." Such personages are easy targets for ridicule; and
both Old and New Comedy, in Greece, joyfully exploited the
satirical opportunities. For Aristotle comedy was, in fact, the same
thing as satire; the "more trivial sort" of writers who later wrote
comedies at first wrote satires, and the iambic measure used in
such compositions was the "lampooning measure." The assumption caught on; for Sir Philip Sidney, "comedy is an imitation of
the common errors of our life, which [the poet] representeth, in
the most ridiculous and scornefull sort that may be"; for George
Meredith, the "volleys of silvery laughter" inspired by comedy
result from the "humanely malign" glance of a writer at persons
who are "overblown, affected, pretentious, bombastical, hypo-
critical, pedantic, fantastically delicate," or otherwise absurd. Lehman was so impressed by the consensus, which he believed to be
mistaken, that he remarked, "The student of literature, reviewing
what has been written about comedy, may well be dismayed. For
what has been written about the subject is, except for incidental
insights, not about comedy. It is about satire." [85] The comedy of

---

84 Maxwell Anderson, "The Essence of Tragedy," in B. H. Clark (ed.), *European Theories of the Drama, with a Supplement on the American Drama* (rev.
ed.; New York: Crown Publishers, Inc., 1947), pp. 548 and 547.
85 Lehman, *op. cit.*, p. 81.

Molière was prevailingly satirical; so also, in spite of the astonishing energy that has been noted, was that of Ben Jonson, at least in intent. The miser, the hypocrite, the unsympathetic father are recognized comic types, although not intrinsically "funny." From one angle of vision, it appears that the essence of comedy is ridicule.

The satirical impulse, like the organic self-indulgence already discussed, has an immemorial ancestry. Primitives as well as modern men feel it. The enemy, the rival, the shamed woman or warrior are made the butts of derisive songs. G. Schweinfurth reports a *Spottlied* sung by African pigmies over the severed head of an enemy: "Bakinda, where is he? Bakinda is in the pot!" Among the Eskimos, quarrels are sometimes settled by competitive insults, the songs being accompanied by drumbeats, while an audience weighs the comparative skill of the singers:

> I was afraid when I heard that you wanted to challenge me to a drum-song! ah-ya-ya!—You wanted to challenge me to a drum-song, since I am alone, and you thought I was unskillful! ka-na-ya-ya!—Oh how forgetful you are! It is very bad to be so forgetful, ha-va-ya. Do you not remember the time when you had no one to live with and we took you into our house?

An Omaha sings of his aging sweetheart, "Pfui! I look on you as on my grandmother! I am disgusted." [86] The examples are typical. "It is characteristic of all the lower peoples," says Grosse, "that they take a particular pleasure in satirical songs." The mockery is often rude and base, as among children. "We met a troop of children one day before the gateway of a school in Berlin who were pursuing a little lame girl with the mocking song:

> Ho! ho! ho!
> Anna has a wooden leg.
> Ho! ho! ho!
>
> Oh, what a leg, oh, what a leg,
> You kangaroo-footed churl!

---

[86] For the examples, see Heinz Werner, *Die Ursprünge der Lyrik* (Munich: Ernst Reinhardt, 1924), p. 20.

sang the Australians on King George's Sound." [87] The roots of satire go very deep, like the roots of the other literary techniques we have studied. It is true that the songs just cited are lyrics, not passages from comedies; but the psychic drive behind them shares something with the drive behind satirical comedy. The desire of the ethical consciousness to correct and reform abuses, like the wish of the primitive mind to assert personal superiority by shaming another, has the affective tonality of attack from a safe distance; and the enjoyment of this feeling is a permanent possibility for human beings.

SERIOUSNESS. The third element in comedy—like the first two, pervasive though not omnipresent—is seriousness. Comedy is not always trivial; perhaps it is so only in proportion as it is weak and ephemeral, the perfume of an hour, not a burnt offering to permanent human attitudes. Lehman says:

> Though we laugh at actions and utterances in comedy, we do not laugh at the comedy as a whole. For the comedy as a whole is a serious work, making an affirmation about life that chimes with our intuitive sense of how things are and with our deep human desire to have the necessary and agreeable prevail.[88]

There is a deep truth in the assertion. Comedy is not, as Hollywood and the television industry believe, mere entertainment. It is re-creation, reinvigoration, rebirth.

Comedy and ritual drama: Francis M. Cornford's analysis

For an understanding of this seriousness, let us once again look back to primitive origins. A convenient "authority" will be Francis M. Cornford, whose *The Origin of Attic Comedy,* though published in 1914 and, like all literary anthropology, vigorously disputed, seems not to have been superseded. We cannot pause to weigh the difference between more and less controversial statements, but must entrust ourselves to the guidance of one among

---

[87] Grosse, *Beginnings of Art,* p. 246.
[88] Lehman, *op. cit.,* p. 82.

many specialists. At the beginning of his researches, Cornford accepted "the current view that Aristophanic Comedy is a patchwork of elements loosely pieced together, and in origin possibly foreign to one another." A closer study convinced him, however, that the view was "almost totally mistaken." Instead, the comedy of Aristophanes emerged from ritual drama: the same drama, surprisingly, "as that in which Professor Gilbert Murray has sought the origin of Tragedy"; [89] and the evidence of such an origin is stronger for comedy than for tragedy.[90] Behind both is the figure of "the dying God whose defeat is a victory, the ironical Buffoon whose folly confounds the pretence of wisdom"—Dionysus, whose cult was both orgiastic and deeply pious.[91] The divergence of tragedy and comedy resulted from the separation of two strains in the rituals, one having the affect of fulfillment, the other the affect of frustration. Each, however, had its serious side. Neither was merely fun, merely entertainment.[92]

Though space is limited, it will be well if the discussion is concrete. The structure of Aristophanic comedy, the earliest that can be studied, is as follows. First comes the *párados,* or entrance of the chorus; secondly, there is an *agón,* "a fierce 'contest' between the representatives of two parties or principles, which are in effect the hero and villain of the whole piece"; next is the *parábasis,* a long and completely undramatic speech delivered by the chorus, standing with its back to the scene of action and addressing the audience directly, all the actors having left the stage; finally there is more action, ending in a festal procession, the *éxodos* or *kômos,* and a union which Cornford calls the "marriage." As Thomson notes in *Aeschylus and Athens,* except for the *parábasis* "this is the sequence we have already identified as the substructure of tragedy"; so it is evident to him, as to Cornford, that "The two artforms go back to a common origin." [93] Cornford's thesis, italicized

---

[89] Francis MacDonald Cornford, *The Origin of Attic Comedy* (London: Edward Arnold & Co., 1914), p. vii.

[90] *Ibid.,* p. 190.

[91] *Ibid.,* p. viii.

[92] Cornford suggests that a difference of emphasis "was already present, at the religious stage, among the various local forms of the ritual." See *ibid.,* pp. 212–13.

[93] Thomson, *Aeschylus and Athens,* p. 242.

for emphasis, is *"that this canonical plot-formula preserves the stereotyped action of a ritual or folk drama, older than literary Comedy, and of a pattern well known to us from other sources."* [94] The *párados* is easily recognized as equivalent to the tragic *pompé,* and the *kômos* as the tragic *éxodos.* Between the two, in both tragedy and comedy, comes the *agón.* We are left, therefore, with the *parábasis,* which requires special examination.

Cornford's explanation of the *parábasis,* briefly, is that it developed out of a formal gap left in the ritual when a contest of abuse, which at one time accompanied the *agón,* replaced it. The chorus was originally the audience itself; when rite, which needs no audience, became spectacle, the spontaneous utterances of worshipers not directly engaged in the ceremonial actions were absorbed into the comments of a formalized group standing between actors and spectators. During the aboriginal combat, the sympathies of spectator-participants would have been divided; each of the antagonists would have had his partisans, who would have encouraged him and jeered at his opponent. Hence the curious doubling of the comic chorus and its division into two groups, which sometimes wore different masks. Later, however, although preserving traces of dramatic action, the *agón* itself tended to become debate (the ancestor of the medieval *débat*); and the chorus then partly lost its function. In compensation, it turned to abuse of the audience. This abuse, in combination with an anapestic prologue, constitutes the *parábasis.*[95] The degree to which the explanation is satisfactory must be decided by specialists; but the reconstruction is not implausible.

The comic *agón* itself Cornford believes to have sprung from the phallic ceremonies alluded to by Aristotle. These ceremonies appear to have had three main parts:

> (1) The procession of the worshippers of Phales [a barely personified phallus] moves on its way, carrying the emblem of the God on a pole and the instruments of sacrifice. (2) It pauses at some fixed place for the sacrifice, accompanied by a prayer to Dionysus.

---

[94] Cornford, *Attic Comedy,* p. 3.
[95] For Cornford's discussion, which contains much that I have been unable to summarize, see *ibid.,* chap. vi, pp. 105–31, esp. p. 129.

(3) The procession moves on again singing the Phallic Song. . . . In the *Agon* which regularly precedes the *Parabasis* we now have come to see the equivalent of the sacrifice which precedes the Phallic Song. The *Agon* is the beginning of the sacrifice in its primitive dramatic form—the conflict between the good and evil principles, Summer and Winter, Life and Death.

In Aristophanic comedy some elements of the sacrifice—notably the cooking and communal eating of the dismembered agonist— have been transferred to the second comic plot, which appears between the *parábasis* and the *kômos* or *éxodos*.[96] The first plot, however, is lineally descended from the ritual slaying of the Dionysian *pharmakós,* or "scapegoat."

The structural element which Cornford named the "marriage" is also, he believes, residual from serious worship, though worship not without a strong Bacchic ingredient. In the *kômos* or *éxodos* the chorus conducts the chief character triumphantly from the orchestra, singing as it does so. The hero, in Aristophanes, is accompanied by a curious figure who is nearly always mute—a nameless courtesan or, again, an allegorical personification. She exists solely for the purpose of becoming the hero's temporary partner "in what is, in fact though not always in the legal sense, a marriage." [97] This is the more to be wondered at because, in Aristophanic comedy, the hero is usually a grown man already provided not only with a wife but with children, and the plots have no love interest whatever. Since the marriage is structurally nonfunctional, it must be ritual in character, "the survival of one moment in a ritual action older than any form of comic literature." [98] The bride and bridegroom, in fact, represent divine beings who, through sexual union, promote terrestrial fertility; they are "the Earth-mother and the Heaven-father, whose rain falls in a life-giving stream into the womb of Earth." [99] Since the Aristophanic protagonist sometimes, or possibly always, wore an artificial

[96] *Ibid.,* p. 103.
[97] *Ibid.,* p. 8.
[98] *Ibid.,* p. 18.
[99] *Ibid.,* p. 19.

phallus, it is not difficult to infer that the comic hero was originally either Dionysus or Phales, the personified phallus itself.[100]

One additional point may be made. We have seen in our examination of tragedy that the Dionysian sacrifice culminated in a *sparagmós,* or "rending," of the victim, whose members were then distributed and eaten. In Cornford's opinion, the scattering of such sweetmeats as figs and nuts to the lower tiers of spectators, hinted at in the *Plutus,* the *Peace,* and the *Ecclesiazusae,* may have been a survival of an earlier ritual intended to spread the divine benefits to the whole community.[101]

OTHER EVIDENCE. All this evidence and much more—for example, the obvious relationship between satyr dances and the savage *Tiertanz,* performed by persons dressed as animals—suggests a very strong probability that comedy indeed derived from religious ritual and preserved many ceremonial forms at a relatively advanced stage of development. Jessie Weston, in *From Ritual to Romance,* has noted a statement by a Christian bishop of the early part of the third century, Hippolytus of Portus, to the effect that, according to the Naassenes, a performer comes on the stage "clad in a robe different from all others, with lute in hand on which he plays, and thus chants the Great Mysteries, not knowing what he says." [102] It thus appears that some recognition of the ritual origins of drama was preserved well into the Christian era. Although the strength of the ritual influence must have declined progressively, the essential conservatism of literature resulted in the retention of many elements of form. For instance, the original set of stock comic masks consisted of those required for the performance of a set ritual; but, as the mystery lost status, the impersonated characters gradually became grotesque. The antagonist, *qua* villain, became contemptuous; the medicine man who previously had resuscitated the dead king became a humbug doctor, a quack whose speels were gibberish; and so on. In a similar way, Pontius Pilate, whose role in the Easter drama is basically serious, became a comic

---

[100] *Ibid.,* pp. 19–20.
[101] *Ibid.,* pp. 100–102.
[102] Jessie L. Weston, *From Ritual to Romance* (Cambridge: University Press, 1920), p. 147.

personage in the medieval mysteries.[103] Once having become the butt of ridicule, such a character as the doctor tended to become a comic fixture; he appears not only in the English mumming plays but also, repeatedly, in Molière. In literature there can hardly be creation *ex nihilo*. Each writer starts with ideas and images either inherited as biological potentiality or absorbed through acculturation. In either event, his materials are in large part those of his predecessors; and his formal combinations of them are less original than he may try to believe.

---

[103] Cornford, *Attic Comedy*, pp. 201–2.

7

The Major Literary Types: Epic and Lyric Poetry

Antiquity of Greek epic

When we pass from drama to epic, we encounter formal tendencies that in Greece, if not everywhere, were more ancient still. If Cassirer, among others, was right in thinking that "myth is the *epic* element in primitive religious life; rite is the *dramatic* element," [1] the ultimate origins of the two are identical; but Greek epic attained an aesthetically sophisticated development well in advance of drama. Aristotle clearly recognized drama as

---

[1] Ernst Cassirer, *The Myth of the State* (New Haven, Conn.: Yale University Press, 1946), p. 28.

derivative. Homer's *Margites,* he says, "bears the same relation to Comedy that the Iliad and Odyssey do to Tragedy"; and "the Epic poets were succeeded by Tragedians." [2] In general, Greek tragedy drew its materials from heroic saga: the Homeric poems together with shorter epics or lays like the *Cypria* and the *Little Iliad.*[3] But the meters of tragedy appear to have been taken from the sung or chanted lyric,[4] which, as we shall see later, has some claim to being the oldest literary form of all. On the whole, it will be sufficiently accurate to regard epic as immensely ancient. Common sense would suggest that stories must have been told, with or without meter, before they were acted out. Common sense, however, is an unsafe guide. In some parts of the world, group gestures, either accompanied by ritual words from the beginning or gradually fitted out with them, may have become formalized into art in advance of the tales told by individuals in front of campfires or in shady resting places.

Epic as Heldensage

Epic as we know it may or may not be continuous with cosmological myths similar to those which have been discovered in most of the primitive cultures studied by anthropologists. If continuous, such epics as the *Iliad* and the *Odyssey* resulted from a partial humanization of legends once wholly divine; but the possibility is by no means negligible that historical occurrences, involving real human beings, were gradually mythologized. Again, of course, both processes may have gone on at once and become inextricably mixed. In any event, the typical Western epic is basically a *Heldensage.*

> Here it is no longer a matter of the fate of sun and moon; here, instead, is the *hero,* and in him the individual man is discovered as acting and suffering subject. . . . As on one side the hero, the

---

[2] Aristotle, *Poetics* 4. 9, 10 (S. H. Butcher's translation).

[3] Cf. Margarete Bieber, *The History of the Greek and Roman Theater* (Princeton, N.J.: Princeton University Press, 1939), p. 4: "Drama, then, derives its material from the epic, that is from heroic saga, which remained always, with few exceptions, the subject-matter of Greek and Roman tragedy." Cf. also Aristotle, *Poetics* 23. 3, 4.

[4] Cf. Bieber, *Greek and Roman Theater,* p. 4.

human personality, appears raised into the circle of the godly, so on the other the gods are intimately involved in the circle of human happenings, in which they take part not as mere spectators, but as warriors and fellow-strugglers.[5]

The heroes live in a legendary past, not in the present. They often have divine forebears and frequently receive divine aid, yet they may be connected with specific localities (as Achilles with Thessaly, and Agamemnon with Argolis) and be claimed as ancestors by living persons. In abilities also they stand between ordinary men and gods. They can, perhaps, throw stones heavier than a dozen modern men could lift, and in all their actions they are more than life-sized; but although the beneficiaries of miracles they work no miracles themselves, and although godlike they are distinctly not gods. Such is the character not only of the Greek heroes but also of the Roman Aeneas, the Teutonic Beowulf and Siegfried, the Frankish Roland, and even the Miltonic Adam. In a more remote past still, the recitation of legends may sometimes have had a magical or religious purpose.[6] For our ends, however, it will suffice to begin with the *Iliad* and *Odyssey* as the earliest poems in a still-living—if now obsolescent—Western tradition.[7]

Dating of the Homeric poems

When were the Homeric poems composed? The question is important, since it bears on the antiquity of the Western tradition and thus, necessarily, on the inclusion in the tradition of "primitive" elements; but unfortunately it cannot be answered either directly or with precision. Several reasonably trustworthy conclusions have emerged, however, from a century or more of painstaking investigation.

The *terminus a quo* is the date of the Trojan War, or whatever

---

[5] Ernst Cassirer, *Philosophie der Symbolischen Formen,* Vol. II (Berlin: Bruno Cassirer Verlag, 1925), p. 243.

[6] Cf. Heinz Werner, *Die Ursprünge der Lyrik* (Munich: Ernst Reinhardt, 1924), p. 39: "So sehen wir, wie die *Epik* in rein magisch-*lyrischem* Sinne (dem Gefühls-Willenmotiv entsprechend) verwendet wird," etc.

[7] E. M. W. Tillyard is undoubtedly right, however, in suggesting that the modern novel is the successor of metrical epic. See *The English Epic and Its Background* (New York: Oxford University Press, 1954), *passim*.

historical event may have been metamorphosed into it. The ancients themselves were inclined to date the war in or near the years 1195–1185 B.C. On the basis of archaeological evidence, including excavations of the presumed site of Troy (Hissarlik VI), the ascription is entirely satisfactory; the Mycenaean culture seems to have been breaking up at about that time, and the siege described by Homer may well have been an incident in the disintegration.[8] The *terminus ad quem* ought apparently to be put in the sixth century, when Peisistratus—or Solon, or Hipparchus—is said to have ordered Homer's poems to be collected; but, in fact, such writers as Lycurgus and Isocrates, in the fourth century, speak rather vaguely of the origin of rhapsodic recitation at the Panathenaeic festival as having been ordained by "the fathers" (οἱ πατέρες) or "the ancestors" (τοὺς προγόνους) and perhaps knew no more than that the custom had existed in the fifth century.[9]

Illiteracy of the Greek Dark Ages

The actual composition of the *Iliad* and the *Odyssey* must in all probability, then, have been a work of the period between, roughly, 1200 and 550 B.C., or a little later. Before the question *when* can be asked, however, it is necessary to consider *how;* for the greater part of this period was illiterate. The Dark Age which followed the dissolution of the elaborate Mycenaean culture—imposing relics of which are still to be seen at Mycenae, Cnossus, Pylos, and elsewhere [10]—was so complete that our knowledge of

---

[8] Erich Bethe has argued, however, that the Homeric war actually was fought on the Greek mainland. See *Die Sage vom Troischen Kriege,* Vol. III of *Homer: Dichtung und Sage* (Leipzig: B. G. Teubner, 1927). Rhys Carpenter, in *Folk Tale, Fiction, and Saga in the Homeric Epics* (Berkeley, Calif.: University of California Press, 1946), has suggested that Homer's battles may include memories of an unsuccessful Achaean raid on Egypt and possibly also of an Aeolic defeat of Etruscans at Pergamon-Teuthrania. See chap. iii, esp. pp. 60–67.

[9] Cf. C. M. Bowra, *Tradition and Design in the Iliad* (Oxford: Clarendon Press, 1930), p. 41; also J. A. Davison, "Peisistratus and Homer," *Transactions and Proceedings of the American Philological Association,* LXXXVI (1955), 1–21.

[10] For an early, but rich, collection of photographs, see Engelbert Drerup, *Homer: Die Anfänge der hellenischen Kultur* (Munich: Kirchheim'sche Verlagsbuchhandlung, 1903).

it depends entirely on archaeology and legend. Not a single scrap of writing has been preserved from a period lasting several centuries.

This is surprising, since writing was in use among the Mycenaean Greeks. The script known to scholars as "Linear B," when deciphered only a few years ago (it proved to be not alphabetical but syllabic), was discovered, however, to have preserved merely "inventories, lists, military operation-orders and identification marks." [11] Apparently it had been mastered by only a limited number of professional scribes, who used it in the service of a highly bureaucratic central government addicted to the keeping of records. After the Mycenaean order had disintegrated, such records ceased to be kept, and knowledge of the syllabary was lost. The single reference to writing in the Homeric poems is bafflingly and perhaps intentionally vague, as if letters, although known by rumor, were believed to have magical power.[12] There is thus inferential evidence that the poet Homer may himself have felt for writing an awe something like that of the savage who learns that white men can enclose words in bits of paper.

Homer and oral composition

This conclusion will be resisted, for the belief in unitary authorship of the poems dies hard, and the composition by an illiterate bard of works which extend to several hundred pages even in close modern print seems impossible. If by "composition" we mean the determination of a single invariable text and not merely the development of an ability to extemporize, on demand, poems about a more or less predetermined series of incidents,[13] the establish-

---

[11] For the remark, see Sir Maurice Bowra, *Homer and His Forerunners* (Edinburgh: Thomas Nelson and Sons, Ltd., 1955), p. 2. For a detailed account of the script and its uses, see Michael Ventris and John Chadwick, *Documents in Mycenaean Greek* (Cambridge: University Press, 1956).

[12] Cf. *Iliad* vi. 168–70: King Proitus, wishing to cause Bellerophon's death, "gave him tokens of woe, graving in a folded tablet many deadly things, and bade him shew these to Anteia's father, that he might be slain." The translation is by Andrew Lang, Walter Leaf, and Ernest Myers and is now published by Random House, Inc.

[13] Cf. the description, in Joyce Cary's *Mister Johnson,* of an African Negro poet who gained fame for a poem which, however, he never recited twice in the same form.

ment of Homer's illiteracy implies the denial of unitary authorship; unless, of course, we attempt to imagine that some single recitation was painfully taken down by scribes. For our present purposes, however, the matter is relatively unimportant. Homer—by whom we shall mean henceforth whatever person or persons originated the *Iliad* and *Odyssey* that we know—whether literate, partly literate, or wholly illiterate, composed by an oral method, not like a modern writer who can make an unlimited number of corrections in a tentative draft.

What this means has been described by an American scholar, Milman Parry, in two brilliant monographs which have been given an extraordinarily enthusiastic reception by scholars.[14] Rhys Carpenter spoke no more extravagantly than others when he called Parry's arguments "unanswerable and unassailable" and added that the truth of his conclusions "abides almost as surely as Euclid's demonstrations." [15] The nature of the oral technique is implied by the Greek word *rhapsodós*, which means "song-stitcher": [16] the poet strung together traditional epic formulas, of which he had memorized hundreds or thousands, in such a way as to form a continuous narrative. There were such formulas for every part of the verse—the beginning, the end, the middle—so contrived, as the result of generations of manipulation by professional bards, as to be susceptible of easy combination. Whole blocks of ready-made lines were no doubt also a part of the rhapsodic stock in trade. "The genius of Homer," says Parry, "displayed itself in the expression of traditional ideas by means of equally traditional expressions." [17] Homer did not invent; he put together. He might, perhaps, at times venture on the substitution of a new word in an old phrase, provided it fitted metrically, but his use even of this liberty appears to have been sparing. The literary treasure genera-

---

[14] Milman Parry, *Les Formules et la métrique d'Homère* and *L'Épithète traditionelle dans Homère* (both published Paris: Société d'Éditions "Les Belles Letters," 1928). Although an American, Parry took his degree in France.
[15] Carpenter, *Folk Tale, Fiction, and Saga*, p. 6.
[16] *Ibid.*, p. 15.
[17] Parry, *Les Formules*, p. 23.

tions of readers have found in his poems is a rich accumulation of small coins.

ARCHAIC FORMULAS. The point is worth illustrating, since its full import cannot be grasped in an instant. In the *Odyssey* Odysseus is called ταλασίφρων (patient, long-suffering) twelve times, but *only in the genitive;* he is called μεγαλήτωρ (great-hearted, magnanimous) six times, but only in the dative and accusative (three times each).[18] The formulas were restricted not only as to diction and word-order, but often also as to case. Again, Homer is so content to accept the "regular" epithets that he uses them even in situations where they are not suitable: ships are "swift" even when drawn up on the beach, the sky is "starry" by day as well as by night, a mother is "lady mother" even when the son in question is the beggar Irus.[19] The modern reader is likely to perceive a fine irony in such passages or to justify them as deepening the poem's perspective in time; and certainly, when it is said that Castor and Pollux are "laid in the life-giving earth" (*Iliad* ii. 243-44), it is hard to believe that the irony was both unintentional and unnoticed. On the whole, however, the preservation of traditional epithets in contexts where they may appear ironic is probably due less to genius than to willing acceptance of such ready-made phrases as were at hand. When poets become literate, they vary the regular description oftener: as Bowra has pointed out, the fifth-century poet Antimachus speaks differently of the pouring of wine on seven different occasions.[20] In Homeric epic, we have to do with a poetry which was astonishingly traditional, not only in subject matter but also in diction and syntax.

It follows directly from what has been said that "Homer" is older than the man Homer—that, in fact, nearly every detail of the *Iliad* and *Odyssey* is in some degree archaic. If this is so, the actual date at which the poems were set down in writing has less to do with their age than has usually been thought. At present, there seems to be a tendency to date the extant poems from the eighth

---

18 Parry, *L'Épithète traditionelle,* p. 239.
19 I draw the examples from Bowra, *Homer and His Forerunners,* p. 2.
20 *Ibid.,* p. 11.

century or even later.[21] Most of the elements, however, are older, and some may go back almost to Mycenaean times. Some of the archaic forms were perhaps Mycenaean, but survived because "they were essential parts of formulae which would be destroyed if they were brought up to date, and the formulae were sufficiently important to be worth preserving." [22] The metrical form itself may have developed in Mycenaean times, when the Greek language had more uncontracted vowels than later and therefore fell more naturally into dactyls.[23] By Aristotle's period, the iambic measure was at least in Attica, "of all measures, the most colloquial" (*Poetics* iv. 14). At any rate, the Homeric poems evidently grew during the course of several centuries by a process of gradual accretion; so the reply to the question about *how* virtually deprives the question about *when* of meaning. If we are right in concluding that virtually all Homer's phrases, as well as most of his incidents, *came down to him* through an oral tradition, the poems' antiquity does not depend on a year to which the establishment of an authoritative text is assigned. We should remember that the early Greek bard places responsibility for his poetry on the Muses, who, in a phrase of Hesiod's, were "the daughters of Memory." [24]

TRADITIONAL INCIDENTS.   When we turn to the content of the poems, we find that this was as traditional as the phraseology. We may begin by noticing examples of overlapping and contradictory traditions. The story of Odysseus' self-revelation to Penelope and her suitors at the end of the *Odyssey* seems to have existed in at least two pre-Homeric versions, in one of which Penelope learned the identity of her beggarly visitor in time to help him take revenge on the suitors, whereas in the other she did not. Again, in one version Odysseus apparently was not at once recognized, because Athena had changed his appearance, whereas in another he was

---

[21] Carpenter, in *Folk Tale, Fiction, and Saga,* decides on the second quarter of the seventh century for the *Iliad* (pp. 179–80) and the last quarter for the *Odyssey* (p. 101). His opinion seems to be shared by the majority of recent scholars; cf., e.g., Cedric Whitman, *Homer and the Heroic Tradition* (Cambridge, Mass.: Harvard University Press, 1958), p. 85.

[22] Bowra, *Homer and His Forerunners,* p. 33.

[23] *Ibid.*, pp. 35–36.

[24] Cf. Gilbert Murray, *The Rise of the Greek Epic* (Oxford: Clarendon Press, 1907), p. 94.

disguised merely by his rags and the changes wrought by twenty years of warring and hardship. Traces of both versions—or of all four, if they are not interconnected—appear in Homer and confuse the alert reader. Did Penelope arrange the trial of archery merely to discourage the suitors, or did she do so to permit her returned husband to declare himself by succeeding? How, if Athena had withered Odysseus' flesh, made waste his yellow hair, aged his skin, and dimmed his eyes (end of Book xiii), could he display goodly and great thighs, broad shoulders, and mighty arms, so that the wooers were amazed, when he prepared to wrestle with the beggar Irus (Book xviii)? [25] The probability is that incompatible versions were awkwardly combined. But this implies alternative traditions worked out by earlier groups of rhapsodes.

Märchen *elements*

Still further back than the variant traditions lie, among other things, certain *Märchen* elements, often so disguised as to suggest a long effort at rationalization. Rhys Carpenter has written of these at length in *Folk Tale, Fiction, and Saga in the Homeric Epics.* The Circe story, he conjectures, has been transferred to a rocky Mediterranean island from an original forest setting.

> "Hearken now unto my words," says Odysseus . . . , "we know not where is darkness nor where is dawn, nor where the sun, who lightens mortals, goes under earth nor yet where he moves aloft." No Grecian mariner on the midland sea could thus have lost his celestial bearings. These are the words of a landsman wandering vaguely in great dark woods.[26]

In the usual form of the tale, the witch's house is sighted from a tall tree, or a helpful animal leads the way. Odysseus sees smoke from a craggy eminence, but then he meets a stag, which he knows no better than to kill.[27] Again, alternative versions are mixed, and one version is misunderstood. Further, Homer seems not to understand

---

[25] Cf. the discussion of these points by Denys Page in *The Homeric Odyssey* (Oxford: Clarendon Press, 1955), chap. v.
[26] Carpenter, *Folk Tale, Fiction, and Saga,* pp. 18–19.
[27] *Ibid.,* p. 19.

that Circe intends to eat the swine into which she has transformed
her visitors; and the protective herb, moly, which is given to Odysseus by Hermes—instead of by the usual "little, bearded old man
or a dwarf, as fairy lore would have told it" [28]—is immediately forgotten and never used. Once more, why did not Odysseus blind
Polyphemus with his sword instead of going to considerable pains
to heat the monster's cudgel in the fire? Although the presence of
the cudgel in the cave is beautifully motivated, Carpenter believes
the ultimate reason for its use to have been "a certain folk-tale
motif that the monster cannot be slain by ordinary human means,
but only by some special weapon of his own, which by good luck
or superior knowledge may be discovered somewhere in his fearful haunt." A well-known occurrence of the motif is in *Beowulf,*
at the point where the hero kills Grendel's mother with her own
sword.[29] Carpenter discusses a variety of similar instances,[30] which,
however, we may skip over in order to reach his conclusion: "In
Homer, despite the obvious opportunity, *Märchen* is heavily disguised or deliberately converted." [31] What we find is not *Märchen*
themselves, but motifs from them—"the trappings of *Märchen*
rather than *Märchen* fully formed." [32] The implication is clear.
These are *Märchen* themes not in the process of formation but
well along in the process of decay. They had existed long enough
for the rationalistic Greek mind to have repudiated some of the
magical elements while retaining others whose origins and meanings it had forgotten.

Treatment of time

Another archaic element appears in the treatment of time. Denys
Page observes:

It is the general practice not only to narrate simultaneous events
successively, but also *to represent them as if they had actually oc-*

---

[28] *Ibid.*
[29] *Ibid.*, p. 21.
[30] See esp. a summary, *ibid.*, pp. 70–71.
[31] *Ibid.*, p. 71.
[32] *Ibid.*

curred successively. It was not permissible to take a step backwards in time (or to leave any space of time unoccupied by events; though the poet might leave to the understanding an event or series of events which must have occurred in one place while he was narrating what occurred in another).[33]

Thus, in the fifteenth book of the *Iliad,* Zeus delivers messages to both Iris and Apollo, who stand before him together; but Iris is made to go and perform her mission before Apollo is given his message. Page adds:

> It is not correct to say that the poets took this particular path in order to avoid an obstacle: the truth is rather that they act as if they had no conception of an all-embracing Time to which different events might be related. They treat time simply as the measure of the duration of particular events.[34]

In the *Odyssey,* the journey of Telemachus described in Books i–iii is certainly simultaneous with at least part of the wanderings of Odysseus, as related in Books v–xiii; but the overlapping events "must be (and are) narrated as if the action was continuous throughout." This procedure gave rise to no special difficulty at the beginning; but at the other end things become awkward, for "after Odysseus has arrived home we must go back to Sparta and fetch Telemachus, pretending not to notice the long interval of time which must have elapsed since we last saw him." [35] To the poet, the question, "How long is it since we last saw Telemachus?" is meaningless. For the Homeric character, time exists only in so far as he is portrayed as active in it.[36] But it has already been seen (Chapter 5) that precisely this treatment of time is common among primitives, some tribes going so far as to consider "dead," and therefore wholly outside the calendar, whatever days or weeks are marked by a ritual suspension of activities.

---

[33] Page, *Homeric Odyssey,* p. 65. The classic treatment of time in Homer is in Thaddeus Zielinski, *Die Behandlung gleichzeitiger Ereignisse im Antiken Epos* (Leipzig: Dieterich'sche Verlagsbuchhandlung, 1901).

[34] Page, *Homeric Odyssey,* p. 65.

[35] *Ibid.,* p. 66.

[36] *Ibid.,* p. 67.

Sacerdotal elements

By accepting considerable risks, we can move back further still. If there is any truth in the assertion that "myth is the *epic* element in primitive religious life," careful scrutiny of so old an author as Homer should disclose elements which can be suspected, at least, of being the detritus of religious rituals.

The most detailed attempt yet made to connect the Homeric epics with such rituals is recorded in a three-volume work by Charles Autran, entitled *Homère et les origines sacerdotales de l'épopée grecque.*[37] The epic, says Autran, is

> not solely a literary manifestation. One may say conclusively that it became that chiefly by extension. In fact, such a manifestation consists essentially of a prolongation into a semi-profane area of a type of production which, having been originally associated with incantation, hymn, and rite, is, in origin as in structure, a regular sacerdotal "instrument." [38]

In the beginning was the rite. The epic developed from the rite only gradually.

The first five hundred lines of the *Iliad* offer an illustration of this thesis: an insult to the priest Chryses is described as resulting in a pestilence which ends only after reparation has been made and the priest has instructed Apollo to discontinue the punishment.

> Whether the matter is one of vengeance or of clemency, Apollo accedes without delay to the injunctions of his pontiff. Noteworthy proof of the power of the priest, whose word suffices to awaken the scourge as well as to suspend it. . . .
>
> Thus the first five hundred verses of the *Iliad,* an indisputably ancient part, and a part on which all the rest of the epic decidedly rests, are, in reality, only an edifying story, a true narrative hymn,

---

[37] Charles Autran, *Homère et les origines sacerdotales de l'épopée grecque* (3 vols.; Paris: Les Éditions Denoël, 1938–1943). Autran later extended his investigations eastward in *L'Épopée indoue: Étude de l'arrière-fonds ethnographique et religieux* (Paris: Les Éditions Denoël, 1946). In the following quotations I have omitted most of the Gallic italics.

[38] Autran, *Homère et les origines,* III, 155.

which has as its essential object—and nearly its sole object—the glorification of Apollo's power and that of his priests.[39]

The modern reader, who feels no awe of Apollo, is not likely to be impressed by the demonstration that pagan priests must be respected. Let us substitute Pharaoh for Agamemnon, however, and Moses for Chryses; it then appears more probable that the introductory incident should have had intrinsic meaning besides motivating the wrath of Achilles.

RITUAL ORIGINS OF ACHILLES. If we shift our attention from the happenings to the personages, we find other traces of ritual origins. At first glance the heroes appear to be basically warriors —men who have distinguished themselves in many battles, sackers of cities, victors in earlier campaigns. On closer inspection, however, they become indued with other qualities. By an investigation of their corporal and material relics, of their tombs, and of pious foundations inspired by their memory,[40] Autran has been led to inquire whether "this war-like character did not result mainly from exigencies imposed on the bards by the literary taste—certainly a laical taste—of the courtly and popular audiences of epic stories." [41] We can afford space to examine this view in relation to one character only, Achilles, pre-eminent among the fighters, and the one whose position in the *Iliad* has always been recognized as central.

Achilles, it will be remembered, is the son of Peleus and the sea goddess Thetis. He is associated especially with Thessaly, his kingdom, like that of his father and his son Neoptolomus, being Phthiotis, which borders on Mt. Pelion. The name of his father, Peleus, seems very probably to mean "the one of Pelion"; and the mountain had a second claim to notoriety, since it played an important role in the mythical war of the gods and the giants. More significantly for our purposes, it was known to produce herbs of strange powers. *A Description of Greece,* written in the fourth or third century B.C. and sometimes attributed to the Athenian Dicæarchus, gives considerable information about these herbs:

---

[39] *Ibid.,* III, 235–36.
[40] See *ibid.,* II, esp. chaps. viii, ix, and x.
[41] *Ibid.,* II, 69.

some repel or kill snakes and have, in addition, the virtue of making snake bites harmless; others are a sure remedy for gout or swollen ligaments; others, again, give an almost total immunity against heat or cold; and so on. A careless use of the simples is attended, however, by peril. One γένος, or family of the locality, and one only, is in possession of the medical secrets, which it hands down from generation to generation, while accepting a pious duty to treat ill persons without payment. The patriarch of this "lignage thérapeutique," as Autran calls it, was the centaur Chiron; and Chiron was the tutor not only of Achilles, whose spear had a curative virtue, but also of Asclepius, god of medicine. We recall that Asclepius, in turn, was the son of Apollo, also god of medicine as well as of music, poetry, and the arts.

At the top of Mt. Pelion, according to the ancient *Description,* stood a temple dedicated to "Zeus of the Mountain-tops" (Ζεὺς ἀχοαῖος). Autran believes there are excellent reasons to consider this "an authentic survival of the great cult of mountain-dwelling and water-dwelling gods of prehellenic times." If the guess is correct, Achilles' famous prayer to the "Pelasgian" and "flowing" (νάιος) god gains new meaning, since it was in the shadow of this temple and on the sides of the god's well-watered mountain that the hero had spent his boyhood.

Up to this point, we have seen that Achilles is connected with "a priestly legend associated with a sanctuary, with a cult-spot, and with a local holy archaeology," all of which allow "ample epic extension." But more is to come. As elsewhere, we stumble upon a liturgy inherited from an immemorial past. Every year, during the dog days, youths are chosen by the priest from among the most distinguished families of the district. These clothe themselves in the fleeces of sheep, climb to the mountain's summit, and there celebrate traditional rites. The age of the ritual is attested by the choice of a date. The dog days took their name from the ascendancy of Sirius; and O. Gruppe, among others, has drawn attention to the importance of Sirius and the constellation Orion, of which it is a part, in the oldest calendar of the pre-Hellenic period.

Continuing to push backward at even greater risk of error, we find that Sirius was described in the *Avesta,* under its Zoroastrian name of Tištriya, as "the liberator of fructifying waters." The reason for the designation seems to have been given correctly by Polybius when he noted that the dominance of the star coincided with the melting of snow in the mountains and the consequent release of water for irrigating the fields. At an earlier time still, a Sumerian name for Sirius, *a-edin,* meant "water" (*a-*) "of the field" (*edin*); and an Accadian text speaks of Sirius as "the one which produces masculine seed." In the light of all this, the costume of the youthful celebrants appears to have been inherited from earlier *mystai,* "initiates," who disguised themselves as sheep in order to enact an ancient fertility ritual. The marriage of Peleus to the sea goddess Thetis thus becomes understandable: Peleus is the personified mountain god himself, and Thetis is the spirit of the waters whose release was so important to the welfare of the district's inhabitants. If Achilles has acquired as part of his patrimony the curative spear cut from among the medicinal plants on the side of Mt. Pelion, he has inherited from his mother, the hypostatized spirit of rapid mountain streams, the fleet-footedness so often insisted on by Homer.[42]

SIGNIFICANCE OF THE FINDINGS.   How far may such a reconstruction be trusted? It is necessary to pause for the question once again, since otherwise the whole purport of the inquiry might be misunderstood. First, it is not suggested here that Homer was aware of all or even a part of the background which has just been sketched for his Achilles. When he called Achilles "swift-footed," he probably had no desire to remind his hearers of a connection with the fast-running streams of well-watered Mt. Pelion; and Peleus himself may have been for Homer either a half-legendary ancestor of Achilles or an actual father about whose history only certain rather remarkable details were known. The point is that, if the reconstruction should happen to be correct, there was a long past, leading back ultimately to an origin in fertility ritual, behind the Achilles whose lineaments and actions were known to Homer from earlier bardic poems. "Homer," in the sense in which that

---

[42] The above reconstruction rests mainly on *ibid.,* III, 328–33.

word has been defined, stepped into a tradition and did something to it which determined its future; but there is no necessity to imagine that in order to fix the tradition he must have been completely informed about its origins and gradual development.

Secondly, the significance of the reconstruction for a fuller understanding of Homeric epic does not depend on its detailed correctness. Once more I must make the difficult and perhaps unwelcome point that my effort has been not to indicate what necessarily happened in prehistory but the *kind of thing* which must have happened. It is possible, perhaps even probable, that many or even most of the details in Autran's elaborately worked out hypothesis are false. What I wish to insist on is that this is roughly the *way* in which ancient literature came into existence. *Something like this,* if not precisely this, must have happened. The incidents, personages, themes, and techniques of literature must come from somewhere, however freshly they are combined; and my answer to the question "From where?" is often quite simply, "From the past." We do not know, and no doubt will never be able to know, exactly how the *Iliad* and *Odyssey* were born; but since they sprang into the light of history from prehistoric darkness, one must infer that they grew in minds whose methods of working were preliterate and therefore, in an even greater degree than those of our own minds, nondiscursive.

One additional comment is appropriate. The instinct of some readers will be to retort, "If we can never discover the truth, why not forget the whole matter?" My reply is that even a faint understanding of real backgrounds is better than no understanding at all. One may, of course, choose to restrict one's attention to questions which can be answered confidently: for example, one may become an expert on Homer's Aeolic forms, or on his grammar generally, or on his total "style," or on what a New Critic might term very broadly the "form" of—let us say—the *Iliad,* with the intention of isolating one's special interest as sharply as possible from every other conceivable interest. The difficulty, however, is that insight into backgrounds often calls into question the preassumptions underlying specialized studies. I cite a single illustration. Let us suppose that our formalist, having found Achilles regularly called "swift-footed," is disturbed at Hector's equal or superior fleetness when Achilles pursues him. Here, he may say, is an obvious structural fault. The swift-footedness of Achilles should not have been insisted on if it was not to become functional; yet, at precisely the point where it might have been used, it is implicitly denied. What, then, is to be the formalist's reply if it is urged that the epithet was traditional merely, having been derived from association with a water spirit, and that no more is to be demanded of it than of other epithets; that the greaves of the well-greaved Achaeans are not described as deflecting spears or arrows, that the loud war cry of Diomedes turns no rout into an attack, that Odysseus sacks no cities, that no raging animals descend from Mt. Ida, the mother of wild beasts? Unless qualified by historical references, the formalist's observation will seem to the better-informed reader otiose or misleading; modern expectations, such a reader will say, should not be read back into an ancient poem. If the frame of reference is so narrow as to exclude such objections, the findings are likely to have small literary relevance.

OTHER SACERDOTAL ELEMENTS. I return, after this digression, to the consideration of other sacerdotal elements in Homer. Of many which are visible, only two or three can be granted mention. The whole expedition against Troy may have had a religious purpose; Autran notes that the war and the terrible revenge wreaked upon the compatriots of Paris "result[ed] from an impiety [the rape of Helen] detested by all." In the same way, "it is an act of religious purification and of devotion which end[ed] the long train of Odysseus' misfortunes." [43] The duel arranged between Paris and the outraged husband, Menalaus (Book iii), must also have had a ritual function. Éliade has observed: "War or the duel can in no case be explained through rationalistic motives." A. M. Hocart, he adds, "has very rightly brought out the ritual role of hostilities." [44] Observations by Gilbert Murray suggest a whole complex of still different ritual implications.

---

[43] *Ibid.,* III, 348.
[44] Mircea Éliade, *The Myth of the Eternal Return,* trans. Willard Trask (Bollingen Series XLVI, Bollingen Foundation, Inc., 1954), p. 29.

If Odysseus had 360 boars, one of whom died every night, one cannot but think of the sun or the year, as described in ancient riddles: one cannot help noticing with interest that the day on which Odysseus and Penelope met was the exact day in which ancient astronomers considered that the sun cycle and moon cycle coincided: the day called "the meeting of sun and moon" in Meton's *Eikosieteris* or 20 year cycle. . . . One must remember that Helen was, in historical times a marriage goddess in Sparta, and as such must herself go through the marriage ceremony, which comprised in Sparta the carrying off of the bride. Hence Helen in saga is constantly "carried off"—to Sidon or Troy by Paris, to Egypt by Hermes, to Deceleia by Theseus or the Apharetidae, to Parmon by "a robber." [45]

Finally, we are shown unmistakable rituals from point to point in the poems. A clear example is the sacrifice by Nestor in *Odyssey* iii. Since the ox was considered a member of the family and was even thought to have a common blood with its owner, it was not slain lightly—unless, of course, it had been captured in a raid, like those on which the Argives feast in the *Iliad*. Its slaughter was therefore accompanied by ritual lamentation. After Nestor had performed a number of preliminary rites, the ox was killed, and "the daughters and the daughters-in-law and the august wife of Nestor all wailed aloud." [46] The description here is detailed enough to permit a modern re-enactment; but few readers, perhaps, fully appreciate the incident's religious significance.

Influence of military dynasties

We may attempt, then, if we will, to visualize the ultimate source of Homeric epics as songs or hymns connected in some way with religious rituals. Whether, as Thomson believes, "behind Greek epic there probably lies the custom of collective chanting, such as we find among some of the North American tribes," [47]

---

[45] Gilbert Murray, "Homer," in *Encyclopaedia Britannica* (1957 ed.).

[46] Cf. Murray, *Rise of the Greek Epic*, pp. 59–62.

[47] George Thomson, *Aeschylus and Athens* (London: Lawrence & Wishart Ltd., 1941), p. 64.

we can perhaps never be sure. If so, Thomson's further guess may also be correct:

> The decisive stage in the evolution of epic was the rise of the military dynasties, which furnished the art of song with new themes and a new technique. The new themes were the wars of conquest, and the new technique was the lay sung by a trained minstrel at the feasts to which the king entertained his vassals.[48]

Such a development would have required that at some point a leader begin to sing by himself; he would then, in course of time, have abandoned strophes for the long dactylic verse, the musical accompaniment of the group or choir being replaced by the rhapsode's lyre or some other instrument. C. M. Bowra reviews Erich Bethe's somewhat similar theory with approval, noting particularly the heroic songs still sung in Herzegovina, Dalmatia, and Old Serbia, where the instrument, the *guslé,* is a kind of fiddle and the lines are grouped into units of five to ten verses. Remnants of the earlier Greek form can still, Bethe thinks, be found in the poetry of Corinna and of Stesichorus.[49] If the theory is sound, the Homeric epic derives ultimately from lyric, very possibly the oldest form of verse; and lyric, in turn, may have begun in the rhythmic excitement of religious ritual.

Summary

Much of this, I repeat, has been conjectural. What is not conjectural is the continuity of epic with a remote past. It did not spring into being in a single moment, or even in a single lifetime or century, but grew organically from small beginnings, transforming its cultural heritage steadily but never entirely destroying it. "The continuity of human works," remarks Austran, "defies every denial. At no place, at no moment, does the present cease to communicate with the past"; and, he adds:

---

[48] *Ibid.* An interesting modern parallel, having to do with African minstrels who serve chiefs, is described by Richard Wallaschek in *Primitive Music* (London: Longmans, Green, & Co., Ltd., 1893), p. 66.

[49] For the summary, see Bowra, *Tradition and Design in the Iliad,* pp. 33–35.

The secret fecundity which is hidden in the archaic works of the classical period comes to them precisely from the fact that, in their time, they were the magnificent and weighty result of an immense past. In origin, their deepest life is a religious life.[50]

The almost religious awe of historical Greeks for Homer thus was natural enough. The atmosphere of epic remained hieratic; Homer came to them reeking, in some not altogether comprehensible way, with sanctity. The poems contained *mana,* and their holiness was enhanced by the ritualistic trappings of recitation at the Panathenaea or elsewhere. By historical times, no doubt sophisticated hearers felt some doubt about the accuracy of epic history. Livy felt a similar doubt about Roman mythological traditions; nevertheless, he said in the Preface of his great history, "Datur haec venia antiquitati, ut miscendo humana divinis primordia urbium augustiora faciat." The spirit at least was right, and the most skeptical Greek felt stronger after breathing it.

It remains to be added, finally, that an art form of this kind, having a connection, at one end of its long career, with religious ceremonies not less sacred than a Catholic mass, and perpetuated, at the other end, by recitation at a patriotic festival not wholly unlike an old-fashioned Fourth of July celebration held in a medium-sized football stadium, had an exceptional opportunity to test itself against basic human responses.

> The recitation took place before a variegated audience which included men with all sorts of backgrounds and of every kind of culture.
>
> Can there be conditions more propitious for the maintenance of the healthiest literary traditions: humanity, naturalness, simple and strong sentiments? Everything, including the formulary professional style, offered a capital advantage. . . .
>
> Thus the essential character of Greek literature, as long as it remained "Homeric," was the exceptional richness of its humanity, its information, its imagination: the vigor with which it affirmed normal and deep sentiments.[51]

---

[50] Autran, *Homère et les origines,* III, 340.
[51] *Ibid.,* III, 338–39.

To this source can be traced the durable appeal of Greek epic: it rose from communal feelings and continued to the end to address itself to them. In a sense, it was not the work of any individual, but the precipitation of deep-seated group emotions into a complex aesthetic construct.

The Homeric influence

The question now arises whether the Homeric tradition, and with it, inevitably, some of the prerational elements embodied in its matter and texture, persisted in later epics. So far as the literate epic is concerned, no detailed answer is necessary. Everyone knows that the "great" epic tradition runs from Homer through Virgil (whose first six books are a Roman *Odyssey,* and the second six a Roman *Iliad*) to Dante (who was guided through hell and purgatory by Virgil) and Milton, who was said by John Toland to be able to repeat Homer's two poems almost without book [52] but was even more deeply soaked in the Latin classics than in the Greek. After Milton, the epic impulse weakened until, finally, epic was mainly absorbed into the novel.[53] To the latest towering exemplar of this tradition, Milton, we shall recur shortly; but first it is necessary to consider very briefly two other groups of epics which stand largely outside the Graeco-Roman tradition. The first consists of works which are "primitive" in much the same way— though not always in the same degree—as Homer's; the second includes "irregular" epics like those of Ariosto, Tasso, and Spenser.

Teutonic epic

From the point of view adopted in the present study, the remarkable thing about such Teutonic epics as those which concern Beowulf, Waldhere, Siegfried, Dietrich von Bern, and other legendary or only semihistorical personages is their similarity to Homer. The parallels were studied in detail nearly half a century

---

[52] John Toland's biography of Milton was first published in 1698. For the remark, see Helen Darbishire, *The Early Lives of Milton* (London: Constable & Co., Ltd., 1932), p. 179.

[53] Cf., again, Tillyard, *English Epic.*

ago by H. Munro Chadwick, who concluded that "the resemblances in the poems are due primarily to resemblances in the ages to which they relate." The comparative study of heroic poems thus became in considerable part "the comparative study of 'Heroic Ages' "; and this required the use of anthropological methods.[54] Since Chadwick's discussion is readily accessible, it will suffice here to mention a sufficient number of similarities to indicate that the discoveries made about Homer might be paralleled by others based on epics which were influenced only at a considerable distance, if at all, by Homer's example.

To begin with, the custom of bardic recitation among the Germans strongly resembled that which seems to have obtained among the prehistoric Greeks. The Greek historian Priscus describes as follows a declamation given before the Hun Attila in the year 448:

> When evening came on torches were lighted and two barbarians stepped forth in front of Attila and recited poems which they had composed, recounting his victories and his valiant deeds in war. The banqueters fixed their eyes upon them, some being charmed with the poems, while others were roused in spirit, as the recollection of their wars came back to them. Others again burst into tears, because their bodies were enfeebled by age and their martial ardour had perforce to remain unsatisfied.[55]

The Huns were not, of course a Germanic people (so that at this point our view widens to include an Asiatic custom); but similar recitations are authenticated among the tribes into whose realms the Huns had penetrated. Tacitus reports that the Germans of his time had no other means of preserving history than songs (*carmina*);[56] the author of the Anglo-Saxon *Deor* tells us that he had formerly been the bard (*scop*) of the Heodeningas; and there are other references to court minstrelsy in both vernacular and Latin sources.[57] If Thomson was right in his guess about the influence

---

[54] H. Munro Chadwick, *The Heroic Age* (Cambridge: University Press, 1912), viii.

[55] Quoted *ibid.,* p. 84.

[56] *Ibid.,* p. 78.

[57] For a fuller discussion, see *ibid.,* pp. 77–100.

of military dynasties on the rise of Greek epic, it is evident that Germanic epic may have responded to a similar opportunity.

Next, there are mythical elements in the Teutonic epics, as in Homer; and these—again as in Homer—are sometimes mixed with folk-tale motifs from which they are hardly extricable. Let us take the Anglo-Saxon *Beowulf* as an example. The conflict with Grendel's mother appears to draw upon folk-tale sources, since the notion of a monster who can be killed only with something belonging to himself is very widely disseminated. We have recognized the same motif in the Polyphemus story of the *Odyssey*. The Danish royal line, on the other hand, seems validly mythical, at least in its upper reaches: Shield (*Scyld*) the son of the Sheaf (*Scēfing*), who was, however, as a child, found destitute (*fēasceaft funden*), looks like a war god descended from an agricultural deity. Beowulf himself seems to fluctuate between a historical king and a bear-man of the kind with which Carpenter attempted to identify Odysseus.[58] He was "made nephew to King Hygelac of the Geatas, an indisputably historical character, and the troll adventures were laid at the court of an equally famous contemporary, Hrothgar of the Danes";[59] yet his name, Bee-wolf, suggests "bear," his prowess in wrestling reminds us of the bear's hug, and other details, such as his capacity for staying under water and the legend of his slothful youth, are appropriate to a bearlike character.[60] A similar mixture of myth, folk tale, and history has been detected in other Germanic epics.[61] Behind all this lies something generically, at least, similar to what has been detected, or suspected, in Homer. To be sure, the absence of frequent reference to sacrifice in the Germanic poems marks a difference. It is known that in pagan times sacrifices were made: Bede speaks of the killing of oxen *in sacrificio daemonum* in his *Historia ecclesiastica gentis Anglorum*.[62] The

---

[58] See Carpenter, *Folk Tale, Fiction, and Saga,* chap. vii.

[59] William Witherle Lawrence, *Beowulf and Epic Tradition* (Cambridge, Mass.: Harvard University Press, 1928), p. 247.

[60] *Ibid.,* p. 248.

[61] See Chadwick, *Heroic Age,* chap. vi, "Supernatural Elements in the Heroic Stories," and chap. vii, "Mythical Elements in the Heroic Poems."

[62] I take the reference from Fr[iedrich] Klaeber, *Beowulf and the Fight at Finnsburg,* (3d ed.; Boston: D. C. Heath and Company, 1950), gloss to lines 175–88.

extant Germanic epics are all, however, comparatively late, and most or all have undergone Christian influence. On the whole, the relations of this second tradition to prehistory seem remarkably like those of the first. If anything, the proportion of the total work accomplished by the discursive part of the mind is less.

Finally, there are notable similarities between Graeco-Roman and Teutonic epics in point of form. These have been drawn out by Chadwick in a chapter entiled "The Common Characteristics of Teutonic and Greek Heroic Poetry" (chap. xv). Among these characteristics are the following: the frequent repetition of formulas; a love of minute description; a tendency to describe in some detail the movements of royal persons in their palaces; the elaboration of various stages in the reception of visitors; the use of formulas in greetings; a fondness for dwelling upon the emotions felt as greetings and farewells are spoken; similar epithets and turns of poetic expression; the holding up of glory as an incitement to bravery; martial boasting; a feeling of family pride; the exhortations offered by princes to their followers; fame as a "leading idea" (*dōm* among the Germans, κλέα ἀνδρῶν among the Greeks); love, revenge, or bravery as a basic motif; and "strength, courage, resourcefulness, generosity, hospitality" as traits of the epic heroes.[63] In combination with the other traits already noted, these resemblances produce a rather startling likeness between two widely separate traditions. If the first reading of *Beowulf* holds some technical surprises for a reader already familiar with the *Iliad* and the *Odyssey*, he also frequently feels at ease. He has been over ground of the same kind before.

"Irregular" epic

The "irregular" Renaissance epic of such men as Ariosto, Tasso, and Spenser—to cite only the most distinguished names—lies at one side of the dominant tradition. The vogue of such works was temporary, and their materials were often those of romance. If the modern successor to the typical epic is the serious novel, that of the irregular epic is the story of exotic setting and marvelous

---

[63] See Chadwick, *Heroic Age*, esp. pp. 320–33.

incident. Yet the irregular epic too was rooted in the subrational in the proportion in which it trafficked with marvels. For example, the Arthurian legends upon which Spenser drew seem to have included many pre-Christian elements. Jessie L. Weston studied some of these in *From Ritual to Romance,* a book which has achieved a certain fame because of its connection with Eliot's *Wasteland.* "My aim," says Miss Weston, "has been to prove the essentially archaic character of *all* the elements composing the Grail story"; [64] and her conclusion was that at the root of the Grail stories "lies the record, more or less distorted, of an ancient Ritual, having for its ultimate object the initiation into the secret of the sources of Life, physical and spiritual." [65] Her view had already been generalized by E. K. Chambers, whom she quotes with approval:

> If the comparative study of Religion proves anything it is, that the traditional beliefs and customs of the mediaeval or modern peasant are in nine cases out of ten but the *detritus* of heathen mythology and heathen worship, enduring with but little external change in the shadow of a hostile faith.[66]

The pagan mystery which Miss Weston believes to have been Christianized into the Grail quest need not be described here. It has no very direct bearing on *The Faerie Queene;* and *The Faerie Queene,* in turn, has only a tangential relation to the usual modern concept of epic. It is useful, however, to observe that even a comparatively minor literary genre is not exempt from the usual tendency of art works to have a substratum in the irrational.

Paradise Lost, *the end of a tradition*

The last great epic in the dominant tradition is Milton's *Paradise Lost.* After the seventeenth century, it became more and more difficult to construe history in epic terms, and the affections, ceasing to pull meaningful elements of experience together as

---

[64] Cf. Jessie L. Weston, *From Ritual to Romance* (Cambridge: University Press, 1920), p. 10.

[65] *Ibid.,* p. 191.

[66] *Ibid.,* pp. 62–63.

myth, began increasingly to express themselves in the more sur-
reptitious ways already partly described in other sections of this
study. Milton's epic is remarkable because it is at once archaic
and modern, mythic and conceptualized. It spans an enormous
cognitive area and comes, perhaps, nearer than any other major
literary work to fulfilling the demand of its most influential recent
depreciator, T. S. Eliot, that poetry be simultaneously primitive
and sophisticated. That *Paradise Lost* is fundamentally mythical
hardly needs to be argued: the universe coalesces in it not as
atemporal law or as verifiable historical process but as divine
drama. Many details of the etiology, however, are consciously
fictitious; Milton committed himself to implications which he did
not literally believe. When the archangel Raphael acceded to
Adam's request that he describe the war in heaven, he did so by
"measuring things in Heav'n by things on Earth" (VI, 893); and
his account of the creation was a parable, not very truth.

> Immediate are the Acts of God, more swift
> Than time or motion, but to human ears
> Cannot without process of speech be told,
> So told as earthly notion can receive.
>
> (vii, 176-79)

So much every attentive reader must have noticed. The principle
goes further, however, and cuts deeper; the whole of divine revela-
tion is "accommodated" to human understanding. In *De doctrina
Christiana* Milton said that the Scriptures portray God "not as he
really is, but in such a manner as may be within the scope of our
comprehension"; and again, "Let us be convinced that those have
acquired the truest apprehension of the nature of God who submit
their understandings to his word; considering that he has accommodated his word to their understandings" (Book I, chap. ii). How
far everything in the story of the Fall is subject to the same limitation is not easy to say; perhaps everything, perhaps not very much.
At any rate, at the very core of Milton's epic is an intellectual
reservation. Yet the myth is nonetheless true for being figurative.
As God's metaphor, not man's, the vehicle has a one-to-one cor-
respondence with its tenor.

This conjunction and reconciliation of opposing thought ways has a special significance. For the first and only time in the present study, we see a major literary tradition at the point of coming to a dead stop because psychic habits had been transformed. After Milton, real mythologizing was gradually to become impossible. John Bunyan's *Pilgrim's Progress,* almost exactly contemporary, was allegory, not myth; so also was Joseph Addison's *Vision of Mirzah* in the eighteenth century, and so have been, so far as I know without exception, the nearest post-Miltonic approaches to Miltonic narrative. Even the cosmic trilogy of C. S. Lewis,[67] brilliantly effective as it is, is in its author's eyes rather metaphor than very truth. The contingent belief granted the incidents is qualitatively different here. To be sure, one may say that the epic, having been diverted underground, has emerged as something apparently different: the realistic novel, such portentous and aspiring histories as those of Edward Gibbon and Sir Winston Churchill, and the like. To this view I would myself be inclined to assent. But this is to say that the epic has ceased to be what it formerly was—that, in fact, it has virtually ceased to exist *qua* epic. Tragedy is still tragedy, comedy still comedy, the lyric still lyric. Epic has become something else. One may wish for more epics in the future, but, as things are, one is not likely to get them. The connection of epic with the irrational seems, therefore, likely to be permanent. From Milton the line runs straight back to Homer, whose connections with prehistory have been traced; and this side of Milton the impulse falters. The connection thus remains frozen in the past, and, barring an abrupt change in the direction of social development, nothing in the future is likely to affect it.

Antiquity of lyric

We come finally to the lyric, which I have already more than once suggested may be the oldest literary form of all. The question of priority is, of course, really unanswerable except in terms of probability; but even within those limits much depends on defini-

---

[67] The three volumes of C. S. Lewis' trilogy are entitled *Out of the Silent Planet, Perelandra,* and *That Hideous Strength.*

tion. At what point do cries expressive of feeling become "lyrics"? And at what point do ritual or other gestures become "drama"? A child, certainly, expresses emotions very early by screams, gurgles, and other noises, which at a later stage of development will become language; but he also begins very early to indicate his feelings by nonvocal movements capable, in time, of modification into dramatic posturing or dancing. Since we are engaged in a search for roots, it will be sufficient to urge that subjectivity is ontogenetically prior to objectivity and that, in one sense at least, lyric is therefore a less "advanced" form of art than the more impersonal drama or epic. Yet the statement is in a way arbitrary, even meaningless, for, in the earliest stages, song, dance, and gesture seem to occur together. In separating out one part of the total activity for special emphasis, we subdivide what was aboriginally one.

Fortunately, at this point we may draw upon Heinz Werner's *Die Ursprünge der Lyrik,* a systematic and careful study based on an enormous mass of anthropological evidence.[68] So far as I have been able to discover, in breadth and circumstantiality the work stands virtually alone, and we need not, in a brief survey, pass far beyond its conclusions.

Diffuseness of primitive lyric

First, we may note in primitive lyrics the diffuseness which was remarked earlier in primitive perceptions. Among the Melanesians of the Bismarck Archipelago, for example, *ciki,* "drop" means

> not only the little drop of water which falls from a tree, but also the spots which it leaves behind; also the noise of the dropping itself, as well as the regular time-intervals within which the drops fall from the roof; and finally also the sudden, unexpected dripping.[69]

There is thus an extraordinary complexity of reference in primitive lyrics, so that interpretation is difficult in a language which isolates meanings more sharply.

---

[68] Heinz Werner, *Die Ursprünge der Lyrik* (Munich: Ernst Reinhardt, 1924).
[69] *Ibid.,* p. 2.

More is involved, however, than this. The distinctness of feelings, movements, perceptions, imaginings, and concepts appears to modern Westerners to be *given;* but

> in the primitive condition, feeling, for example, as a definite kind of activity, is not a closed-off whole, but is bound up on one side with the action of moving, and just as closely, on the other side, with perceptions and imaginations.[70]

All the varieties of psychic activity occur together and are not separated by rational analysis. Accordingly, it is not surprising that the aesthetic is often inextricably mingled with the religious and practical. "One must free oneself altogether," says Werner, "and on principle, from the idea that in all circumstances the forms which at our cultural stage are recognized as aesthetic have been aesthetic from the beginning." [71] The further back we go toward the beginnings, "the more poetic form dissolves into a relationship with non-aesthetic wishes and is interwoven with aesthetic tendencies of other kinds, especially musical and mimetic." [72] In what follows, accordingly, we isolate for a special purpose what in fact is by no means an autonomous activity. Yet in one respect lyric is more easily recognizable among savages than among modern sophisticates; it is often marked by a special mode of utterance, which Westerners associate with singing. Even Western song, however, is sometimes less distinct from ordinary speech than is primitive lyric characteristically. The Omaha Indians say that "the whites speak a good piece, when they sing"; and, among many tribes, clear articulation of the words is avoided as unlyrical.[73]

Meaningless lyric

Ontogenetically, the earliest element of lyric is probably mere noise produced by motor affect. At any rate, Werner notes meaninglessness as a mark of one of the two most primitive lyrical types,[74]

---

[70] *Ibid.,* p. 3.
[71] *Ibid.,* p. 6.
[72] *Ibid.*
[73] Cf. *ibid.,* p. 8.
[74] *Ibid.,* pp. 8–9.

and Richard Wallaschek, in *Primitive Music,* asserts without qual-
ification that "the most striking feature of all the savage songs is
the frequent occurrence of words with no meaning whatever." [75]
The cause, says Werner, is a preponderance of the motor impulse
in utterance.[76] The poetry of the Ceylonese Veddas, which is
"rather screamed than spoken, in an incomprehensible language," [77] may typify such a preponderance, which is observable
also in the tantrums of young children; but it should be observed
that meaninglessness may result from such other causes as the
borrowing of uncomprehended songs from neighboring tribes and
the preservation, often with accidental changes, of songs composed
in an earlier dialect.

Another variety of meaninglessness appears in lyrics "which
possess apparent sense, although what unfolds itself beneath this
appearance is produced by the accidental and more or less meaningless utilization of particular sensory expressions." [78] Thus children often fill out their songs with nonsense words and sentences
which for adults possess at least hints of meaning. Good examples
can be found among the Brazilian Unauas: "single-toned repetitions of single words in constant rhythms—they are nothing more
than enumerations of objects which play some kind of role in the
dance." [79] Modern analogues would be such songs as the German
Schnitzelbank, the English incremental lyric about Christmas gifts
(on the first, second, third, fourth days of Christmas my true love
gave to me a partridge in a pear tree, two turtle doves, three colly
birds, four French hens, and so on through the twelfth day), and
perhaps also a variation of "Green grow the rashes, O" ("One is
One and all alone . . . Two, two, the lily-white boys, clothèd all
in green, O," and so forth, again through twelve). The underlying
motive for such enumerations, Werner thinks, is not a desire to
say anything in particular, but rather an urge "to create a flowing

---

[75] Wallaschek, *Primitive Music,* p. 170.
[76] Werner, *Ursprünge der Lyrik,* p. 8 (". . . dem Übergewicht des Motorischen
der Lautgebung").
[77] *Ibid.,* p. 9.
[78] *Ibid.,* p. 10.
[79] *Ibid.,* p. 11.

body of sound without special psychic strain." [80] We arrive thus at a paradoxical rule for nonsense lyrics: "The logical form is preferred to the meaningless in order to conserve psychic energy." [81]

Development from interjection
to presentation

The second of Werner's "most primitive" types is "the short interjectional extempore, which springs spontaneously from a predominantly affective mood"; this, he believes, is "the original form of logical poetry, from which higher types develop." [82] A frequent subject for such lyrics is sorrow, which expresses itself as complaint; and the predominance of this mood in primitive lyrics, as in modern, is surprising. At a higher stage, exclamation yields place to description. An image of lost happiness or present calamity is presented, and mere outcry, the more direct motor response to psychic pressure, becomes less important. This, however, is a development; the earliest form of complaints is "everywhere the lyrical interjection." [83] Other lyrical subjects likely to be treated interjectionally are the yearning for food or for sexual satisfaction. These too can give rise to description, as in the following Malay song: "Fat, our fruit, at the end (of the) branch; they climb up, they tear it off, at the end (of the) branch; fat, bird, at the end (of the) branch; fat, young squirrel, at the end (of the) branch." [84] Although here the description is still rudimentary, the movement from interjection to description has clearly begun. The interjectional "Fat!" inspires the addition of a localizing phrase, "at the end of the branch"; and as the process develops further, the impulse to exclamation will weaken. Attention is diverted from the subjective affect to the desired object, which then can be contemplated, in the mind's eye, as an actualization of the wish.

The development from exclamation to presentation can be observed in the death lament also. "The primordial form of the death-

---

[80] *Ibid.,* p. 12.
[81] *Ibid.*
[82] *Ibid.,* p. 8.
[83] *Ibid.,* p. 13.
[84] *Ibid.,* p. 14.

song," says Werner, "is perhaps mere interjection. The interjection may consist, in part, of quite meaningless syllables; but when it becomes expression instead of the release of inner feeling, it has already reached the first stage of logic." The first step is toward specification of the affect's cause.[85] Successive stages might be illustrated as follows: "Ah!" (completely unreflective outburst); "Woe!" (the oppressive affect is named); "My dear father!" (the source of the affect is named); and, finally, "Skillful hunter! Lion-voiced warrior!" (objectification begins and can proceed to any length). Since the development of human consciousness from one primitive stage to another cannot be observed directly, the historical basis of the analysis is less sound than the logical; but such a speculative reconstruction is at least orderly.

Lyrical symbolism

A still later stage is that of lyrical symbolism. There may seem to be a qualitative break between the specification of a poetic object by a listing of its qualities and meanings, on one hand, and the substitution for the object of something which is affectively adjacent or shares some aspect of its structure, on the other. Yet Werner believes there is no discontinuity. The inner states of feeling flow into and color objects adjacent to that which provoked the original affect; and, at the same time, the aesthetic universe tends spontaneously to become autonomous.

> A special world of aesthetic contemplation develops, with its own laws and peculiar meanings. The object is adjusted more and more thoroughly to this aesthetic sphere . . . is clarified and defined. The special lawfulness of the artistic image separates itself ever more sharply from the lawfulness of natural objects.[86]

Comparisons creep into the lyric statement and assist in the work of definition and clarification: "The mood is itself symbolized in the aesthetic object—that is to say, is given visual form. . . . The less symbolic an art work is, the less sharply it is presented in the

---

[85] *Ibid.*, p. 16.
[86] *Ibid.*, p. 32.

aesthetic-visual sense, the more fragmentarily, the more casually." [87] The aesthetic impulse, once born, develops a momentum which results in a constantly increasing transformation of its object. The bridge from statement to symbol is provided by just such a comparison as slipped unintentionally into the example given a moment ago; the subject of a death lament, I wrote, may be described as a "skillful hunter, a *lion-voiced* warrior." Thus there is no deep gulf between the poetry which merely names (*Benennungspoesie*) and poetry which symbolizes. The one is capable of leading by natural stages to the other.

The steps toward symbolization, Werner thinks, can be distinguished, though the analysis ought once again, no doubt, to be conceived as rather ontogenetically than historically accurate. The first stage is that of symptomizing: "If instead of a happening or an object a characteristic or a part is named, the naming is symbolical in a primitive way." Thus the simpler, "Oh, my husband, why are you dead?" may become, "Who will fetch cocoanuts for me? Who will work for me?" [88] The second stage consists of the substitution of a whole for another whole, as, for example, in a satirical poem of King George's Sound: "What legs, what legs! Kangaroo-hipped fellows!" Somewhat more complicated is the Melanesian description of the female *pudendum* as a tree at whose roots poisonous midges swarm.[89] In the third stage, which comes relatively late, the poet's mood, rather than an external object, is symbolized. At the beginning (says Werner), symbolism of this third kind is prevented by a sharp separation between the expression of feelings and the statement of percepts; but the tendency of savages to regard natural objects as themselves possessed of feelings, hence to personify, to anthropomorphize, provides a transition from one kind of lyric to the other. When the Polynesian speaks of flowers which grieve, he animizes ("Our clothes are grieving grasses and flowers!"). It is otherwise when the poet speaks of "withered" flowers, for "here the aesthetic vision first becomes self-contained, here the complete objectivation of the

---

[87] *Ibid.,* p. 33.
[88] *Ibid.*
[89] *Ibid.,* pp. 34–35.

mood is first achieved." The development can proceed, however, by gradual steps. A phrase in a Tahitian song, "Thick falls the fine rain on the surface of the lake; the drops are not rain, they are tears of the god Oro," is intermediary between the two examples already given; the tears are a true symbol of grief, but they are accounted for anthropomorphically. In general, a tendency is perceptible, as poetry develops, toward "a gradual visualization of the lyrical feelings, a sentimentalizing of the lyrical vision. A constantly more inclusive part of the total content is comprehended symbolically in the expression, until finally the total image symbolizes nearly perfectly the total content." [90] The connection between art and feeling, so often emphasized in the foregoing pages, is thus strongly supported by a study of primitive lyrics.

Formalization of lyric

Since the discussion must be kept brief, we pass finally to a consideration of elements more exclusively formal—particularly rhythm and rhyme (assonance, alliteration), which are present in much poetry but have greatest density, as it were, in lyric. By way of introduction, however, we may observe that the formalization of lyric appears to be accomplished at least partly through the formalized ritual which often accompanies it. Werner, who continues to be our chief guide, reminds us that in magic success depends frequently quite as much on the manner in which an incantation is uttered as on its matter. The omission of a traditional detail may have the most unfortunate results. He believes, consequently, that "the special intention to act *formally* develops from the cultivation of *formulas:* the turning of the lyric poet from mere content to significant expression is grounded in a consciousness of the use of this or that structure, this or that style." [91] The supposition is perhaps unnecessary, although interesting and cogent. So long as lyric remained social, a pressure toward the development of patterns must have resulted from the need for simultaneous motor activity by groups of participants. Yet the influence of

---

[90] For Werner's discussion, see *ibid.,* pp. 35–37.
[91] *Ibid.,* p. 37.

incantation, which in many primitive societies absorbs much energy, may well have been strong.

THE DEVELOPMENT OF RHYTHM.   The development of rhythm in any kind of motor expression is not hard to understand in its essentials. The clapping of hands, the stamping of feet, or the beating of a drum tends to become rhythmic in proportion as it becomes automatic. There is economy in the settling of time intervals, since the alternating concentration and relaxation of effort ceases to require attention. The simplest possible rhythm is perhaps that which results from the mere spacing of activities—let us say blows or cries—in an undifferentiated row, as follows:

$$\prime \quad \prime \quad \prime \quad \prime$$
$$\underline{\quad}\; \underline{\quad}\; \underline{\quad}\; \underline{\quad}$$

From this, more complicated rhythms develop easily, and at times almost or quite independently of consciousness; for example:

$$\prime \quad \backslash \quad \prime \quad \backslash \quad \prime \quad \backslash$$
$$\underline{\quad}\; \underline{\quad}\; \underline{\quad}\; \underline{\quad}\; \underline{\quad}\; \underline{\quad}$$

Such rhythms appear very early in childish behavior, as when, after an outburst of anger or misery, a child's crying becomes patterned.

On this aspect of the subject it is unnecessary to speak further. "Pure movement, unimpeded by external restrictions and in no other way monitored, is rhythmic in its psychically simplest expression." [92] What happens, however, when consciousness of the activity becomes acute and the will is tempted to intervene? Quite simply (says Werner), what happened to the millipede when he was asked about the order in which he moved his feet. The rhythmic flow of activity is disturbed, perhaps destroyed. But no one will wish to argue that lyric poetry, which is usually rhythmical, proceeds independently of consciousness and will. We must therefore look for another source of poetic rhythms than that which obtains in motor processes which permit only a very restricted degree of conscious guidance.

---

[92] *Ibid.*, p. 116; see also p. 115.

An approach can be made through the observation that rhythm tends to establish itself also whenever a stimulus provokes a response sufficiently complex to involve qualitatively different motor impulses; here again the patterning of the response allows a saving of psychic energy.[93] In lyric poetry, the different motor impulses relate—or related—to vocal activity and bodily movements.

> Such a composite movement can proceed completely without differentiation, as a stream of movements, which break out simultaneously and indiscriminately in as many parts of the body as possible; but they can also proceed in a conscious articulation, since a mutually related duality of locomotor and acoustic-motor content is clearly experienced. In this latter instance, only two important possibilities can be stressed and distinguished: the general bodily movement may become the center, the acoustic activity being mere dependent accompaniment; or the contrary may happen.[94]

When bodily activity takes the lead, what develops is dance; when acoustic activity predominates, the movement is toward lyric. The complexity of the activity becomes sufficiently great to permit a degree of conscious direction without the forfeiture of rhythmic potentiality.

From this point on, development is in the direction of greater differentiation and refinement. Differentiation appears in the separation of song rhythms from speech rhythms and in the establishment of sensed connections between particular rhythms and particular moods, subjects, aims, and even people. Refinement consists in a more or less irresistible drift (in the "higher" cultures) toward perfection and significance, inasmuch as "in these differentiated media the rhythm expresses itself more definitely and less fragmentarily, according to its own nature." [95]

The importance of some degree of control, of guidance, becomes still more apparent in the recognition that rhythmic expression does not occur in connection with the most intensely charged emo-

---

[93] Cf. *ibid.:* "Rhythm establishes itself automatically as soon as bodily movement aims at the psychically simplest form of expression."
[94] *Ibid.*
[95] *Ibid.,* p. 117.

tional states. Like children, primitives do not cry rhythmically when very deeply moved; the appearance of rhythm coincides with a drop in affective pressure. When a child's wails become regular, the worst part of the crisis is over. The affective mood which is rhythmically optimal lies between maximal and minimal intensity. For example, after a boat accident in which several paddlers were drowned, a group of savages at first ran to and fro, gesticulated, wept, held their heads, and jerked their bodies forward and backward, but later began to lament rhythmically under the leadership of the chief bearer; in about half an hour their emotion subsided and cheerfulness was restored.[96] Thus the existence of form in lyric regularly bespeaks some mastery of the motivating affect. Mere outcry is never art. If there were no affective pressure, lyric rhythm would be purely mechanical; but the emotion must be in some degree controlled before it can be given patterned expression.

Mechanical rhythms may, of course, arise spontaneously in special communicative situations—for instance, when words must be shouted instead of spoken. When speech rises to a shout, it becomes rhythmical in order "to bring the meaningful intensities of the sound-stream to expression in the most economical way possible." [97] Such rhythms develop when messages must be delivered from a distance; when heralds make their announcements in a loud voice (as among the Loango Negroes, where herald speech "is completely distinct from ordinary speech"); and even when ship captains converse through megaphones.[98] Such activities would seem to have little bearing upon art forms. Yet one remembers the enormous audiences of Greek dramas and epics and wonders whether this influence alone might not have produced poetic rhythms. Moreover, a familiarity with *Rufsprache,* which is often used when psychic pressure is relatively low, may conceivably have led to the development of a cognitive interest in rhythm and thus have encouraged linguistic experimentation.

THE PSYCHIC EFFECTS OF RHYTHM. So much, very briefly and partially, concerning the primitive background of lyric rhythms.

---

96 *Ibid.,* p. 118.
97 *Ibid.,* p. 119.
98 *Ibid.*

But what of their results? Of much that Werner has said on the subject, we can notice, in passing, only a series of observations which tend to confirm an analysis by Max Rieser summarized in Chapter 4. Besides having a power to awaken emotion in quiescent minds, rhythm has a concomitant and synchronous ability to allay already-aroused feeling, to reduce its scope and limit its intensity. In rhythmic structures "one part always determines another," so that "the second always points back toward the first. Accordingly, rhythm is a closed circle within which the inner concatenation of an A with a B appears perceptually to the ear." The capacity of rhythm to arouse—since the A *demands* the B, and the B, reciprocally, the A—is therefore balanced by a self-sufficiency in the rhythmic structure itself. The pattern has a sleep-working effect because of its "closed-offness." Thus lullabies are found in virtually all primitive communities, and among the Apaches "song is used consciously, in its relaxing effect upon the will, to induce beneficent sleep in ill persons." [99] We must remember here the extraordinary prevalence of repetition in primitive lyric: in proportion as repetition is frequent, the song's power to soothe (or, conversely, if the occasion has a different emotional tilt, to arouse) is increased.[100]

RHYME. Even less can be said here about rhyme, which we shall construe very loosely to include assonance and alliteration.[101] At first, primitive rhyme is "an exclusively sensory activity which answers the affect-motor character of its origin." At this stage, there is a complete separation between rhyming but nonsensical lyrics, on the one hand, and sensible but unrhymed lyrics, on the other. This finding, which is "indubitable," contradicts a theory supported by Biedermann and Wundt: that rhyme developed from the gradual shortening of repeated lyric units, the initial repetition of the whole song giving way gradually to the repetition of half sentences, words, and finally parts of words. Empirical research leads, rather, to the following discoveries.

---

99 *Ibid.,* p. 123.

100 For remarks on repetition in primitive lyric, see Wallascheck, *Primitive Music,* pp. 175–76.

101 For Werner's discussion, see *Ursprünge der Lyrik,* pp. 182–223. The brief summary given below is drawn chiefly from pp. 221–23.

1. Rhyme begins in songs which express a motor or an affect-motor state. Its higher forms result from a "constantly stronger intrusion of sense, of meaning, since between syllables that express affects and have a rhythmic and rhyming function other words multiply, which, to be sure, have an affective intent, but yet possess linguistic and objective functions."

2. A second development crosses this, beginning in the sense-making song. Here rhyme breaks into and at first disrupts the meaning; and thereafter, for a long time, change can proceed only in the direction of a compromise between meaning and sound. In the process, the influence of a magical world view is not to be underestimated, since, for the magically oriented consciousness, acoustic resemblance is not accidental but significant. The highest possible function of rhyme is attained, however, only when rhyming becomes a technique for the emphasizing of real and not merely coincidental relationships—that is, when the acoustic climaxes coincide with climaxes of meaning. Rhyme then becomes "not merely unexceptionally *sens*-ible, but . . . sense-*full,* sense-concentrated." [102] This final development appears only in cultures which have fostered aesthetic self-consciousness to a degree not possible among savages. In such a poet as Goethe, the unity of song, sacrificed when the enticement of rhyme and other acoustic echoes produced an apparently irreconcilable struggle between sense and senselessness, is triumphantly restored.

Continuity of modern lyric with the past

The foregoing discussion of lyric poetry has not only been hurried but has also been fragmentary. A fuller treatment can be found in Werner's book, upon which I have relied because of its rich anthropological documentation and its empirical approach. Although difficult, it deserves to be better known; it is cited by German scholars but almost never by British or American. More extended consideration of it here is prohibited by the intention

---

[102] *Ibid.*, p. 222 (". . . nicht nur vollgültig *sinn*voll, sondern bald und später *sinn*voll, sinnkonzentriert").

of treating two of the major literary forms in some detail and the other two more briefly. Enough has been said, however, to indicate that, like tragedy, comedy, and epic, lyric poetry has an astonishingly long history and continues to have contact with its roots.

That the contact has not been broken need not, I think, be demonstrated at length. The subjectivity of primitive lyric, emphasized in the early part of the discussion, continues in modern lyric to such an extent that it is signalized in handbook definitions. If symbolization has gone further in art lyrics than among savages, and if cognitive domination of the affect has increased, a basic relationship to mood is nonetheless still evident. Rhythm and rhyme (or assonance, or alliteration), although now highly subtilized, have by no means been abandoned. Finally, in all lyric poetry, as in all art, patterning is achieved only partly by rational means.

The last point deserves brief illustration, since, in a way, it includes all the others but has not yet been distinctly asserted. The importance of irrational elements in the total lyric structures, evident everywhere upon close examination, sometimes appears very starkly in subliterary song. I choose as an example a song recently popular among Berkeley teen-agers:

> Oh, the horses run arou-ound,
> Their feet are on the grou-ound,
> Who will wind the clock when I'm awa-ay, awa-ay?
> Go get the axe, there's a hair on baby's chest,
> And a man's best friend is his mother.

When enthusiastically rendered to a simple tune, the lines give youthful singers obvious gratification; and a sympathetic adult can recognize that, despite apparent incoherence, the doggerel is *right,* within the evidently very narrow limits of its intention. Why do the inconsecutive lines make curious sense? Because the images express symbolically a desire, prudently qualified in proportion as it becomes violent, to break through habitual repressions and give the instinctual part of the self, the id, a gaudy day. In the first and third lines, and most wildly and destructively in the fourth line, the images suggest freedom, irresponsibility, a lifting of reins, and a joyous smashing of objects which arouse distaste—for the baby, because it has diverted much of the parents' attention, is an object of unconscious hostility. But another part of the psyche, the superego, which has absorbed a cautionary ethic from its environment, is made uneasy by the id's boisterousness and reacts by the projection of images which, although partly satirical on the manifest level, on a deeper level soothe and reassure. In the second line, the imagining of the horses' feet as firmly on the ground gives comfort; in the third, pretended anxiety about the winding of the clock implies, antisatirically, some residual acceptance of responsibility; and in the last a retreat is made from the symbolic murder of the baby to the security and warmth of the mother's presence. In other ways, too, the lyric has the logicality not of discursive thought but of fantasy and dream experience. The "round" in which the horses run suggests the roundness of a clock face, which then becomes the "ground" upon which the clock's hands revolve. As an entity, the lyric has some power to satisfy because it permits a harmless indulgence of destructive impulses, fenced off from the "real" world both by the fact that the song is "only" a song and by the fact that within it the superego moderates or rejects the id's claims for self-expression.

Most lyric poetry, I submit, no matter how artful, shares some of the song's irrationality, some of its primitiveness. If it did not, it would gratify us less deeply. We seek from lyric poetry, as from other lyric forms, not the rationality of cool logic but the expressiveness of dream, of myth, of a symbolic structure. The symbolic structure may of course be accompanied, and perhaps very skillfully hidden, by a façade of hard rationality; but if it is wholly absent we lay the poem aside as "routine" or "uninspired."

8

Conclusion: Literature
and Feeling

The hypothesis: review

Having come a long and circuitous way, we
pause for a glance backward. In Chapters 1
and 2 reasons were given for believing that
during creative excitement and, reflexively, in
"good" aesthetic contemplation the whole psyche is awakened into activity, not the discursive intelligence only. In Chapters 3–7 an
attempt was made, on the assumption that
nonrational cognition is residual from earlier
psychic tendencies—those of the racial and
individual past—to achieve some understanding of how the subrational parts of the mind

work. Similarities between primitive languages and the language of literature were observed in Chapters 3 and 4; the tendency of story to substitute for causal analysis in primitive thought and in literature was examined in Chapter 5; and in Chapters 6 and 7 the four major literary types, tragedy, comedy, epic, and lyric, were discovered to have perpetuated psychic habits which originated in an immemorial past.

Nothing of all this is in the least mystical. Whatever was intuited (for the mind makes sudden leaps in all inquiry) was empirically checked, so that scaffoldings can be hacked at in the open air. The effort has consistently been to obtain a rational grasp of what in its nature is irrational. The basic investigative method has, in fact, been the thoroughly tested and academically popular one of genetic study. Neither is there real ground for astonishment that psychically as well as physically "ontogeny recapitulates phylogeny." To be sure, the evidence is certainly incomplete and, here and there, may be unreliable. The extrapolations from observable facts may have prolonged as smooth curves lines which, if they could be followed visually from beginning to end, would appear to make sudden dips or leaps and to turn sharp corners. Yet this is the nature of extrapolation; on the principle of Occam's razor, one dares not invent corners and swerves which are not accessible to observation. What has emerged is admittedly hypothesis, not irrefragable fact. Hypotheses, however, not only can suggest directions for future research but, in being disproved, can give birth to more accurate syntheses.

PARALLEL BETWEEN BIOLOGICAL AND PSYCHIC RECAPITULATION. The plausibility of the hypothesis is (I think) enormously enhanced by a parallelism with biological fact. I have just reminded the reader that man's physical development recapitulates his racial —even his preracial—history; why should his psychic history not do the same thing? Charles Roberts Aldrich, in *The Primitive Mind and Modern Civilization,* has drawn a striking picture of the history of a fifty-year old man. Let us, he suggests, imagine such a man standing beside a six-foot tree. If the height of the tree is understood to symbolize the man's individual human experiences, eleven miles of root will be required to represent the "collective, racial psychic structure of the man." We must not, however, imagine that human life is wholly discontinuous with life in a lower form; and, to symbolize the period of time required for human beings to develop from the lost ancestors of apes and men, some additional forty-five miles of root must be conceived.[1] What wonder if the puny individual sucks energy from the illimitable root, if the inertia of the race presses on into the individual? The belief that this occurs demands no commitment to Jungian psychology but rests on the improbability that there is a sharp disjunction between the individual and the species. At birth, modern man is not essentially different from his primitive ancestors. His education is a coating, beneath which he remains simply man—the same kind of creature as his remote forebear who wore skins or leaves and, for want of sophisticated knowledge, read his own consciousness into natural phenomena. There is no irrationality, not even much speculative daring, in the guess that at times—especially when he is moved by excitement—he reverts, at least in parts of his psyche, to patterns no longer so richly sanctioned by his society's institutions as they were by those of former ages.

To use another of Aldrich's metaphors, the human consciousness is like a house with a basement in which many things are stored, some easily accessible, others not. But beneath the basement is a subterranean labyrinth which belongs to no individual's house but is common to all.[2] The artist, I have urged, descends often into this subbasement and brings from it things which, although puzzling to the reason, seem to persons who themselves have a little of the artistic temperament strangely familiar, also vaguely "real" and unaccountably important.

SUPPORT FROM CRITICS. Further credibility is given the hypothesis by the fact that theories resembling it have repeatedly been advanced, not always, clearly, as the result of borrowing. My own formulation, resulting from a sudden realization that descriptions of the savage mind applied with remarkable accuracy to states of aesthetic contemplation, thus turned out not to be

---

[1] Charles Roberts Aldrich, *The Primitive Mind and Modern Civilization* (London: Kegan Paul, Trench, Trubner & Co., Ltd., 1931), p. 29.

[2] *Ibid.*, p. 21.

original. Frederick Clarke Prescott, writing in 1927, quoted George Edward Woodberry as saying still earlier that the poet's mind is a "highly developed mind working in a primitive way" and then himself added that the peculiar fascination of poetry is always due to nonreasonable elements coming from feeling and imagination but tracing their "clear descent" to ancient myth.[3] In 1936, Émile Cailliet, in *Symbolisme et âmes primitives,* remarked that "in spite of inevitable differences, there is not an author known to us *who does not connect symbolism with elementary psychic activity.*"[4] In 1949, Richard Chase said: "To the student of myth the important general conclusion of psychoanalysis is that the artist and the neurotic and the dreamer have much in common both with one another and with the primitive magico-mythical psychology."[5] Northrop Frye declared in 1957 that "in myth we see the structural principles of literature isolated";[6] and in the same year Edward G. Ballard, in a notable work on aesthetics, asserted that the artist's imagination is "much more primitive and childlike" than the scientific imagination. The artist's mental processes are dreamlike and are "in closer touch with the irrational depths of his being, the dark forests of the mind where tigers burn and which shelters one from the tigers." "Beyond a doubt," he adds in another passage, "art has sprung from archaic forms of expression and still retains an intimate and subtle kinship with them."[7] And yet again:

> The primitive in human nature is relevant not only to a special early stage of mankind's history, but it is relevant to all men at all times. Our archaic history and our childhood are not something like a snake's skin, a growth shed after its allotted time. Rather it is like the inner rings of a tree, something which is in-

---

[3] Frederick Clarke Prescott, *Poetry and Myth* (New York: The Macmillan Company, 1927), pp. 9 and 35.

[4] Émile Cailliet, *Symbolisme et âmes primitives* (Paris: Boivin & Cie., 1936), p. 174.

[5] Richard Chase, *Quest for Myth* (Baton Rouge, La.: Louisiana State University Press, 1949), p. 92.

[6] Northrop Frye, *Anatomy of Criticism* (Princeton, N.J.: Princeton University Press, 1957), p. 136.

[7] Edward G. Ballard, *Art and Analysis: An Essay toward a Theory in Aesthetics* (The Hague: Martinus Nijhoff, 1957), pp. 55 and 146.

cluded within later growth and determines its shape. The experience of beauty appears to be the means of maintaining a healthy interchange with this primitive being, and an understanding of this commerce should throw light upon the nature and meaning of beauty.[8]

These quotations are only a selection. The realization that an insight arrived at privately, then checked by a long course of reading, has been shared by men whose studies had different points of departure and dealt with different materials is reassuring.

SUPPORT FROM ANTHROPOLOGISTS.   Anthropologists as well as students of literature and aestheticians have often proclaimed the continuity of modern man and the primitive. R. R. Marett has said that "something of the primeval man lurks in us all." [9] "I am assuming," wrote Aldrich in an introductory passage, "that there is no difference in kind between our psychic structure and processes and those of the savage and the primitive; also that the primitive psyche and all its ways survive in the most highly cultured modern man and woman." [10] Psychic illness often causes regression to ancient thought ways, "whereupon the ancient mystic, myth-making interest is revealed to be still alive and flourishing riotously." [11] The demonstrations by such developmental psychologists as Heinz Werner and Ludwig von Holzschuher that the mental patterns of savages, children, and psychotics share similar traits tend to bear out such generalizations, as do also, less directly, the clinical experiments of Jean Piaget and others with children.

Most striking, perhaps, is an affirmation by Lucien Lévy-Bruhl, who has been accused of drawing too hard and fast a line between the "prelogical" psychic patterns of savages and the "logical" thought processes of adult Westerners. In a French lecture given at Oxford in 1931 he denied emphatically that the distinction was meant to be absolute and concluded his remarks as follows:

---

[8] *Ibid.*, p. 151.
[9] R. R. Marett, *Anthropology* (New York: Henry Holt and Company, ?1912), p. 186.
[10] Aldrich, *Primitive Mind*, p. 3.
[11] *Ibid.*, p. 72.

In our country districts, and even in our large cities, one would not have to search far to meet people who think, feel, and, indeed, act like primitives. Perhaps we must . . . recognize that in every human spirit, whatever its intellectual development may be, an ineradicable base of primitive mentality remains. It is improbable that this will disappear or even weaken beyond a certain point, and no doubt it is not desirable that it should do so. For with it, perhaps, would disappear poetry, art, metaphysics, scientific invention—in short, almost everything which makes the beauty and grandeur of human life.[12]

Although anthropologists differ about the mechanics of the "low" consciousness, probably no contemporary anthropologist of distinction would deny that the most highly cultivated Westerner retains primitive impulses and is liable, especially when relaxed, fatigued, or excited, to some degree of psychic regression.

SUPPORT FROM PSYCHOLOGISTS.   The same tendency would be asserted by depth psychologists in terms even more directly relevant to literature. Erich Fromm, in *The Forgotten Language: An Introduction to the Understanding of Dreams, Fairy Tales and Myths,* says that irrational symbolism is "the one universal language the human race has ever developed, the same for all cultures and throughout history. It is a language with its own grammar and syntax, as it were, a language one must understand if one is to understand the meaning of myths, fairy tales and dreams." [13] The language of fiction is at bottom the same as the regressive language of dreams.

It would be a mistake to regard such statements as prejudicial to the dignity of literature. Fromm quotes Henri Bergson on the difference between the waking and the sleeping states:

You ask me what it is that I do when I dream? I will tell you what you do when you are awake. You take me, the me of dreams, me

---

12 L[ucien] Lévy-Bruhl, *La Mentalité primitive: The Herbert Spencer Lecture, Delivered at Oxford, 29 May, 1931* (Oxford: Clarendon Press, 1931), pp. 26–27.
13 Erich Fromm, *The Forgotten Language: An Introduction to the Understanding of Dreams, Fairy Tales and Myths* (New York: Rinehart & Company, Inc., 1951), p. 7.

the totality of your past, and you force me, by making me smaller and smaller, to fit into the little circle that you trace around your present action. That is what it is to be awake. That is what it is to live the normal psychical life. It is to battle. It is to will. As for the dream, have you really any need that I should explain it? It is the state into which you naturally fall when you let yourself go, when you no longer have the power to concentrate yourself upon a single point, when you have ceased to will.[14]

The state into which you naturally fall when you let yourself go: our racial thought patterns are prerational, and, no matter how thoroughly we are trained to avoid them, they continue through life to exist as psychic potentialities. "Fiction speaks to us," declares Simon O. Lesser, "in a language more natural to us, more intimate, more readily understood, than our native tongue."[15] Anton Ehrenzweig's *The Psycho-Analysis of Artistic Vision and Hearing* is based on a similar insight, though his terminology is peculiar. The first phase in creating the "abstract" aesthetic vision is "a return to the undifferentiated thing perception of the child or to the lack of thing differentiation in primitive thought."[16] Ehrenzweig, too, regards the lower levels of consciousness as important and prizes highly the externalization they achieve in art.

SUPPORT FROM CREATIVE WRITERS. The basic thesis of the present essay is thus substantiated by the conclusions of literary theorists, anthropologists, and psychologists. It is supported also by the intuitions of creative artists. Joseph Conrad's "Heart of Darkness" takes as its theme the existence of repressed savagery in every human heart. As Marlowe, the narrator, works his ship slowly into the African jungle, he is disturbed to find that he responds to the mysterious wilderness. The black savages glimpsed suddenly, when the ship came round a bend in the river, seemed —well, not inhuman.

---

[14] See Henri Bergson, *Dreams,* trans. Edwin E. Slosson (New York: B. W. Huebsch, 1914), p. 49.

[15] Simon O. Lesser, *Fiction and the Unconscious* (Boston: The Beacon Press, 1957), p. 146.

[16] Anton Ehrenzweig, *The Psycho-Analysis of Artistic Vision and Hearing: An Introduction to a Theory of Unconscious Perception* (New York: The Julian Press, 1953), p. 168.

That was the worst of it—this suspicion of their not being inhuman. It would come slowly to one. They howled and leaped, and spun, and made horrid faces; but what thrilled you was just the thought of their humanity—like yours—the thought of your remote kinship with this wild and passionate uproar. Ugly. Yes, it was ugly enough; but if you were man enough you would admit to yourself that there was in you just the faintest trace of a response to the terrible frankness of that noise.[17]

The heart of darkness is not only the African jungle but also the soul of man. Kurtz yielded to his primitive impulses—the recognition that he had done so provoked his dying exclamation, "The horror! The horror!"—and Marlowe, who could understand and perhaps partly sympathize with his actions, associated himself with the guilt by speaking falsely to Kurtz's fiancée. There is not, I think, any distinct recognition in the book that the accessibility of this primitive substratum to the artist is a major source of his power. Yet Conrad, perhaps because his maritime career had taken him to odd corners of the earth, anticipated, in one of his most powerful and least finicky works, a discovery which was to be more and more widely disseminated in our century.

As frequently happens, others writers have also sensitively registered the implications of scientific exploration. In the last few decades, literature has often sought deliberately for the quality of myth—for example, in such semiclassical works as T. S. Eliot's *Wasteland,* James Joyce's *Ulysses,* and several of Thomas Mann's works, most notably the Joseph series and *The Holy Sinner.* Less-known writings have shown the same tendency, among them J. R. R. Tolkien's *The Lord of the Ring,* C. S. Lewis' *Till We Have Faces,* and, most recently, Mary Renault's fascinating *The King Must Die.* The artist's understanding of *why* mythological quality is a literary good is no doubt often vague; but the movement of art toward primitive techniques and subjects has been massive enough to evoke protest.

POSSIBILITY OF ERROR. If the general thesis of the study wins acceptance, doubts may still arise about the analysis of primitive

---

[17] Joseph Conrad, "Heart of Darkness," in *Youth and Two Other Stories* (New York: Doubleday, & Company, Inc., 1924), p. 96.

thought patterns. Here, I confess, the footing is less sure. One may discover a general principle without obtaining a firm grasp of the way it works in detail. Anthropologists are just now very reluctant to analyze the primitive mind; and psychologists and literary critics, apparently the only remaining "authorities," notice different phenomena and arrive at varying, if not finally incompatible, conclusions.

In my own view, the likelihood of error has been markedly reduced by the effort made in Chapters 3–7 to move on the plane of comparatively high-level abstraction. It is not really doubtful, for example, that both primitive and literary thought is frequently animistic, that story as well as analysis can satisfy the desire for explanation, that the four major literary types had prerational origins which continue to be discernible behind whatever logical façades obscure them. Moreover, it is significant to me, though it must be less so to the reader, that continued study, instead of creating uneasiness about what has been said, has tended to confirm it. Thus the discussion in Chapter 4 of an animistic drift in literature is strengthened by an analysis of animated cartoons which I found later in Hanns Sachs' *The Creative Unconscious,*[18] and certain views of tragedy recommended in Chapter 5 are supported strongly, if indirectly, by Simon O. Lesser's *Fiction and the Unconscious,*[19] a modest but penetrating work which had not been published when the chapter was written. Such substantiations are not (it seems to me) astonishing, since in the more explicitly anthropological sections the discussion was kept, for the most part, deliberately on the level of the clearly apparent—one might almost

---

[18] Cf. the following: "The [animated] cartoons revive the primitive concept of the world, called 'animistic.' . . . This was the world of our forefathers thousands of years ago and our own world when we were children."—Hanns Sachs, *The Creative Unconscious: Studies in the Psychoanalysis of Art* (Cambridge, Mass.: Sci-Art Publishers, 1942), p. 178.

[19] Cf. Lesser, *Fiction and the Unconscious,* p. 275: "Above all, [the ego] benefits from letting desire and inhibition, id and superego, engage in a mock but violent battle under the strict terms which tragedy proposes. One may suppose that the ego sometimes becomes weary to the point of bitterness from its incessant efforts to moderate and reconcile the claims of its unreasonable psychic partners. 'Very well,' one can imagine it suggesting in such a mood, 'within the framework laid down by tragedy let us have the pitched battle for which you both seem to be aching.' "

say the obvious and the banal. Nevertheless, it is gratifying to find new information falling gracefully into place.

Implications for literary scholarship

On the assumption that the basic thesis and many (not necessarily all) of the inferences are sound, what are the implications for academic scholarship and for aesthetic theory? Let us begin with scholarship, which can be conceived here in a very narrow way, with relation merely to investigative emphases.

First, although a major purpose of the study has been to relate to literature bodies of relevant anthropological data, it would be unwise to conclude that, in the future, anthropology and literary scholarship must be sister sciences. A little knowledge of anthropology—better still, a great deal—has broad educative value because it opens the eyes to previously undreamed-of human possibilities. It shows us that our own institutions and patterns of behavior are not, as we had thought, exclusively valid, uniquely right; in consequence, we become able to understand much more sympathetically the widely varying cultural backgrounds of the world's great literature, hence the literature itself. To offer only one illustration, Greek mythology ceases to baffle and revolt the intelligence, and we read Greek drama and epic with quickened interest. Again—and this value is the converse of the first—an acquaintance with anthropology reveals to us an enduring sameness in human nature. If we learn that Greek (or Roman, or Celtic, or ancient Germanic) society was less like our own than we had imagined, we discover also, as our knowledge deepens, that "progress" has not after all carried us very far from the psychic bedrock upon which both Greek and modern institutions were built. Yet the business of the literary scholar is of course literature, and he will use or ignore anthropology according to his needs. The rare scholar who elects to make the anthropological backgrounds of literature his specialty instead of such other more conventional backgrounds as the sociological, the political, the rhetorical, or the linguistic ought not to be read out of the profession. Anthropological knowledge is no more degrading than other knowledge, nor does it, in certain of its guises, lack literary relevance. It is appropriate, however, to say categorically that I neither foresee nor wish a mass movement of scholarship toward anthropology, or even toward the study of myth. The anthropological approach is one approach of many, not exclusively or even preeminently valuable.

Much the same comment can be made about depth psychology. The dangers of amateurism here are perhaps even greater, and the reliability of the professional findings may be less. Not improbably, some of the Freudian and Jungian theories have the structure rather of useful myth than of objective truth. Indeed, it has already begun to seem that Freud's belief in the necessary hatred of the son for the father, his incestuous desire to mate with his mother, and so on, may owe a good deal to the conditions of late nineteenth-century Austro-German family life. Moreover, psychoanalytical interpretations of literature, like the Oedipal reading of *Hamlet,* usually seem grossly oversimplified to the literary scholar; and reductionism of any kind is to be deplored. Yet, unquestionably, many psychoanalytical insights are profound, and no adequate reason can be given why a literary scholar who has received special training in psychology should not bring his knowledge into play. The literary situation is bipolar—here is the work, there is the reader or hearer—and behind the work is the personality of its creator. Psychological analysis can be directed profitably either to the relation between the book and its author or to that between the book and its audience, though I should myself urge that the best focus of attention is the psychic patterns *embodied* in the work by its creator and *accessible* to the empathizing reader. Beyond this, it is much too late for literary scholars as a group to doubt the existence of a subconscious (preconscious, unconscious) mind whose workings can astonish the rational intelligence. An insistence on taking into account only the rationally articulated relationships in literature is programmatic, not truly empirical. It imposes limitations upon the materials instead of taking methodological hints from them. I do not urge all literary scholars to become psychoanalysts, but I solicit greater awareness of the nonrational elements in literature and more tolerance of the occasional scholar who chooses to specialize in them.

For the rest, our findings suggest, as does philosophical aesthetics, that many traditional assumptions about art are mistaken and that much scholarship focuses on what Konrad Fiedler, a nineteenth-century aesthetician who just now has great prestige in Germany, called *Nebenseiten,* or "incidentals." The Aristotelian aesthetic still basic to much scholarly thought (because it was official doctrine during several "great" literary ages) has been sufficiently called into question in earlier chapters; I repeat merely that art is as often expressionistic as imitative, and that even imitations, if they are to be artful, must be expressive. "That elementary human need, the impulse to imitate," wrote Worringer in a study which quickly ran through three editions and fifty years later was still attracting favorable attention, "stands outside aesthetics proper, and . . . the satisfaction of it has, in principle, nothing to do with art." [20] There is, of course, a realistic expressive mode, but the artist may, and often does, elect to do something other than imitate sensory (or archetypal) realities.

Regarding the usurpation of attention by *Nebenseiten,* much might be said without convincing scholars already committed to favorite investigative methods. Yet a feeling that institutionalized methods ignore some of the most important characteristics of literature has provoked many rebellions and is still a source of dissatisfaction both inside and outside the universities. What happened, apparently, was that certain literary *Nebenseiten* proved easier to cope with scientifically than literature itself; the exploiters of these became established in the academies and attracted followers eager to do the safe thing, whereas "belletristic" discussion, because it appeared to be irresponsible, came to be thought a gentlemanly amusement. It ought (I hope) by now to be clear that my own instincts are all for responsible methods; moreover, no candid person would deny that the industrious and patient study of *Nebenseiten* led to immense bodies of indisputable data both highly

---

[20] Wilhelm Worringer, *Abstraktion und Einfühlung: Ein Beitrag zur Stilpsychologie,* (3d ed.; Munich: R. Piper & Co. Verlag, 1911), p. 12.

pertinent to literature and valuable in their own right. I propose no excommunication of accepted disciplines. Yet the question remains whether scholarly attitudes ought ever to become frozen. Much is perpetually over the horizon—but not necessarily all of it permanently there. With tolerance from scholars who stand aloof, and at the price of a good deal of initial doubt and probably many false starts, I believe that we can get nearer to literature, to its vital principles, to *what really makes it tick,* than we have hitherto succeeded in doing.

The effort, at least, is worth making. It behooves those who make it, however, to adopt no hieratic airs and to claim no transcendence of facts or logic. Though the materials which they turn over are partly irrational, their handling of data must strive for consistent rationality and be vulnerable to empirical disproof.

Implications for aesthetics

We come at last to a consideration of the meaning of our findings for aesthetic theory. Let us suppose that the "good" writer's mind adopts, at moments of highest creative tension, perceptive and reflective patterns characteristic of the primitive and the child —so what? How ought our most fundamental ideas about literature to be affected?

It need not follow, and I am convinced does not, that literature is a less valuable human activity than its lovers believe. The point is worth dwelling on, for the conclusions reached in the foregoing chapters will be resisted quite as strongly by persons who feel that the dignity of literature has been compromised as by those who think that the investigative methods have been unsound. Nonetheless, literature unquestionably has truth value in spite of its more or less pervasive irrationality; and it performs other psychic functions so effectively, and so uniquely—or nearly so, since other art forms have a somewhat analogous power—that its total service to humankind is inestimably great.

TRUTH IN LITERATURE.   The truth value not only of literature but of all art began to receive a distinctively modern emphasis at least as early as the end of the last century in the writings of

Konrad Fiedler, an art-intoxicated man whose interest was chiefly in painting.

> It must be constantly realized that the hand does not express something which could be imaged previously in the mind; instead, the process carried out by the hand is merely the further stage of a unitary and indivisible transaction which, to be sure, is invisibly prepared in the mind, but can reach a higher stage of development in no other way than just through painterly manipulation.[21]

The remark rests on a valid insight. Aesthetic creation does not, typically, consist in giving material form to the results of a process already completed in the imagination. The point was made earlier and need not detain us now. Two inferences drawn by Fiedler are more important. First: "It leads to confusion to wish to explain the artist's condition by calling it a kind of madness; for madness is a clouding of the consciousness. The artist's ecstasy is a heightening of the consciousness." [22] Secondly, and still more penetratingly: "The highest task of the plastic arts is that of raising into the sphere of consciousness, by their peculiar means of presentation, certain things which are accessible to no other means of presentation." [23] Art is profoundly cognitive, though its techniques are not those of the reason.

That this is so is scarcely any longer a matter of doubt. "There is such a process as non-discursive thought," says Sir Herbert Read, "and . . . the mind develops, and apprehends reality, as much by imagination and dream, by myth and ritual, by art, in short, as by practical intelligence." [24] This we can take as certain, this we can accept as proved. Such masses of empirical evidence cooperate to support it that it has become axiomatic for philosophical aesthetics and for much nonaesthetic thought—for example, Ernst Cassirer's whole philosophy of symbolic forms. The serious question involves not the "whether" but the "what." *What* does art

---

[21] Konrad Fiedler, *Vom Wesen der Kunst: Auswahl aus seinen Schriften* (Munich: R. Piper & Co. Verlag, 1942), p. 135.

[22] *Ibid.,* p. 122.

[23] *Ibid.,* p. 69.

[24] Sir Herbert Read, *Art and the Evolution of Man* (London: Freedom Press, 1951), p. 47.

raise to consciousness which can be cognized in no other way?

TRUTH IN DREAMS.   Many varying answers can be offered to the question, none adequate in isolation, all together no more than approximate and perhaps partial. Sir Herbert's remark contains one hint that can be taken up immediately. If art shares some of the characteristics of dreams, it may sometimes express similar meanings. Fortunately, the existence of truth value in dreams is beyond question. The difficulty is merely in reading the symbols. Throughout most of history, dreams were recognized to have meanings; and everyone knows that psychoanalysis now relies heavily on them for knowledge about mental states. The manifest confusion often *presents* latent sense. That this is so should awaken surprise only among persons who disbelieve in the principle of causality. Behind apparent nonsense there is always some meaning—if not about external reality, then about the originating mind.

ART AND PERCEPTIONS.   But dreams contain truths about external reality also, as Erich Fromm has shown in *The Forgotten Language.* Very often they embody facts which have been not thought but perceived: for example, a person who is consciously admired but has been recognized by the subconscious to have socially undesirable traits may appear in an unflattering guise. The dreamer is puzzled, but the dream portrait is subsequently proved to have been more faithful than the waking concept.[25] The instance is symptomatic. Much, perhaps most, of our truest knowledge comes to us directly through our senses. The human ability to reason is inexpressibly precious; it not only leads us to form concepts but sometimes to revise false impressions. Yet intuited knowledge is a larger part of our total knowledge than most of us realize; and a major source of intuitions is nonconceptualized perception.

From this point of view the artist would appear to be, among other things, a specialist in perception, a man whose senses are keener than those of the average person and more resistant to the

---

[25] See Fromm, *The Forgotten Language,* pp. 36–46, for a discussion. The example is taken from pp. 36–38.

reason. His impressions are often stronger, and his reliance on them more confident. Such an image of the artist accords far better with his observable social traits than the alternative picture of him as sage and philosopher that has been promulgated recently by critics eager to glorify their calling. Because he sees much that is hidden from dull eyes, his works are rich with true experience. "Have you noticed now," asks Browning's Fra Lippo of the captain of the guard, "Your cullion's hanging face? A bit of chalk, / And trust me but you should, though!" Most of us pass through life half-blindfolded, half-deaf, our noses stopped, and our fingers in our pockets. The artist can give us the use of his senses, and because he does so we know the world better. He may be wise with a wisdom of the flesh, if not—though he may be this too—with rational intelligence. That his sensory keenness is more important to his art than conceptual profundity is indicated by the fact that although there is much art of pure sensation there is no art of pure thought. Here, then, is one source of truth in literature. The world has a sensory surface, and the artist can tell us more than any other man about the surface, which is as "real" as what lies beneath it.

ART AS EMBODIMENT. It does not follow from what has been said that every person with sharp senses is an artist, or even that all artists have especially sharp senses. We pass on, therefore, to a further implication of what has been said about dreams. We have observed that the truth in dreams is not rationally articulated but presented; and the artist must also have the gift of presenting, of embodying what he perceives or thinks in images. How he accomplishes this is by no means easily understood; and scholars who collect factual data about literary backgrounds sometimes allude, in awed tones, to the "final mystery of creation." Scientific criticism must aspire to the resolution even of final mysteries, and one purpose of the present work has been to dissipate a little of the fog by suggesting that the artist's mind relapses into the habits of minds which necessarily presented because they had not yet been trained to analyze every experience into elements. The immediate point, however, is that art loses none of its claim to truth value because it stimulates direct insights instead of laying down trains of syllogisms.

The foregoing observations are not new. According to Lesser, the fiction which is so important to literature

> *quickly and effectively transmits almost any kind of material without requiring the reader to put what he understands into words.* Though composed of words, so far as its reception is concerned the language of fiction is an instrument of non-discursive communication.[26]

A similar assertion might be made about most art, which, indeed, one might define as "pure" art in proportion as it is nondiscursive. A comment of Fromm's about dreams is also relevant. The dream

> has no "but," "therefore," "because," "if," but expresses these logical relations in the relation between the pictorial images. The dreamer may, for instance, dream of a person standing up and raising his arm and then being transformed into a chicken. In waking language the dream thought would be expressed as meaning, "He gives the appearance of being strong, *but* he is really weak and cowardly like a chicken." In the manifest dream this logical relation is expressed by a sequence of the two images.[27]

Presented truth, I insist once more, is not necessarily less truthful than explicated truth, although it may have more ambiguity (which is one reason why science has mainly eschewed presentation). We must learn to read its language, which, in these rationalistic and positivistic times, is all too "forgotten"; but the truths are there to be recognized.

TRUTHS OF THE MIND.   We have not yet done with our consideration of presented truth, for not all aesthetic knowledge has a perceptual basis. If it had, the methods of this essay would have been badly chosen. A very large part of the cognitive value of literature depends on its capacity to raise into consciousness truths not of the external world but of the human mind. Poems, plays, and novels show a profounder knowledge than either psychology or anthropology of *what we are really like,* of nonlogical processes which go on inside us below the threshold of awareness but are

---

[26] Lesser, *Fiction and the Unconscious,* p. 153.
[27] Fromm, *The Forgotten Language,* p. 71.

really *there*, really important. Indirectly, but sensitively and, in a sense, *accurately*, literature gives us an understanding of aspects of our nature that escape nonaesthetic formulation.

That this is so has been argued eloquently by Lesser. First of all, the presentation of truths about human consciousness does not necessarily involve a false reflection of external reality. (If it did, the cogency of what has just been said would suffer.)

> Whatever appearances may suggest, in fact the reading of fiction implies no reluctance to face or struggle with the real world. While fiction alters the facts of experience, a fundamental purpose of those alterations, as the first and greatest esthetician, Aristotle, realized, is the achievement of an imaginary world more lifelike than life itself, more directly and honestly concerned with essential problems, more supple in its expression of every aspect of man's nature, less burdened by distracting irrelevancies.[28]

In judging literature, "we give the highest place precisely to those works which ignore no aspect of man's nature, which confront the most disagreeable aspects of life deliberately and unflinchingly": [29] to *Oedipus* and *Hamlet,* to *The Brothers Karamazov* and *The Divine Comedy,* not to *Pollyanna* and *The Magnificent Obsession.* From such works we obtain, paradoxically, more satisfaction, even more immediate pleasure, than from works which restructure the external world in such a way as to flatter and approve our aspirations. The principle holds even of comedy; we rate *Gulliver's Travels* and *Le Misanthrope* higher than *You Can't Take It With You.* Why?

The answer brings us directly to the forms of human consciousness. Fiction seeks presentations which not only mirror the world truthfully but also reflect the total human psyche, not timidly chosen parts of it merely.

> Fiction gives our conflicts a much more thorough airing. Directly or indirectly it tries to represent every consideration which might be advanced to justify or oppose the satisfaction of a given impulse—to give the impulse its full measure of attraction and yet

---

[28] Lesser, *Fiction and the Unconscious,* p. 54.
[29] *Ibid.,* p. 55.

remind us of everything which whispers that we should not yield
to it. . . . Moreover, in keeping with its willingness to hear all
sides, it strives for resolutions based upon maximum fulfilment,
rather than the illusory kind achieved by denying or slighting certain claims; it seeks resolutions which, to use a happy word of
Robert Penn Warren's, are "earned" rather than "forced." [30]

The greatest literature gives us "the impression of having over-
looked nothing, no relevant consideration, no possibility of har-
monizing apparently incompatible elements." [31] Its value systems
(which of course have their seat in the mind, though the *objects*
which are valued may be in the world) "are all pervaded by what
I like to think of as *a sense of the opposite,*" and its attitude is
"one of poised and sustained ambivalence." [32] Its constructions
leave no part of the psyche, conscious or unconscious, rational or
emotive, unrepresented and dissatisfied.

DISTANCING OF PSYCHIC CONFLICTS.   The tendency of good
literature to formalize psychic activities which ordinarily are repressed from consciousness because they awaken anxiety raises a
problem. If in everyday life we try to deny or ignore psychic conflicts, why do we not resent having them forced upon our attention
by the writer? The reply is that in literature the conflicts are
distanced. We view their image across a gulf, securely, and obtain
from the experience a relief analogous to that felt by the psychotic
when he is induced to express his inhibitions.

> It is our fears, obviously, which lead us to evade and falsify our
> problems. *But in reading fiction we do not have to be afraid;* there
> honesty is possible and welcome. We turn to fiction because we
> know that there we will find our problems imaged in their full in-
> tensity and complexity, everything faithfully shown, the desires
> and fears we have slighted drawn as distinctly as anything else.
> Unconsciously we want to see justice done to those neglected con-
> siderations—they are a part of us too.[33]

---

[30] *Ibid.,* pp. 78–79.
[31] *Ibid.,* p. 79.
[32] *Ibid.,* p. 87.
[33] *Ibid.,* p. 81.

The gulf between the real and imagined worlds is wide enough to permit the normal reader to do much to minimize its existence—to send emanations of himself across the void, to empathize.

> We cannot have the experiences for which we turn to fiction if what we read does not possess the momentary authority, the hallucinatory vividness, of our fondest dreams. . . . Yet we cannot have the experiences either unless we are aware that we are engaging in make-believe.[34]

If the awareness falters, as it may sometimes do for neurotics, guilt feelings arise and anxiety may become unbearable.

DISPLACEMENT.   A second reason why inhibitions can be released in literature is that their manifestations are often skillfully disguised. Such fictive characters as Hamlet and Prince Myshkin are tormented, Lesser thinks, "by impulses so violent and so repugnant to their idealistic nature that they are never acknowledged." How, then, are the impulses made known to the reader?

> The answer is a curious one: we never become consciously aware of them either, at any rate not before we have put down *Hamlet* and *The Idiot* and begun to dissect them as critics; the repudiated impulses are communicated to our unconscious minds while their existence is safeguarded from awareness; the illicit satisfaction is procured secretly and subterraneously, without the participation of consciousness.[35]

The device is known to psychologists as displacement: "Feelings are divorced from their real source and associated with something else in connection with which their avowal becomes permissible." [36]

Displacement is common in emotional experience and need only be described to be recognized. Dissatisfaction with the purpose of a trip may express itself as annoyance at the train service. A businessman displaces when he scolds his secretary because he is angry with his wife, the secretary when she slams down on her desk a notebook filled with dictation which she must work overtime to

---

[34] *Ibid.,* p. 143.
[35] *Ibid.,* pp. 107–8.
[36] *Ibid.,* p. 108.

transcribe. Similar displacements permit the release of pent-up energies as we read.

> Desires so repugnant to us that they cannot be acknowledged, and our anxieties themselves, constitute perennial themes of fiction. Even to deal with such material in fantasy entails a certain amount of risk. If there is not everywhere the suggestion of order and control, if the potentially offensive material is not softened and disguised, and if—especially in the absence of such disguise—its connections with our own impulses and fears is not carefully concealed from view, we will experience so much uneasiness that we will be unable to enjoy what we read and in all probability will feel repelled by it. A driving purpose of form is to transform that which might inspire terror into something which can be contemplated and experienced without fear.[37]

We arrive thus at an insight into the importance of form and also of style. By giving the impression of control, these "orient our interest not toward action but toward perception and understanding"; [38] hence they are important in proportion as the anxiety potential of the material is greater.[39]

COGNITIVE VALUE OF LITERATURE.   Much of this explanation may seem strange. I have said that the truth value of literature depends partly on a capacity to raise "truths of the mind" into consciousness; is it not contradictory to add that the truths are not recognized? No, for what most resists recognition is that they are truths of *our* minds. They are less difficult to cognize within the fictive framework. Professional critics, and even students, write perceptively of characters and incidents in literature, and in doing so reveal an awareness of many complexities, including exactly the "sense of the opposite" and the "poised and sustained ambivalence" about which Lesser has remarked. The displacements are seldom noticed; and perhaps it is as well that they are not. The point here is that *because* there are displacements what is

---

[37] *Ibid.,* p. 128.

[38] *Ibid.,* p. 134. Lesser uses the phrase in a somewhat different context.

[39] Cf. *ibid.,* p. 182: Stylization is determined by the "anxiety-potential of the material. . . . Innocuous subject matter requires very little; tragedy, because it deals with our most rigorously repressed impulses, requires a great deal."

learned about the fictive universe is learned also, in an extremely indirect but not ultimately mysterious way, about ourselves. We analogize (thinks Lesser) as we read, down to the smallest details of the story. "Ralph Touchett's deep and selfless adoration of Isabel Archer may remind a reader of his feeling for a beloved child"; Robinson Crusoe's desire "to venture over for the main," which "increased, rather than decreased, as the means for it seemed impossible," may perhaps "recall an episode in which our longing for someone grew long after we became aware that she was too dear for our possessing." [40] In empathizing the frightening adventures described in Tolkien's *The Lord of the Ring,* we become better acquainted with the structure of dread—*our* dread, wherever and however it may occur, not merely the dread of elves and hobbits.

All this, I repeat, corroborates the dogma that literature, though "unreal" and in a sense "false," yet has cognitive value. The incidents and feelings develop at a distance, within a frame, under conditions which facilitate learning. "Issues are posed and resolved, event follows upon event, and all the while nothing is asked of us: no action, no decision, not even, in any physical sense, any response. The very quality of the movement of fiction tends to make us spectators." [41] The writer, moreover, differs markedly from the daydreamer in not being his own hero. According to Hanns Sachs, "he is not guided by a wish for self-glorification, but for self-investigation." [42] The narcissism of daydreaming is displaced by the narcissism of the work itself, its inward-turning structure. This tendency to turn inward is one of the most highly significant elements of aesthetic form and deserves to be noticed separately. In a continued effort to avoid originality, I turn to Edward Ballard's discussion of reflexive form in *Art and Analysis.*

REFLEXIVE FORM. In Ballard's opinion, the persistent straining of art objects to point inward instead of outward, to return constantly upon themselves, is due to a condition of aesthetic experience. In nonaesthetic contemplation objects "are attended to as

---

[40] *Ibid.,* p. 247.
[41] *Ibid.,* p. 167.
[42] Sachs, *Creative Unconscious,* p. 42.

passing phases in some more inclusive experience," as parts of a larger whole.

> If the object is to be attended to for itself, then some especially effective device must be used by which the object is, so to speak, continually re-presented and by which it continually draws attention back upon itself when attention tends to stray away. The kind of object which can be regarded aesthetically therefore, is the object whose formal construction insures that it continually represents itself to be enjoyed or valued.

Aesthetic form is dynamically unified form "just because only this form leads the percipient to confine his response to just that object and hence, if it is valued, to value it for its own sake." [43] The word "temple," Ballard remarks, "meant originally to 'set apart' (the Greek etymon means 'to cut out'). The notion of the qualitative difference in space is conserved in the term *contemplari*, a meaning to be conserved, I think, in the aesthetic usage of this word." [44] From the point of view adopted here, the apparent (though of course illusory) separateness of the art object from everything not itself is valuable because it permits a certain cognitive objectivity. We can perceive within the fictive framework truths which would disturb us in an ordinary context.

That reflexivity is characteristic of art need not be shown at length. Why should the end of a novel or poem reflect the beginning, the coda of a sonata incorporate the themes of earlier movements, the curve of a statue's elbow reciprocate that of a knee, the gaze of one painted figure be directed toward the contrary and reciprocating gaze of another, if not to keep perception within the aesthetic frame? In fiction one of the most recurrent of all motifs is that of the journey and return. "Any writing," says Ballard emphatically, "is poetry if it imitates this cycle," [45] and again, "The master principle of aesthetic form, the journey home, the return upon itself, is the rule of organic unity." [46] The outward sweep of the statue's elbow, instead of carrying the observer's eye

---

[43] Ballard, *Art and Analysis*, p. 90.
[44] *Ibid.*, p. 148.
[45] *Ibid.*, p. 85.
[46] *Ibid.*, p. 87.

into the surrounding space, is sensed to be balanced by a compensating curve elsewhere, so that the eye travels from one to the other, and back again, instead of outside the work's limits. So also with the other reciprocations. Attention thus dwells within the art work, and what is discovered within it mingles with other knowledge at a very deep level in the mind, where anxiety is unlikely to be awakened.

ART AS CONSUMMATORY. By this series of reflections we are prepared to understand the emphasis of many distinguished aestheticians—for example, John Dewey—on the *consummatory* nature of aesthetic experience. It is quite right, in a sense, to insist that aesthetic value is terminal and not instrumental, that we need not go through art to something else in order to establish its value. The reader of the *Divine Comedy* or of *Pilgrim's Progress* can, and usually does, stop short at the work's edges and not continue into Catholicism or Protestantism. Yet it is absurd to deny that his attitude toward religion in workaday life can be affected by his literary experience. The atheist may look at his Catholic friends with more respect after emerging from Dante's imagined universe. Art is *both* autonomous and continuous with nonaesthetic life. As *distant* it is consummatory, self-completing; but at the same time it can be nearer and more intimate than consciousness itself.

The place of feeling in nonrational psychic states

It is time now for this work, which is not art, to return upon itself and end (though not quickly) where it began. Our subject has been irrationality in art, and particularly in literature; and in the greater number of pages evidence has been offered for a belief that the source of the irrationality is a tendency of the artist's mind to recapture the perceptual and reflective habits of primitive men and of children. From the beginning, however, it has been implicit that nonrational psychic states are impregnated with *feeling*—that, in fact, they depend heavily upon it, that their dynamic structure is largely determined by it. When the mind does not stand coolly off from experience to conceptualize it but instead flows into it undivided and whole, as among children and savages, the resulting image of the world derives in considerable part from the patterns of the affections themselves. In the remainder of the chapter, it will be my purpose to show that literature takes as its primary, though unacknowledged and often unrecognized, task the creation of symbols which articulate human feelings and attitudes.

Nothing said hitherto conflicts with this view. The perceptual truths presented by dreams are truths not so much of the non-human world as of impacts made on the mind by experience. We *feel* in an acquaintance qualities which would make him an un-satisfactory friend, though our reason may tell us there is no ground for the suspicion. Such an item of knowledge, which has come to us through peripheral sense impressions, registers in the sub-conscious mind as an affective bias, which the intelligence may or may not prevail on us to resist. Similarly, the writer's perceptions of the nonhuman world do not often seem to us to have specifically literary quality if they are not in some degree impregnated with feeling. A meteorologist's description of the weather, which has no affective overtones (temperature 91°, stratus clouds, humidity 85, 6-mile SW wind), seems to us less perceptive than the novelist's (hot, dull, muggy, still) because, without translation, it has no leverage on the feelings; yet the meteorologist is a trained observer. The referents of his terms are nonhuman criteria of measurement; those of the novelist's terms are psychic impressions touched with emotive meanings. This is the hardest case. The other varieties of aesthetic cognition described earlier involve subconscious layers of the mind more directly; and it is axiomatic in depth psychology that such layers are rarely or never affectively neutral. I have spoken of emotional conflicts, repressed anxieties, displacements, consummations: the acquaintance with these which literature can give us may constitute true knowledge, but the knowledge is neces-sarily of ourselves and other people like us, and predominantly of our emotional nature. Everything that has been discovered hitherto converges upon the realization that the importance of feelings to literature is far greater than is acknowledged by domi-nant literary theories.

This is not to say that the place of feeling in art has not historically been accepted. "Applauding hands, and dry eyes (which during *Dryden's* theatrical reign often met) are a satire on the writer's talent, and the spectator's taste." Thus Edward Young, almost exactly two centuries ago, in *Conjectures on Original Composition*. The emphasis here is different—and I think mistaken—but, in the Age of Reason itself, a vital commerce between literature and the feelings was signalized. Until recently, indeed, there has seldom been a time when a connection between art and the affections was not emphasized by a dominant popular or learned aesthetic. The ancient doctrine of inspiration (or possession) marks another, more mystical, way of cognizing the role of excitement in the creative process. I am acquainted with no important historical aesthetic, with the possible exception of the Thomist (such as it was), which did not grant and in some way justify the presence of feelings in art. The idealist system of Bernard Bosanquet, which made much of felt qualities in aesthetic materials, was perhaps the last that had a continuous descent from classical and medieval notions. More recently, literary theory has turned a corner, and at present academic and literary journals rarely admit critical analyses which focus on embodied feelings. Emotive theories, like that of Yrjö Hirn, are regarded as faintly disreputable.

> The work of art does not claim to give us, nor do we expect to receive from it, increased knowledge as to the real nature or predominant characters of things and events. We only wish to get the clearest and strongest impression of the feelings with which an object has been contemplated by the artist.[47]

In general, academic stress is on historical backgrounds or, among critics who are interested "in art as art," on cognitive or formal values other than affective.

Within the last few years a salutary reaction has begun. Susanne Langer, in *Feeling and Form*, called attention to Otto Baensch's essay, "Kunst und Gefühl" ("The aesthetic value of an art work lies merely in the power with which it forms and binds and makes

---

[47] Yrjö Hirn, *The Origins of Art* (London: Macmillan & Co., Ltd., 1900), p. 120.

generally communicable a definite feeling-content" [48]) and herself said decisively, "Art is the creation of forms symbolic of human feeling." [49] Rudolf Arnheim has discussed art works as isomorphs of human feelings. The thesis of Ernest Ballard's *Art and Analysis,* which, like Mrs. Langer's work, draws on the symbolic philosophy of Ernst Cassirer, is that "the aesthetic object is a certain sort of symbol to which the appreciator responds in a characterizable manner, these responses being precisely the thing which the aesthetic object symbolizes." [50] Simon Lesser, in *Fiction and the Unconscious,* declares that "any kind of problem must be invested with a great deal of feeling before it becomes a suitable object for fiction," and again that "literature gives us forms for our feelings —often a variety of forms; as Krutch puts it, 'a repertory of roles amongst which we have only to choose.' " [51] The readjustment of emphasis is promising, for it permits us to approach an understanding of the strange "vibrations" awakened in us by good literature, and also noticed by Ballard: "In addition to excellent character portrayal, a well developed story, and full technical command of language, we find also in the greatest art 'a strange unanalyzed vibration below the surface, an undercurrent of desires and fears and passions, long slumbering yet eternally familiar, which for thousands of years (have) lain near the root of our most intimate emotions and been wrought into the fabric of our most magical dreams.' "[52]

Character of the artist

If, in the light of these observations, we inquire how art is produced and what it contains, at least a partial answer is accessible. No doubt the answer is neither exhaustive nor wholly accurate, but it will serve as a rough preliminary guess and perhaps also as a stimulus to further analysis. To begin with, the artist differs from

---

[48] Otto Baensch, "Kunst und Gefühl," *Logos,* XII (1923), 26.

[49] Susanne K. Langer, *Feeling and Form: A Theory of Art Developed from Philosophy in a New Key* (New York: Charles Scribner's Sons, 1953), p. 40.

[50] Ballard, *Art and Analysis,* pp. 1–2.

[51] Lesser, *Fiction and the Unconscious,* pp. 67 and 44.

[52] Ballard, *Art and Analysis,* p. 36. The quotation is from Gilbert Murray's "Hamlet and Orestes."

the ordinary man in at least two notable respects. His perceptual and reflective processes, however sophisticated on one level, have contact with other, more instinctive and less intellectualized, processes which predominate in primitive men and in children—he is a *whole* man, not an emotionally emasculated thinking machine —and he has retained control of the "forgotten language" of presentational symbols, the language of ritual, of myths, of dreams. In addition, he has the creative instinct. He likes to "make things," as a salesman may enjoy building a dog house or a housewife mixing up a batch of divinity fudge. (So defined, the creative instinct is not a prerogative of artists only.) Finally, if he is to be a writer, he must have an unusual sensitivity to language, to the meanings of words and to the shapes and affective colors of linguistic units, from syllables to paragraphs and chapters. Such a man, at a time (let us say, without any desire really to dogmatize about the nature of creative impulse) when he is dissatisfied, fidgety, without an adequate outlet for his energy, or when pressure is put upon him by a mood ("With me," wrote Johann von Schiller, "the sensation is at first without a clear and definite object" [53]), happens to observe, or to think about, or to image, something which engages his interest. It may be anything: person, landscape, thing, event, phrase, gesture, expression, movement, and so on indefinitely. His interest is aroused. He begins to play with the object, to build a fantasy about it, to surround it with imagined causes and effects. The structure grows, spreads, acquires complexities, develops feeling tones. ("The magnetism of a soul-filling interest," wrote Thomas Mann in a book about the writing of a book, "is strong and mysterious. Without conscious help from its bearer, among men it will guide conversation, draw talk irresistibly into its sphere. It directs, forms, and colors outer experience and social encounters." [54]) An aesthetic universe emerges, apparently distinct from that of everyday contemplation, with laws and limitations of its own. (The "virtual" world of art, said Cassirer,

---

[53] Quoted in Friedrich Nietzsche, *Die Geburt der Tragödie aus dem Geiste der Musik* (Leipzig: E. W. Fritzsch, 1872), p. 20.
[54] Thomas Mann, *Die Entstehung des Doktor Faustus: Roman eines Romans* (Amsterdam: Bermann-Fischer, 1949), p. 49.

"has its own truth . . . , its own lawfulness." [55]) To the creator, it may appear after the work has been completed that it has been produced through him but not by him. ("For years," remarked George Moore of what is perhaps his most remarkable work, "I believed myself to be the author of *Hail and Farewell,* whereas I was nothing more than the secretary." [56]) Many of the connections which seem to the author to be implicit in the materials are, however, in actuality implicit *in himself.* When the writing is done and the piece is cut free from its creator to lead an apparently autonomous life, it will be held together, in very large part, by the forms of the author's feelings. If he has been successful in probing to lower strata of the common human psyche, these will be forms also of his reader's psyche, therefore strong enough to support an aesthetic structure which must issue into the world and awaken responses.

The mechanisms responsible for this process require brief explanation, and the value of the accomplishment further comment.

The embodiment of feelings in art works

The process of embodying feelings in art works need be sketched only in its essentials. It is a common observation that certain colors clash, that pairs of musical notes jar, that angular shapes conflict with curves. Some such statements have an ascertainable physical basis; for example, harmonious notes are produced by a string vibrating as a whole, as two equal halves, in thirds, and so on. Other impressions of objects are harder to track down to physical laws. A tall, thin vase may appear to be light, a short, squat vase heavy, though the two in fact have identical weights. Here one may suspect an unconscious inference from known properties of gravity, which pulls more strongly on denser masses. What are we to say, however, about such a human illusion as that the right-

---

[55] Ernst Cassirer, *Philosophie der Symbolischen Formen,* Vol. II (Berlin: Bruno Cassirer Verlag, 1925), p. 320.

[56] George Moore, *Hail and Farewell* (Edbury ed.; London: William Heinemann, Ltd., 1937), Preface.

angled handle of a softly curving vase "wants" to spring out into a curve? What nonpsychic justification can be offered for the careful "balancing" of a group photograph or the tendency of choreographers to have successive ballet dancers enter from opposite corners of the stage? It would "feel wrong" to put all the illusory weight on one side of the photograph, and the soaring appearance of the première danseuse from upstage left seems to "call for" that of the leading male dancer from upstage right; but the reasons behind such forms are purely human. Arrangements like these accord neither with material necessities nor even with intrinsic physical conveniences. On the contrary, certain members of the photographed group may be put into uncomfortable positions, and the dancers must often squeeze behind backdrops in order to start from formally satisfying positions.

So, I suggest, with many or most of the formal elements in art. They are worked out, often at great expense of spirit, in accordance with psychic promptings in which the role of the affections is more important than that of the reason. In contemplating the curved vase with the angular handle, the psyche is disposed by its appreciation of curves in the greater portions of the presented surface to desire curves in the smaller portions also. To speak metaphorically, the affective tilts of curves and angles get in each other's way, and the most obvious way of relieving the psychic distress is to allow the stronger tendency to swallow the weaker.

No doubt, if it were wanted, a less metaphorical explanation could be hammered out: for example, that inside the mind as well as outside it conflicting energies tend by a natural law to seek either reconciliation or balance. A steel ball ejected laterally across an inclined plane is pushed forward by its initial momentum at the same time that it is drawn downward by gravity; the resulting path is a smooth curve which permits the ball at every instant to satisfy both impulses. Condensed gas inside a balloon causes the balloon to expand until inner and outer pressures are equal. Similarly for psychic forces. If the weight of the angles in the vase exactly balanced that of the curves, the part of the mind which responded to the angles might not wish for an opportunity to obtain relief from pressure; the halves of the psyche would stand in dynamic equipoise. Or, again, the psychic tension initiated by the contrast might be resolved, as in the case of the steel ball, by a prominent design—let us say on a central boss—in which a shape transitional between the curves and the angles, but nearer to the angle, was several times repeated. The possibilities are endless. Angles and curves might balance and yet be reconciled in a boss consisting of a square inscribed inside a circle. What must be avoided is precisely the confusing and upsetting of nonrational responses, the apparent effort to balance unequals or to provoke an affective movement which is then resisted and frustrated.

The illustration has been simple; in a complex art work there may be many overlapping and apparently (to the intelligence but not to the feelings) conflicting structures. Contradiction may itself be formalized, so that the alternation from one kind of affective reaction to a second qualitatively different kind becomes rhythmic, hence can be anticipated and enjoyed. If the art work is successful, however, the reason is always that the artist, by following the hints given him by his feelings—as well, certainly, as others given him by his rational intelligence—has in the end produced an object which is the material equivalent, or symbol, of an organized psychic pattern.

The importance to creative activity of nonrational states of the mind can be illustrated by a dialogue in Joyce Cary's *The Horse's Mouth* in which a painter and a sculptor consider a work half finished by the sculptor.

> "Look at what I've done with it—slop, just slop. Lost all the monumental. And that corner, oh my God—"
> "Well," I said, "what did you mean—knocking that hole in the left side? What's it doing, that hole? What's it for?"
> "Don't ask me," he said, throwing his hammer on the floor and making a bit of the parquet jump right out of its socket. "I thought I saw one of the dead there, sitting up with his head on his shoulder. I could feel him this morning. . . . And so I cut into the block above it, cut out the whole corner. But it went soft. And it goes on getting softer. However sharp you make the edges. And now I can't even see the next vertical. . . . But Christ, look at

it now—it's gone soft—it's rotten. You could put your bloody fingers through it like bad butter." And he gave the stone a prod as if he really expected his finger to go through it.[57]

So artists talk about art—if they are articulate and center their attention on their own work instead of trying to be impressive for a public. They *respond* to their images and materials with the whole psyche, not with a coldly calculating reason alone. When the responses conflict, or, worse still, cease, they fall into black depressions from which they can be rescued only by a vision in which everything is again ordered. The vision, moreover, may be almost totally nonrational. The sculptor whom we have just seen frustrated disappeared for a week, after which he returned with a beard, with green face, and with crimson eyes, but again full of enthusiasm. " 'It's a feeling of declivity,' he said. 'I had just been sick,' he said, 'and I was looking at the bowl when it came to me. That's what I've been feeling after—declivity.' " [58]

The writer, who is an artist in an especially complicated medium, is also a creature of strong and sensitive feelings. Since he manipulates words, which often have not only feeling tones but also referential and conceptual meanings, he must take more account of ideas than the painter, the sculptor, the musician, the choreographer. Yet he is not primarily and basically a thinker. He does not act like one. In social groups he tends usually—though there are exceptions—to give the impression of being perceptive and emotionally volatile. He does not appear to possess the cool wisdom of the philosopher or the exact and impersonal knowledge of the scientist. Neither—and this is more important—does he work like the thinker. His dissatisfaction with his words and paragraphs differs fundamentally from that of the ploddingly rational scholar who has only ideas to manipulate. To be sure, he aims at exactness; but the exactness is seldom merely or even mainly conceptual. One of his words is "too thin," another "too hard," a third "too sticky"; an imagined incident may be "sickening" if it is not "sensational" or "terrific." He is a specialist not so much in rational

---

[57] Joyce Cary, *The Horse's Mouth* (New York: Harper & Brothers, Publishers, 1944), p. 209.
[58] *Ibid.*, p. 216.

thought as in affections and affection-provoking notions. His sensitivity may of course be limited to *his* feelings and notions and the structures which effectively symbolize *them,* in which event he will be a bad, because uncatholic, critic. Whether wide or narrow, however, a sensitivity to psychic weights is his distinguishing trait. More than most of us, he knows what is going on in his mind-body and can externalize his affective states in presentational structures.

On April 6, 1958, Harvey Breit reviewed in the *New York Times Book Review* a volume called *Writers at Work,* edited by Malcolm Cowley and consisting of interviews with sixteen more or less distinguished writers: E. M. Forster, Joyce Cary, Dorothy Parker, James Thurber, Thornton Wilder, William Faulkner, Frank O'Connor, Georges Simenon, Alberto Moravia, William Styron, Nelson Algren, Truman Capote, Robert Penn Warren, Angus Wilson, François Mauriac, and Françoise Sagan. The book, said the reviewer, was an excellent one of its kind, since the questions asked the writers were more than usually pertinent and searching; but the reader would be hard pressed to discover any common element in the subjects. There is no common dedication to work, certainly no common skill at graceful conversation, probably no common thoughtfulness or even common articulateness. "My own notion," he concludes, "is that E. M. Forster holds in common with Françoise Sagan, and the fourteen others in between, only a tough awareness of the minute particulars of his own special thought and feeling."

Modern art: hindrances to production and a way of overcoming them

In our day, the writer is in an especially difficult situation because emotions are less socialized than ever before, and the artist's affective patterns are therefore more likely to be idiosyncratic and hard to communicate. Moreover, the prestige of reason is so great that the presentational language of aesthetic symbols is becoming less and less generally understood. Still a third source of trouble is the attempt of critics and aestheticians, often alluded to in these pages, to justify art in terms of its cognitive value, a procedure which has resulted in a misconception by writers themselves of the direction in which they ought to exert their energy. In the past, there have been cultures in which art was one of the most powerful forces for social solidarity—in many primitive tribes, in ancient Greece, in medieval Europe, in pre-Restoration Japan. In the West today, candor forces the acknowledgment that art has little social importance. It is the solace and delight of individuals, the preoccupation also of cliques and professional groups, but hardly meaningful to society as a whole. Can a readjustment of our ideas about art help to remedy the deficiency? "People generally assume," remarked Fiedler, "that without art, as without religion and other spiritual and ethical forces, life would suffer a loss; that, however, is unimportant; the actual fact is that without art our picture of the world would be incomplete." Art is not simply a kind of knowledge, "but rather one of the means by which man tries to release himself from his isolation and regain coherence with nature." [59] It is a commonplace that for modern man, as for John Donne, all coherence is gone, the solidarity of man with man destroyed because the solidarity of man with nature has been shattered. Is it conceivable that art should once again perform its old function?

I believe it is possible—at a cost. Artists must value their individualities less highly and must come to regard as inestimably precious the psychic traits which mark them as *men,* as *human beings,* as representatives of a culture, the race, and the whole world. They must aim at the projection not of eccentric private feelings—much less of peculiar ideas—but of human feelings as such. In the present situation, however, since education aims almost exclusively at disinterested comprehension and the emotions of cultivated men and women are allowed to develop more anarchically than when they were institutionalized by religion and deep patriotism, the only way this end can be achieved is by the artist's descending to psychic levels too deep to have been affected by a highly conceptualized training. He must regress, as it has been the

---

[59] Fiedler, *Vom Wesen der Kunst,* pp. 51 and 88.

purpose of most of the foregoing pages to show that historically he has in fact regressed, to the mental patterns potential in his own biological constitution and in that of all his normal readers. He must do this on principle and willingly, not fitfully and grudgingly, when his aesthetic instincts get the better temporarily of a conscious intent to be "fresh" and "original"; not, of course, by saying to himself, "Now I will animize," "Now I will use story as a substitute for analysis," but by allowing common human affections to seek suitable presentational forms, by taking them seriously. Since his materials will be mainly contemporary, we may hope that in time the intellectualized universe of modern experience will become naturalized to the social affections and the gulf which separates men from an unfeeling and indifferent nature will be bridged.

The place of art in culture

The wholeness and depth which are missing from a culture in which common feelings are denied conceptual validity can be suggested by an observation of Joseph Campbell:

> The hogan, or mud hut, of the Navahos of New Mexico and Arizona, is constructed on the plan of the Navaho image of the cosmos. The entrance faces east. The eight sides represent the four directions and the points between. Every beam and joist corresponds to an element in the great hogan of the all-embracing earth and sky. And since the soul of man itself is regarded as identical in form with the universe, the mud hut is a representation of the basic harmony of man and world, and a reminder of the hidden life-way of perfection.[60]

Here one recognizes nostalgically, almost achingly, a continuity between man and nature. For the Navaho, the building of a rude hut becomes an act of religious worship which results not only in the sheltering of the body but also in the gratification of the soul. Campbell adds:

---

[60] Joseph Campbell, *The Hero with a Thousand Faces* (Bollingen Series XVII, Bollingen Foundation, Inc., 1949), p. 385.

A transmutation of the whole social order is necessary, so that through every detail and act of secular life the vitalizing image of the universal god-man who is actually immanent and effective in all of us may be somehow made known to consciousness.

But this is not a work that consciousness alone can achieve.

Consciousness can no more invent, or even predict, an effective symbol than foretell or control tonight's dream. The whole thing is being worked out on another level, through what is bound to be a long and very frightening process.[61]

The task of art is to *ingest* whatever can be learned objectively about the world of the non-I and then to *give out* an image which will accord not only with nonhuman truths and idiosyncratic notions but also with the forms of universal human feelings.

Only in some such way as this, *through art,* can the soul-chilling breach between man and the universe be healed. The transaction will be between mind and what it must absorb from outside itself, what it must somehow, if the world is to be made spiritually habitable, come to terms with. The aim of the rational sciences is to adjust consciousness to external nature; that of art is to adapt external nature to consciousness. The activities are complementary and equally important. In the end, the universe may again be impregnated with shared human meanings, and the human spirit may be relatively at peace, at bottom if not on the surface—for some pain, some disorientation, are unavoidable in experience. That no bond should really exist between man and his physical environment is unthinkable. On the mechanical hypothesis, man also is mere matter; on the religious hypothesis, his consciousness reflects a consciousness that permeates the universal whole. In either view, he is part of a totality. Without symbols, however, the nature of the binding relationship can never be brought home to the heart. "Der Mensch," wrote Cassirer (who deserves to be quoted last in a work which has derived from his thought), "sein eigenes Sein nur soweit erfasst und erkennt, als er es sich im Bilde seiner Götter sichtbar zu machen vermag." [62]

---

61 *Ibid.,* p. 389.
62 Cassirer, *Philosophie der Symbolischen Formen,* II, 269.